Focus on Sexuality Research

Series editor

Heather Hoffmann, Knox College, Galesburg, IL, USA

More information about this series at http://www.springer.com/series/10132

Eric Anderson · Mark McCormack

The Changing Dynamics of Bisexual Men's Lives

Social Research Perspectives

 Springer

Eric Anderson
University of Winchester
Winchester
UK

Mark McCormack
Durham University
Durham
UK

ISSN 2195-2264   ISSN 2195-2272 (electronic)
Focus on Sexuality Research
ISBN 978-3-319-29411-7   ISBN 978-3-319-29412-4 (eBook)
DOI 10.1007/978-3-319-29412-4

Library of Congress Control Number: 2016932504

© Springer International Publishing Switzerland 2016
This work is subject to copyright. All rights are reserved by the Publisher, whether the whole or part of the material is concerned, specifically the rights of translation, reprinting, reuse of illustrations, recitation, broadcasting, reproduction on microfilms or in any other physical way, and transmission or information storage and retrieval, electronic adaptation, computer software, or by similar or dissimilar methodology now known or hereafter developed.
The use of general descriptive names, registered names, trademarks, service marks, etc. in this publication does not imply, even in the absence of a specific statement, that such names are exempt from the relevant protective laws and regulations and therefore free for general use.
The publisher, the authors and the editors are safe to assume that the advice and information in this book are believed to be true and accurate at the date of publication. Neither the publisher nor the authors or the editors give a warranty, express or implied, with respect to the material contained herein or for any errors or omissions that may have been made.

Printed on acid-free paper

This Springer imprint is published by Springer Nature
The registered company is Springer International Publishing AG Switzerland

Dedicated to John Sylla and the American Institute of Bisexuality

Acknowledgements

We are grateful for many fine scholars, from multiple fields, who have helped to make this book possible. First our appreciation goes to John Sylla, President of the American Institute of Bisexuality. A great source of knowledge on sexological matters, John recruited us to undertake bisexuality research, and funded our multiple projects. We owe John a debt of gratitude for his support of our work, but also for his energy in promoting research on bisexuality within the academy and beyond. Research on bisexuality is in a better place because of his drive, and that of the team at the *American Institute of Bisexuality*.

We are grateful to the many academics from multiple fields, who have helped us develop this interdisciplinary book. Ritch Savin-Williams has been generous with his time and provided astute advice along the way. Our thanks must also go to Heather Hoffmann, President of the International Association of Sex Researchers and our acquisition editor for Springer. Not only did she see the value of our interdisciplinary work, her shrewd observations enhanced our thinking and broadened our literature base we draw on in the book. Our knowledge of sexological research has benefited enormously from our membership of J. Michael Bailey's list-serv SexNet, where he and others have been the source of much important research on sexuality in the fields of psychology, sexology and beyond.

There are many other colleagues who have made important contributions to the book. Adi Adams was a research assistant on the empirical project and was central to that process. Brian Cash and Max Morris have read copious drafts of earlier versions of the work, while Ryan Scoats, Sarah Merrill, Meg John Barker, Mark Ogilvie, Rachael Bullingham, Rory Magrath and Adam White have all contributed in various ways throughout the process.

Finally, we thank our partners, Grant Peterson and Liam Wignall, for their support.

Contents

1	**Introduction**	1
	A Sociological and Sexological Approach to Bisexuality	8
	Overview of the Chapters	10
2	**Bisexuality: It is Complicated**	15
	Defining Sexuality	17
	Examining the Components of Sexuality	17
	Sexual Attraction	19
	Sexual Repulsion	21
	Sexual Behavior	22
	Sexual Identity	23
	Romantic Love	24
	Distinguishing Romance from Bromance	25
	Types of Bisexuality	28
3	**Measuring and Surveying Bisexuality**	31
	Measures of Sexual Attraction	32
	Surveying Bisexuality	34
	Surveying Bisexuality in Our Research	37
	Problems in Estimating the Bisexual Population	40
	Survey Results of Sexual Minority Populations	42
	How Bisexual Are Bisexuals?	44
	Expanding Categories and Sexual Flexibility	45
4	**Bisexuality as a Unique Social Problem**	49
	Biphobia and Bisexual Burden	51
	Characteristics of Bisexual Burden	53
	The Psychological and Health Effects of Bisexual Burden	64
	Bisexual Privilege	65
5	**The Gendering of Sexuality**	69
	Homohysteria	71
	A Stage Model of Homohysteria	72

ix

	Homoerasure	73
	Homohysteria	75
	Inclusivity	77
	The Effects of Inclusivity	80
	An Expansion of Gendered Boundaries	80
	Erosion of the One-Time Rule of Homosexuality	82
	Decreasing Biphobia	85
	Changing Sexual Identities Among Youth	87
6	**Taking Bisexual Research to the Streets**	89
	Situating Our Study	91
	Evaluating the Method	95
	A Controversial Method?	96
	Interview Procedure	96
	Qualitative Analysis	98
	The Importance of Generations	99
	A Note on Women	99
7	**Challenging Identities, Changing Identifications**	101
	Confusion and Denial Among Men in the 20th Century	102
	Young Bisexual Men and Clarity of Desire	105
	Generational Differences in the Value of Identity Categories	106
	Critiquing Bisexuality as an Identity Label	107
	Conclusion	110
8	**Coming Out with 20th Century Baggage**	113
	Coming Out to Friends	114
	The Difficulty of Coming Out to Family	119
	Negotiating Bisexuality at Work	121
	Bisexual Burden on the Scene	123
	Heterosexism	124
	Misogyny	125
	The Importance of the City	125
	Conclusion	127
9	**Coming Out in the 21st Century**	129
	Acceptance and Inclusion Among Friends	130
	Coming Out to School	132
	Inclusive Families	134
	Eroding Heterosexism	135
	Similarity Between City and Countryside	137
	Conclusion	138
10	**Bisexual Relationships**	141
	Increased Personal Acceptance	142
	Remnants of Bisexual Burden Among Romantic Partners	144
	Decreasing Heteronormativity	145

	Gendered Preferences	146
	Monogamism	147
	Conclusion	149
11	**Conclusions**	151
	The Presence of a Generational Cohort Effect	152
	Theorizing the Cohort Effect	155
	Intersecting Factors	157
	Expanding Sexuality and Death of the One-Time Rule	159
	The Benefits of Our Recruitment Procedure	160
	Recommendations for Future Research	161
	Implications for Social Policy	164
	In Conclusion	165

Appendix 1: Participant List 167

Appendix 2: Paradigmatic Perspectives on Sexual Desire 169

References 173

Index 191

About the Authors

Dr. Eric Anderson is Professor of Sport, Masculinities & Sexualities at the University of Winchester. He has published 16 books, over 50 peer-reviewed articles, and is recognized for research excellence by the British Academy of Social Sciences. He is a fellow of the International Academy of Sex Research, and is regularly featured in international television, print and digital media.

His work shows a decline in cultural homohysteria leading to a softening of heterosexual masculinities. This permits heterosexual men to kiss, cuddle and love one another; and promotes inclusive attitudes toward openly gay athletes and the recognition of bisexuality. His sexuality work finds positive aspects of non-monogamous relationships and explores the function and benefits of cheating.

Professor Anderson is also trustee of the Sport Collision Injury Collective, which is committed to examining and removing negative outcomes of participation in contact sports. He also writes about sport psychology, distance running, and the social problems of organized team sports. More can be found at his website www.ProfessorEricAnderson.com.

Dr. Mark McCormack is a Senior Lecturer in Sociology at Durham University, and Co-Director of its Centre for Sex, Gender and Sexualities. His research examines how decreasing homophobia has affected the gender identities of heterosexual male youth, and how this influences their attitudes, social practices and use of technology. He is author of *The Declining Significance of Homophobia*, published with Oxford University Press in 2012, and he has published on these topics in journals including *Sex Roles*, *British Journal of Sociology* and *Journal of Adolescent Research*. He also examines the changing nature of sexual identities and sexual practices, including kinky sex and pornography consumption, and has published on these issues in *Archives of Sexual Behavior*, *Sociology* and *Journal of Bisexuality*.

Abstract

Although bisexual men outnumber gay men, there is very little research concerning their lives. When bisexual men are the topic of inquiry, they are often viewed through a medical lens, or are sociologically pathologized as the victims of multiple forms of oppression. Part of this perspective comes from poor sampling, as research on bisexuals is almost exclusively conducted on those obtained from sexual minority organizations or from organized groups of bisexuals that maintain their own, unique, counter-culture. *The Changing Dynamics of Bisexual Men's Lives: Social Research Perspectives* is designed to ameliorate these issues.

We base this research in the latest scientific research concerning bisexuality, from multiple academic disciplines. We then investigate the lives of 90 bisexual men recruited from non-institutionalized spaces. Instead of finding them through bisexual organizations we recruited them from city streets in Los Angeles, New York and London. Second, although surveys generally fail to measure biphobia explicitly, results from our interview research suggest that as cultural homophobia has decreased, so has biphobia. Our in-depth interviews highlight a cohort effect, whereby younger bisexual men have more rewarding experiences coming out as bisexual than older bisexual men. Finally, we find that younger bisexual men are less troubled by their sexuality, and suggest that their peers are largely unbothered by it as well. These results are generally more positive than what other research on bisexual men suggest.

Chapter 1
Introduction

In 1948, Alfred Kinsey and his research associates published one of the most culturally influential scientific treatises on human sexuality to date. The work, *Sexual Behavior in the Human Male*, was immediately controversial because the findings challenged conventional wisdom about human sexuality; for example, the presumption that everyone was heterosexual. Kinsey showed that 4% of men were exclusively homosexual since adolescence (Kinsey et al. 1948). However, he also showed that sexuality was not a binary category, writing, "The living world is a continuum…The sooner we learn this concerning human sexual behavior the sooner we shall reach a sound understanding of the realities of sex" (p. 639).

Kinsey and his colleagues deployed a huge body of statistical and qualitative evidence to support their arguments. Not just that 10.6% of married men aged 21–25 had once had sex with another man, but that 37% of men reported at least one same-sex sexual experience to the point of orgasm by age 45. They also found that approximately 10% of men between the ages 16 and 55 were predominantly homosexual in behavior for at least three years.

While Kinsey's sampling techniques have been called into question, the cultural effect of his research was profound. Not only was the cultural presumption of heterosexuality called into question, gender exclusivity in sexual desire was troubled as well. Kinsey's team demonstrated that bisexual desire was not uncommon among men. They famously wrote:

> Males do not represent two discrete populations, heterosexual and homosexual. The world is not to be divided into sheep and goats. It is a fundamental of taxonomy that nature rarely deals with discrete categories… The living world is a continuum in each and every one of its aspects (Kinsey et al. 1948: 639).

So radical for the time, Kinsey's ideas are now considered commonsense. But the awareness of homosexual and bisexual attraction and behaviors does not mean that they are culturally acceptable. While contemporary society has generally positive attitudes toward sexual minorities, progress has not been linear or the same for all groups; social understandings of bisexuality have taken a complicated, controversial, and circuitous path to contemporary understandings and levels of acceptance.

© Springer International Publishing Switzerland 2016
E. Anderson and M. McCormack, *The Changing Dynamics of Bisexual Men's Lives*, Focus on Sexuality Research, DOI 10.1007/978-3-319-29412-4_1

In charting these trends, it is crucial to understand that societal attitudes toward bisexuality have been tightly linked with society's disposition toward homosexuality (Hubbard and deVisser 2014; Kangasvuo 2011). Although outnumbering homosexuals, bisexuals have been squeezed within the Lesbian, Gay, Bisexual, and Transgender (LGBT) alphabet soup. Here, bisexuality has frequently been erased both culturally and from academic investigation.

The erasure of bisexuality occurs from both progressives and conservatives alike. While smaller events and groups exist for bisexuals, progressives have the Gay Games, the Gay and Lesbian Anti-Defamation League, and the Gay, Lesbian and Straight Education Network. From the other side, fundamentalist Christians simultaneously rail against the "*homosexual* agenda." Bisexuals have faced a lack of recognition from both sides of the culture wars.

Some of this erasure is by omission, but Barker (2014: 170) suggests that it also exists because bisexuality is sometimes considered problematic within LGBT politics. She states that this is because of "its potential to disrupt some of the foundations upon which lesbian and gay rights have been fought for (essential and dichotomous sexuality on the basis of gender of attraction)." Collectively, it seems fair to say that bisexuality, and the experiences of bisexual people, have been ignored, denied, and made to seem illegitimate by both sexual minorities and those who hold antipathy toward them (Sears 2014; Weiss 2003).

In recent times, some sexologists have been critiqued for seeming to deny the existence of men's bisexuality. Exemplifying this, when Rieger et al. (2005) investigated genital arousal to male and female sexual stimuli in 30 heterosexual, 33 bisexual, and 38 homosexual men, they found that the men who identified as bisexual did not have strong genital arousal to both male and female sexual stimuli. Rather, most bisexual men appeared to retain exclusively same-sex desires in terms of genital arousal, although some appeared to be exclusively heterosexual. Thus, it was argued that male bisexuality was primarily a way of interpreting or reporting sexual arousal rather than a distinct physiological pattern of genital sexual arousal. These researchers privileged physiological measures over self-reported identities. In other words, they did not take the subjects' words that they were attracted to members of both sexes as valid. Instead, they relied on an instrument to measure this. Despite serious limitations of the study, particularly relating to how participants were recruited, its findings were reported in a New York Times article titled *Straight, Gay, or Lying? Bisexuality Revisited* (Carey 2005).

The cultural reaction to the original study by Rieger, Chivers, and Bailey exemplifies the resistance toward bisexuality in society. Despite the authors recognizing the limitations within their study, the world's biggest newspaper was quick to relegate bisexual desires to confusion or untruthfulness. At the time this highlighted that America was a *monosexual* culture — where sexual desire is seen as gender exclusive, with people being either exclusively heterosexual or homosexual. People with monosexual desire often suggest that bisexuals are confused, or are trying to lessen the stigma of coming out as gay. Today, these same researchers have used a fancier instrument (magnetic resonance imaging) and found what they call a bisexual arousal pattern among men. When the findings are released to the media, they likely will, as studies by Rosenthal et al. (2012) have, receive less media than a study suggesting bisexuality does not exist.

Indeed, the cultural resonance of bisexuality "not existing" highlights the privileging of monosexual desire within society. Despite decades of research into the complexity of men's sexual activity and identity categorization, people still tend to think in dualisms about sexuality. We call the privileging of monosexual desires in society *monosexism* because just as society esteems heterosexuality (called heterosexism), it also reproduces a binary conceptualization of society in which the complexity of desire is reduced to gay or (preferably) straight. Exemplifying this, in homophobic cultures, people are often called gay as a way to marginalize them and cast social stigma upon them (Plummer 1999). Yet when this is done, that person is labelled gay—rarely do people speculate that someone might be bisexual. This also explains why there are no pejorative words to describe bisexuals, while pejorative labels for gay people are more than abundant (see Savin-Williams 1998).

Our monosexual culture is deeply troubling for those concerned with equality of sexualities. It denies a person's right to define their own sexual identity, and also imposes a particular way for individuals to interpret their sexual desires and enact them in their sexual lives. It promotes a pathological model of bisexuality, which does not account for the importance of individual's narratives of their own experiences. For us, however, while we draw on sexological research in the first part of this book, our grounding as sociologists means that we view people's lived experiences as paramount in understanding sexuality in society, and that social identities play a pivotal role in this dynamic.

The monosexist erasure of bisexuality occurs alongside a number of unique myths and stereotypes about bisexual individuals that are not attributed to gays and lesbians (Steinman and Beemyn 2014). We discuss these issues as *bisexual burden*, highlighting that they have traditionally influenced bisexuals to selectively disclose their identities to a greater extent than lesbians or gay men (McLean 2007). Pew research (2013) finds that bisexuals are out of the closet to fewer people than gays and lesbians. Indeed, part of the invisibility of bisexuality is the result of self-silencing on behalf of bisexual individuals.

Part of the self-silencing of bisexual individuals is attributable to the fact that remaining in the closet is easier for bisexuals than it is for gays and lesbians. Bisexuals can find fulfilling sex and relationships in ostensibly heterosexual couplings, benefiting from heterosexual privilege in a manner not possible for gays and lesbians. Gay people must come out of the closet in order to find their desired sex and love if they want that to be socially recognized. Bisexuals, on the other hand, live in a heterosexist culture that encourages them to attend to the heterosexual side of their desires, and minimize the homosexual—and this is certainly problematic—but it is also an option that gays and lesbians do not have. Many bisexuals thus have heterosexual relationships, and either silence their same-sex attractions willingly, or fail to contest social boundaries that gay couples do by simply holding hands walking down a street. The result is a lack of visibility that would contest dominant social stereotypes about bisexuality. Thus, as a community of sexual minorities, bisexuals as a group have been far less active in fighting stereotypes about their sexuality than gays and lesbians (Deschamps 2008; Hayfield et al. 2013).

This is not to blame bisexuals for their marginalization. When people come out as bisexual, an overwhelmingly homophobic and monosexist culture has regularly insisted that they were gay. As we discuss in Chap. 4, a 'one-time rule of homosexuality' (Anderson 2008) exists in homophobic cultures that sees any single same-sex experience as evidence of a gay identity. Here, even one same-sex sexual act is socially equated with a homosexual orientation, regardless of how many 'opposite-sex' sexual experiences one has. The absorption of bisexuality within homosexuality – as *evidence for* homosexuality – inextricably links attitudes toward bisexuality with the level of homophobia in a culture.

When mass awareness of homosexuality also exists alongside considerable cultural antipathy for it, the one-time rule of homosexuality becomes particularly relevant (McCormack and Anderson 2014a). Defining this cultural zeitgeist as "homohysteric," our driving thesis in this book is that it is the level of homohysteria in a culture that determines the operation of homophobia and sexual prejudice in that culture. Given that there is no space to recognize sexual diversity, and heterosexuality is privileged as bisexuality is erased (Steinman 2011), homohysteric cultures are monosexist as well.

It is not just sexual identity that is policed in a homohysteric culture—a person's gendered behaviors are socially regulated as well (Anderson 2009; Worthen 2014). The conflation of sexuality and gender occurs because sexuality is not somatically marked in a way that gender, age, and race are. While it is generally possible to tell if someone is male or female by looking at their physical features (see West and Zimmerman 1987 for a discussion of this), or old or young, black or white (all of which are socially constructed dichotomies, too), it is not possible to tell who is gay, straight, or bi just by looking at them. Yet rather than relying on a person's self-identification, gendered behavior becomes the proxy for sexuality in homohysteric cultures.

In this context, gender is seen in part to be a display of sexual identity (Halperin 2012). It is even deemed more 'truthful' than what a person might state their sexual identity to be. This is because in homohysteric cultures it is impossible for heterosexuals to prove they are not gay. The existence of the closet calls into question anyone's self-proclamation of heterosexuality. When self-identification is not effective, men align their gendered behaviors with things socially coded as heterosexual. In addition to esteeming sport, muscularity, and stoicism, they also avoid association with things that are coded as homosexual: they avoid wearing pink, attending the ballet, or saying "I love you" to other male friends for fear of being thought gay (Mac an Ghaill 1994; Plummer 1999).

What makes the contemporary study of bisexuality so interesting is that times are changing. Cultural homohysteria is decreasing quickly, and this has enabled a transformation in heterosexual masculinities among younger men (McCormack

2012a), as well as an erosion of the one-time rule of homosexuality. For example, some young heterosexual men kiss, cuddle, and even engage in pseudo-sexual activities with each other without losing their heterosexual identity.

There is a corresponding trend within the academy, where bisexuality has traditionally been erased from academic investigations, lagging behind homosexuality as a serious topic of academic inquiry. It is for this precise reason that the *American Institute of Bisexuality* sought to rectify this problem. Endowed by the estate of bisexual activist and scholar, Fritz Klein, the organization, today led by John Sylla, has funded empirical research related to bisexuality, including our own.

There are multiple implications for bisexuality in this new social and intellectual zeitgeist. We first highlight that bisexuality has gained considerable social recognition since the last major qualitative investigation of bisexual men twenty years ago (Weinberg et al. 1994). Public discussion of bisexuality has made it easier to come out, to live out, and to have bisexuality accepted as a legitimate orientation (Morris et al. 2014). At the same time, decreasing homophobia has led to an expansion of the definitions of what it means to be bisexual (Epstein 2014). As bisexuality has become more accepted, its definition has become more amorphous. Thus, while we discuss bisexuality as a singular term in this book, it is symbolic of a broad concept of gender non-exclusive sexual desires.

We recruited participants who *identified* as bisexual for our empirical research. However, given that what it means to be bisexual has expanded, it is possible that we have interviewed people who simultaneously identify as pansexual, ambisexual, and many other terms that people with non-exclusive desires use to describe themselves. This is an important component of bisexuality in the 21st century.

We show that bisexualities are forged out of multiple types of attractions: including sexual, romantic, and emotional. Bisexuality is about how a range of behaviors and identities are understood, acted upon, and represented publicly (Steinman and Beemyn 2014). Thus, readers should not think that we propagate just one form of 'bisexual' or that the term is even preferred by the men we interviewed—they just had to have some level of identification with it. We use the term bisexual not to diminish other ways of identifying, but as a sociological concept so that we might say something meaningful about men who are attracted to men and women.

The purpose of this book is thus to critically examine the lived experiences of openly bisexual men, during an age of decreased homohysteria. Whereas stigmatization and discrimination have been documented as endemic characteristics of bisexual individuals' life experience (Herek 2002; Klein 1993; Mohr et al. 2001), we suggest that things have changed significantly in recent years.

It is important to recognize that our data will not speak of the lives of closeted bisexual men: we strategically focused on men who are open about their bisexuality because we were interested in examining their lives and social responses to their bisexuality, not documenting the differences between closeted and open sexual minorities—which would be a book by itself. Our results also only speak of the locations in which data was collected – Los Angeles, New York, and London.

It is important to note that there is very little contemporary empirical sociological research on bisexuals, particularly related to bisexual men. One of our key aims is to address this omission in the literature by providing a substantive monograph grounded in the narratives of our 90 participants. Thus, while we draw on contemporary research, we also refer to older seminal literature as there are many cases in which this older research is more comprehensive and has a greater scope (e.g. Weinberg et al. 1994).

Given the need to provide separate analyses of men's and women's experiences of bisexuality (Brown 2002), and given our expertise as masculinities scholars (Anderson 2014; McCormack 2012a), we examine the coming out and lived experiences of bisexual *men* only. This is not to suggest that the experiences of bisexual women are not equally important, but that our expertise lies within men's gender and sexual lives.

Furthermore, because research on bisexuality is frequently conducted on participants from LGBT groups and networks—which may not reflect the experiences of bisexuals more broadly—in collecting data for this book we desired to avoid recruiting from LGBT activist or community groups. We thus took advantage of the more inclusive cultures that these large, urban cities provide in order to collect data in a way that may not have been possible in the 1980s, or 1990s. We publically recruited bisexual men from busy pedestrian areas of New York, Los Angeles, and London. Furthermore, we recruited participants from parts of these cities that are not recognized as gay neighborhoods.

We found our participants on busy public streets and pedestrian areas in each of these three cities by repeatedly calling out that we were looking to interview bisexual men. Holding clipboards with participant information sheets, bisexual men who fit our criteria were taken to nearby coffee shops or other private areas for in-depth, semi-structured interviews. This is the first large-scale qualitative research that avoids recruiting participants from bisexual or sexual minority organizations, websites, or email lists.

Our methods were intentionally designed to enable a systematic examination of a generational cohort effect. We recruited 90 bisexual men for interview, but these men had to fit particular characteristics. We stayed in each city until we had interviewed 30 men, and stopped recruiting in that city once we had reached our target number. However, within each city we did not just recruit the first 30 men who approached us. Instead, we designated three age cohorts (18–24, 25–35, 36–42) and interviewed ten men from each cohort in each city. This meant that when, for example, we had recruited 10 men aged 18–24 and ten men aged 25–35 in Los Angeles, we turned away men from these age groups, only recruiting 10 men aged between 36 and 42. Our sample thus looks "neat" in the sense that we have 10 men from each group in each of three cities. This was not by chance—it was the result of a carefully designed and executed sampling procedure.

We rely on this categorical and systematic approach to recruitment in order to examine for a cohort effect: to explore generational differences in coming out experiences, relationships, and personal sexual identities across these three age cohorts. The age cohorts themselves were determined to fit significant epochs concerning homohysteria—this is why the age ranges are not the same for each cohort.

Finding that the experiences of the 30 men in the oldest cohort are substantially more negative than the 30 men of the youngest cohort, we argue that the combination of the liberalization of attitudes toward homosexuality (Baunach 2012; Keleher and Smith 2012); the liberalization of attitudes toward sex more generally (Twenge et al. 2015); and the expansion of gendered behaviors for men (Anderson 2014; McCormack 2012a) has improved the social environments for these urban participants in London, Los Angeles, and New York. That these differences are internal to our sample – that we do not have to make comparisons with other research – is strong support for the generational shift we document.

Our sampling method also permitted us to recruit a diversity of ethnic groups. Because attitudes toward sexual minorities have been shown to depend on socio-demographic factors, including race, ethnicity, gender, and religiosity (e.g. Collier et al. 2013), we chose to recruit participants from metropolitan areas where ethnic minorities can be found in higher numbers. As might be expected in these metropolitan cities, our samples were diverse. The participants from New York and Los Angeles were roughly a third each white, black, and Hispanic, with some mixed-race participants. Participants from London were predominantly white, however.

We recognize that these racial categorizations are simplistic terms for what is a complex and socially constructed element of identity (Collins 1999); and we recognize the problems inherent in using these categories—but our use of simplistic categories also helped us highlight the lack of racial effect in our findings. Put simply, race did not prove a fertile way of analyzing the data, as our main findings did not change significantly when examining different racial groups.

Similarly, while our research is deeply rooted in the city, the processes of globalization mean that a taxonomic understanding of geography was not possible (see Ghaziani 2014). While recruiting from metropolitan areas with a density of people enabled us to recruit our desired number of bisexual men, we also recruited bisexuals from the same country but resident in other cities—or who had only recently moved to the city. Perhaps for this reason, while we found differences between rural and metropolitan areas, analysis by city did not produce meaningful results.

Instead, our key finding is that the experiences of openly bisexual men in these three metropolitan cities have improved over the past thirty years in line with our generational cohort framework. With a reduction in homophobia and homohysteria resulting in a softening of masculinity and an expansion of cultural understandings of sexuality, more space has emerged for bisexuality as an identity and as a way of life (see McCormack and Anderson 2014a). Our central thesis is therefore that there is a generational cohort effect in the improving experiences of openly bisexual men. In other words, the experiences of coming out and being bisexual are dependent on the historical context of one's adolescence (Dubé 2000; Pearcey 2005; Plummer 2010) as well as attitudes in contemporary society.

In this book we show that sexualities are generational, and that those whose adolescence was in a period of high homohysteria have far worse experiences than those whose adolescence was more recent and in more inclusive times. Significantly, this is not just about experiences at that time, but that the contemporary world in which all our participants live is mediated differently according to that adolescent experience.

In line with our cohort findings, we also examined for the perseverance of long-standing myths and burdens of bisexuality, even as attitudes toward sexuality have liberalized. We find that as orthodox views and institutional control of sexual behaviors and relationships have eroded in recent decades (Clements and Field 2014; Keleher and Smith 2012), young bisexual men's experiences are markedly better than prior generations.

This book thus contributes toward the sociological understanding of bisexuality by: (1) examining the changing nature of bisexual men's lives through a theoretical lens of decreasing homohysteria; (2) examining how the changing cultural zeitgeist manifests in the lived experience of bisexual men according to their age cohort; and (3) drawing upon an innovative recruitment method to avoid bisexuals institutionalized into gay or bisexual subcultures, thus providing us with an understanding of the increasing ordinariness of openly bisexual men's lives.

A Sociological and Sexological Approach to Bisexuality

The data that we generate for this study is sociological. A sociological approach to sexuality is to examine it from the outside in, not the inside out. That is, we are interested in what culture says about bisexuality, and how men who have sexual desires for both men and women deal with that. We are less interested in what makes someone bisexual in the first place. Thus, our aim is to describe what bisexuality feels like to the men we interviewed, how they navigate their social identity, and what factors are important in influencing these experiences.

As sociologists, we are concerned about the applicability of our findings to other groups. We wish to find dominant, relevant, and important patterns and trends in the data we analyze. So while the 90 men we interviewed are unique individuals, each with an important story to tell, it is only through the collective analysis of stories that we learn something important about our culture, how we think about sexual difference, and how we act toward sexual minorities.

Through rigorous coding of data, logical argumentation, and theoretical development, we are also able to generate predictions about social phenomena. This enables us to extrapolate our results – to take the findings from our data set and suggest how they may be relevant to other groups of urban bisexuals and how they might augment our theoretical knowledge of bisexuality and society. Thus, we cannot guarantee how an individual bisexual man will be treated by his peers and family after coming out in London, Los Angeles, or New York, but our research enables us to make predictions that most will be treated better today than they would have twenty years ago—at least in these urban areas.

To avoid doubt, we are not arguing that our findings are generalizable to all bisexual men. Our data cannot speak of the experiences of those who are closeted, those that fell outside of our age range, or lived in rural areas. Indeed, the three cities selected are particularly large and diverse, and experiences of being openly bisexual will likely be different in smaller cities, or cities in other regions of the US and the UK. These are important caveats, and further research is needed to explore how these issues influence experiences of bisexuality. We hope, however, that the trend of decreasing homophobia throughout western culture means that similar results for bisexual men will be experienced.

While we adopt a sociological and social interactionist approach to the study of the intersection of men's bisexuality and society, we do not wish to convey a belief that bisexuality—or any sexuality—is purely the product of social processes. We are aligned with the vast majority of scientists and even the majority of sociologists who maintain that sexual attraction has biological origins (e.g. Engle et al. 2006; LeVay 2011).

One frequent misunderstanding of this biological framework is that it means we are destined to fulfill our genetic fate (e.g. Buss 1995). This is not our position. It is not possible to willfully change one's sexual orientation, yet sexual desire will not be explained the same way for all people, nor will people with similar desires identify in the same way. But to deny any biological component to sexuality is as deterministic as to argue that biology is our destiny. We thus reject both forms of deterministic thinking, and are frustrated by the polarized nature of these debates within sociology—where one is seen to espouse biological determinism if *any* value is given to biology.

We find sociology a valuable tool for explaining the etiology and operation of stigma but we do not solely attribute the development of sexual identity to society. There is credibility to Wilson and Rahman's (2005) notion that sexual identities are taxonomic – they are socially constructed categories, but they also maintain some resemblance to empirical, biological realities (see also Gangestad et al. 2000). These taxonomies will, of course, vary in their accuracy depending on homophobia, sexual conservatism, and other dynamics of a culture (Burleson 2008), but they are linked in some way to bodily desires. We support Fausto-Sterling's (2000) argument that it is the combination of the biological and the social that result in societal understanding of sexuality (see also Andersen et al. 2000). It is for this reason that while the presentation of our findings is strictly sociological, our discussion of the complexity of bisexuality adopts an interdisciplinary perspective, drawing on sociological and sexological research.

Accordingly, when we say that we are interactionist (or social constructionist) sociologists, we also highlight that we are not social determinists. We examine how culture shapes our identities and desires, but this does not rule out our biological traits as a factor. We find it presumptuous, even fundamentalist, to assume that any one discipline has all the answers to the questions around sexuality. We maintain that the best work comes from examining the weights of evidence from what multiple scholars across multiple disciplines have to offer. These debates are important not because we empirically studied the etiology of sexual desire in this book, but because one's perspective on these issues influences how bisexuality is studied sociologically.

Evidencing this, there has been a tendency for many sociologists to examine sexual identities through poststructural frameworks—where biology is rejected in favor of social and discursive practices. With bisexuality characterized as a "middle ground" between sexualities (Hemmings 2002: 2), the "deconstructive impulse" (Green 2007: 32) of poststructuralism may seem to synchronize with the categorical indeterminacy of bisexuality (Alexander and Anderlini-D'Onofrio 2014). However, this perceived synergy is problematic, as it influences scholars to emphasize issues with personal identifications above the everyday social practices of bisexuals (Jackson and Scott 2010). The notion of bisexuality as a "middle ground" also requires an understanding of homosexuality and heterosexuality as oppositional, a notion we and many sexologists reject; it is something we frame as a zero-sum game of sexuality (see Chap. 2).

We continue to see the value in identity categories as ways of mediating sexuality in everyday life. Identity categories are always in some way fictions, yet it is vital to recognize that people live in and through these identities as if they are real (Crawley et al. 2007). Viewing identities as "necessary fictions" (Weeks 2007: 84), we consider ourselves social constructionists who are also strategic empiricists. That is to say that we know that the identity of bisexuality is a social construction, but as long as people think it exists, live their lives through it, and experience discrimination based on this identity, we remain committed to a perspective of identity that seeks to achieve social justice through identity politics. We encourage you to read Appendix 2 for more on paradigmatic perspectives on sexuality studies.

Overview of the Chapters

In Chap. 2, we begin our exploration of contemporary bisexuality with a discussion of how bisexuality is defined in academic research—a vital issue if we are to have any clear debate about bisexuality more broadly. We demonstrate not just the complexity of defining bisexuality, but sexuality more broadly. We complicate definitions of sexuality that rely solely on identity, attraction, or behavior, arguing that emotional attraction is just as important—particularly in a context of increasing homosocial inclusivity for adolescent males.

We use bromances as a contemporary phenomenon to understand the importance of same-sex intimacy among those otherwise classed as heterosexual, arguing that emotional love between two men can be, and sometimes is interpreted as a form of bisexuality by young, ostensibly heterosexual men. We next use this holistic understanding of sexuality to discuss the different forms of bisexuality that exist:

from situational acts of homosexuality and using bisexuality as a coming out stage into homosexuality, to bisexuality as an enduring and defining feature of one's sexual orientation.

In Chap. 3, we discuss the methods by which bisexuality can be studied. We start with the most famous method of ranking and measuring sexual desire and the sex to which a person is attracted, the Kinsey Scale. Recognizing its value, but also its limitations, we progress to the Klein Sexual Orientation Grid, which provides a more holistic approach to thinking about sexuality, and other measures of sexuality. In briefly analyzing these approaches, we critique them for adopting a zero-sum game of sexuality: the idea that the more homosexual one becomes the less heterosexual they are. We address the situation by incorporating sexual drive and asexuality into a new model for understanding human sexuality, adding to the literature a heuristic tool—the Sexuality Thermometer—that might be useful for undertaking research.

In highlighting the difficulties of using survey measures for estimating the percent of the number of bisexuals in the US, we note it to be a difficult task because of the slippery definitions of bisexuality, the importance of wording on survey measures, and the difficulty of separating out bisexuality from LGBT research more broadly. We conclude that, while it seems safe to say that a minimum of 1.8% identify as bisexual, many more find themselves attracted to both sexes, and sometimes engage in same-sex behaviors. We conclude that for those adopting the label bisexual, their distribution shows that they are relatively in the middle or equally attracted to both males and females. Finally, we explore the literature on the stability of sexuality and highlight research that suggests while men have some sexual fluidity, men's sexualities are more stable than women's.

In Chap. 4, we highlight the unique social problems that bisexuals face, including discrimination from both gays and straights. This chapter thus conceptualizes the forms of marginalization unique to bisexuals. We call this collective *bisexual burden* and suggest that, according to minority stress theory, it has negative social and personal effects. While heterosexism exacerbates these in some ways, the operation of heterosexism also provides a level of emotional health protection to bisexuals, particularly in highly homohysteric times, because it enables bisexuals to retain heterosexual privilege in a way that other sexual minorities cannot.

In addition to stressing the cultural and academic erasure that bisexuals face from a monosexist culture, we also contend that not all of bisexual erasure comes from straights and gays; that there is a significant amount of *self-erasure* that is reproduced by bisexuals themselves. Bisexuals are much more in the closet, and find their sexualities to be less an integral part of their identities than gays and lesbians. Thus, the ability to date opposite-sex partners both privileges bisexuals as a sexual minority while simultaneously contributing to their marginalization.

In Chap. 5, we draw on our expertise as masculinities scholars to look at how men's bisexuality is gendered. We explicate the conceptual tool used in this research – homohysteria – as a cultural condition where men fear being socially perceived as gay through the wrongdoing of gendered or sexual behavior. Key to this operation is the "one-time rule of homosexuality" where even same-same sexual behavior is socially equated with a total homosexual identity, regardless of the number of heterosexual activities one partakes in. Highlighting that homohysteria is germane to a culture with both a high awareness that homosexuality exists, alongside strong animosity toward it, we also suggest that decreasing homohysteria makes bisexuality more visible by opening it up the legitimate sexual identity categories in society.

We argue that the erosion of homohysteria, which we substantially document among male youth, enables men to engage in a much wider range of gendered behaviors, and that this facilitates more benevolent attitudes toward sexuality in society. Thus, with the decrease in homohysteria, the one-time rule of homosexuality dissipates, and bisexuality becomes a legitimate and viable sexual orientation. We discuss the expansion of gendered and sexual behaviors that occurs in a period of inclusivity. It is this social trend of decreasing homohysteria that inspired our work on bisexual men, and is the rationale for a study of bisexual men that takes account of age cohort in these experiences.

In Chap. 6, we discuss the methods we use to undertake our empirical research. We describe the 3 × 3 cell method we used to collect data on 90 bisexual men: 30 each from New York, Los Angeles, and London divided into ten men from each of three age categories in each city (see Appendix 1). We discuss the sampling problems that have beset research on sexual minority populations in the past, arguing that it has led to a skewed understanding of sexual minority experiences.

Instead of rely upon these same recruitment methods, we describe how we took to the streets to recruit bisexual men who are not deeply embedded in bisexual communities, which are not representative of bisexuals more generally. We critically evaluate our method, providing full details of the method, so that the reader can judge the rigor of our study.

Most of the men we interviewed identified as being equally or near-attracted to men and women on all five measures that we categorize as comprising sexuality. No apparent differences in attractiveness or love preferences for bisexual men across the three age groups were observed either. Thus the nature of our methodological inquiry—recruiting by shouting out that we were looking to interview bisexual men from busy city streets—seems to have enabled us to capture a demographic of bisexual men in which the label 'bisexual' implies that they are currently sexually aroused by the thoughts of sex with both males and females near equally. We cannot say how this group of men compares to other bisexual men, but we can state that our participants find significance in being bisexual; yet men who are not necessarily part of bisexual support groups or organizations.

In Chap. 7, we examine how early identifications with bisexuality were harder for the older men than younger. As with other studies, the older men in our study were less able to understand their bisexual desires until adulthood. This was not found among the younger men, however, who had a greater clarity of desire.

We also document ambivalence toward identity categories, with many younger participants not rejecting them but de-emphasizing their importance; talking about their utility rather than having a strong emotional attachment to them. This, we argue, is a privilege that comes with decreased homohysteria. Being that there is decreasing stigma about sexual minority categories, it makes them less important socially and politically.

In Chap. 8, we discuss the coming out experiences of participants who had their adolescence in the 20th century. We find that their experiences broadly mirrored that described in the literature on bisexuality: that is to say that they experienced significant elements of bisexual burden, often facing rejection from their peers and delaying coming out to their family for many years. We discuss the problems of coming out on the scene and at work as well. With this chapter, we add to the existing literature by finding that these men had also internalized a level of heterosexism and misogyny, which we attribute to growing up in a homohysteric culture.

Contrasting those who had their adolescence in the 21st century, we show in Chap. 9 that the collective experience of the 18–23-year-old men have substantially more positive experiences than those in the two older cohort groups. Many participants still felt that coming out was an important milestone in their social lives, but it was frequently experienced as an enjoyable event. The experiences of the bisexual men coming out were diverse, but as a collective, much improved upon compared to the older men we interviewed.

In Chap. 10, we find that there is a substantial difference concerning bisexual relationships: Finding that older men sexualize men and romanticize women more than younger men, often holding quite stereotypical views about women in particular. There was still evidence of bisexual burden in the older men's lives in terms of attitudes of others toward their partners—although we again found a significant improvement among younger men.

We also found that many participants held relatively conservative views about sex and relationships, particularly in relation to monogamy. This contrasts with what the literature has traditionally found about bisexuals being more open to polyamorous relationships (Kleese 2005). We attribute this difference to variations in sampling procedures, given that the bisexuals communities used to recruit participants in other research have dominant discourses of nonmonogamy (Burleson 2005; Klesse 2005).

Chapter 2
Bisexuality: It is Complicated

We begin this chapter with a simple fact: bisexuality exists. Whatever the constellation of sexual and emotional desires and behaviors that constitutes it, scientifically and socially speaking, some people are bisexual (Rullo et al. 2014). Long before there was a cultural awareness that bisexuality exists as a non-pathological and stable orientation among a significant fraction of the population, sexologists were studying the phenomenon. Over a century ago, Freud wrote (1905: 261–262):

> It is well known that at all times there have been, as there still are, human beings who can take as their sexual objects persons of either sex without the one trend interfering with the other. We call these people "bisexual" and accept the fact of their existence without wondering too much about it. ... But we have come to know that all human beings are bisexual in this sense and that their libido is distributed between objects of both sexes, either in a manifest or latent form.

While society now accepts that bisexuality exists, it is less clear, even among sexologists, what exactly it is. If a man generally has heterosexual desire, but has once had sexual thoughts for other men, does that make him bisexual? Is a person bisexual because they once, decades ago, masturbated to the thought of a different sex to their preferred one? Is a person bisexual if they are romantically attracted to males but sexually attracted to females? Or does one have to be equally attracted to men and women to be considered bisexual? The answers to these questions are rooted in social perception and social categorizing. There is no definitive answer.

The social perception of what constitutes bisexuality is also different cross-culturally (Carrillo 2002), as well as historically within any given culture. For example, two men kissing in Britain during the 1980s would have resulted in people thinking that they were gay. Yet research is starting to suggest that kissing between two young straight men in Britain today is not perceived as a gay act (see Anderson et al. 2012); instead, it is a common act of homosocial bonding among hetrosexual men in some contexts. In order to highlight the importance of social and historical context in defining sexuality, consider the following narrative.

Jake is 16. He lives with his mother and sister in a somewhat economically deprived area in England. Jake has a rich network of friends, both male and female. He grew up in the same neighborhood as his best friend, Tom. Jake frequently expresses his love for Tom in a public manner. This is evident when seeing them interact socially, but the frequency of it is also quantifiable through examination of his Facebook posts, where Jake posts on Tom's wall with terms of love—expressions of endearment that Tom reciprocates.

During an interview for a different research project (Anderson 2011a), Jake said that he was preparing to go on a 13-day holiday to Spain with Tom. When he was questioned about whether he feared that they might fight, being together for that length of time, he answered, "No mate, we're too close for that." Highlighting their closeness, Jake added that he was spending Saturday night with Tom. After going out and drinking with friends, Jake and Tom would return to Jake's house, where they would share a bed and cuddle. They have spent many nights, both drunk and sober, in bed together. They regularly express their emotional bond privately as well. Just one example is the text Tom sent Jake after a week apart from each other: "Love you, this week has made me realise how weak I can be without you. And I don't like not being with you :."

At this point, many readers will think Jake is either gay or bisexual, or possibly closeted with same-sex desires. Indeed, the near-impossibility of proving a negative means that we cannot be certain that he does not harbor same-sex desires. But we can say that Jake publically identifies as heterosexual and that his peers perceive him as heterosexual. This is despite them having full knowledge of his intimacy with Tom. Furthermore, Jake is not much different than other heterosexual boys that we have researched in the UK (Anderson and McCormack 2014). He is a normal, typical heterosexual teenager in England. This includes having a girlfriend, Amy. When asked about Amy's views on his going on holiday with Tom, he responds, "She knows how close we are. She's gotta share me."

While Jake still lives in a heterosexist culture, the erosion of homohysteria offers him the opportunity to have the same level of emotional and physical intimacy with his best male friend as with his female partner. Jake does not fear discussing this type of emotional intimacy because there is less stigma about being thought gay. This is something that we have documented empirically; finding that sharing strong emotional bonds, which can manifest into physical affection, such as cuddling with a male friend in bed, is common practice for heterosexual male athletes in the UK (Anderson and McCormack 2014). While this had been the case in earlier times (see Ibson 2002), physical tactility between men had become stigmatized and heavily censured in the late 20th century (see Chap. 5 for a full discussion of this).

For those readers who have not experienced this social dynamic – those who are older, or who live in a setting where young men still emphatically avoid being socially perceived as gay – some element of homosexuality or bisexuality will likely be read into Jake's narrative. This illustrates the importance of cultural perspective in understanding behavior. Those having their adolescence in the 1980s will more likely find Jake's behaviors indicative of homosexuality, while those having their adolescence today, will see it as an acceptable way to express friendship.

We hope this narrative has highlighted that personal frameworks for categorizing people by their behaviors into a sexual identity category are not necessarily accurate —our personal typologies of sexuality are dependent upon the culture we are born in, the time in which we experienced our adolescence, and our own intellectual views of the social world. Individuals' perspectives are tied to cultural norms and social values. Sexualities are generational (Plummer 2010).

Jake's narrative also highlights that regardless of how we define sexual identity categories – be it gay, straight, bisexual or other – our definitions are dependent on a range of social factors, making our task of defining bisexuality all the harder. This highlights the complexity of bisexuality: It is much easier to define what it means to be exclusively gay or exclusively straight. This chapter therefore examines tough, slippery, and, for sociologists, highly contentious question of what, precisely, sexuality is.

Defining Sexuality

Sexuality is a complex and multi-faceted phenomenon. It is not easy to define, and this is exacerbated by the use of different terminologies across academic disciplines. The term *sexual orientation*, for example, has a different meaning in sociology and psychology. Sociologists generally use sexual orientation to describe sexual desires or attractions, regardless of whether those desires are expressed to other people or acted upon. Sexual orientation tends to indicate the gendered-direction of one's sexual desires, rather than other components such as age. Psychologists, however, often use orientation to describe a constellation of factors related to the total umbrella of sexuality. The American Psychological Association (APA: 2008) defines sexual orientation as

> an enduring pattern of emotional, romantic, and/or sexual attractions to men, women, or both sexes. Sexual orientation also refers to a person's sense of identity based on those attractions, related behaviors, and membership in a community of others who share those attractions.

Accordingly, the psychological definition of orientation is muddled, containing a variety of conceptually distinct constructs. Given this, and our grounding as sociologists, we use a sociological definition of sexual orientation as referring to sexual desire. We think Bailey (2009: 44) describes it well by saying, "The term sexual orientation connotes a mechanism, analogous to a compass that directs our sexuality." We then use the term 'sexuality' to relate to our overarching understandings of the sexual: sexual behavior, public, and personal sexual identities.

Examining the Components of Sexuality

While *sexuality* is helpful as an umbrella term to discuss the sexual, it is not sufficient to understand the complexity of human desire. For example, the difference between *identity* and *orientation* is a simple yet fundamental component of sexuality. Savin-Williams (1998: 3) describes it as a "distinction between an ever-present, invariant, biological and psychological truth (sexual orientation) and a historically and culturally located social construction (sexual identity)." Importantly, research shows that while the two are strongly correlated, there is a significant group of people that maintain same-sex sexual desires without identifying as a sexual minority (Savin-Williams 2001a).

The other key component is sexual *behaviors* which are the sexual acts people engage in. Again, while there is close correlation with identity and orientation, there can be significant differences between these—not least people who have taken virginity pledges, heterosexuals that are segregated from the opposite sex in prison or the army, or homosexuals who are in the closet.

There is a social awareness in the US and the UK about the potential differences between a person's sexual orientation, their social identity and the behaviors they engage in. For example, the 'down low' is a popular term that describes ostensibly heterosexual (closeted) men who seek same-sex sex in private (Boykin 2005), where there is a disjuncture between identity and orientation. While the conceptualization of behavior, identity, and orientation are helpful in exploring different aspects of sexuality, they also neglect other integral components—most significantly who one is emotionally, romantically, and even socially attracted to. We discuss these under the umbrella term of *emotional orientation*.

These neglected aspects are particularly important in the context of our research because their erasure also serves to marginalize bisexuality. If emotional, social, and romantic attraction were accounted for, it would increase the percentage of people that could potentially classify as bisexual and provide greater recognition of the complexity of sexuality—making a monosexist culture harder to legitimize. In Table 2.1, we provide a set of definitions that we use throughout the book.

In the following sections, we examine sexuality from a holistic perspective, developing a framework in which bisexuality can be fully realized and incorporated into understandings of human sexuality. We start with a more detailed examination of attraction, behavior, and identity before examining components of sexuality that receive less attention.

Table 2.1 Definitions

Sexuality is an umbrella term for all aspects of sexual direction, including one's attractions, behaviors, identities and emotional orientation.
Sexual orientation refers to the gendered direction of one's sexual attractions.
Sexual attraction refers to the sexual desires a person has. It is assumed to be consistent with one's masturbatory fantasies.
Sexual identity refers to how one views their own sexuality in light of cultural understandings of sexuality.
Sexual behavior refers to what consensual sexual acts one engages in.
Emotional orientation refers to the gendered-direction of one's desires for emotional intimacy.

Sexual Attraction

Sexual attraction serves as the groundwork for defining all other aspects of sexuality (LeVay 2011). Sexual attraction is a fundamental component of one's sexual orientation. While a part of the body or a particular person may elicit sexual arousal, a central characteristic of the organization of sexuality is the gender of the person involved. For most people, whether we are attracted to men, women, or both is a central issue in these desires. Males who have sexual desire for males are described as having "same-sex" attractions and males who desire females have "opposite-sex" attraction.

Research surveying attraction normally asks about degrees of sexual attraction to one's own or the opposite sex. Sometimes these surveys are framed as "sexual feelings" or "sexual desires" and questions about sexual attraction are normally logged on a scale from "entirely heterosexual (attracted to persons of the opposite sex)" to "entirely homosexual (attracted to persons of the same sex)."

However, talk about the "same" sex or the "opposite" sex is problematic as it reproduces a sex binary that does not recognize the diversity of human bodies (Fausto-Sterling 2000). Indeed, Fausto-Sterling (1993) has argued that there are five sexes, taking account of various forms of intersex bodies. Diamond simply describes attraction as being person-based, rather than being a binary assessment (2009). Despite this, the use of same and opposite continues, partly because it is cumbersome to do otherwise. In this book, we try to avoid reproducing binaristic norms while recognizing the issue of readability. To this end, we use the vocabulary of "same," and "different," or "other," where possible, and "opposite" only when it refers to specific literature that uses the term.

We recognize that this approach is flawed by its focus on attraction to people with normative gender identities. That is, by focusing on attraction to men and women, attraction to trans people is not positioned as legitimate within the scientific literature (Weinrich 2014a). In a wide-ranging and insightful discussion of multi-dimensional ways to measure sexual orientation, Weinrich (2014b) discusses important new methodological approaches that can incorporate sexual desire for non-cisgendered people in ways that do not prove unwieldy in practice. Recognizing the limitations of the current context, he frames this as an ideal component of sexualities research: we had not encountered the methods Weinrich discusses when we collected data, and thus we use an adapted model of the Klein Sexual Orientation Grid. We discuss further the implications of using such approaches in the conclusion.

We also highlight that part of the centrality of sexual attraction is attributable to how humans have evolved. This explains why sexual attraction toward an individual is determined almost instantly. Research shows that it is possible to determine someone's gender, age, and race in milliseconds (Brewster et al. 2010). Attraction to the face occurs at a similar speed (Thornhill and Gangestad 1998), although it is extremely difficult to describe verbally what is found attractive in a face.

In order to understand the phenomenon of speed of facial attraction, scientists have focused on facial symmetry (Thornhill and Gangestad 1998; Gangestad and Simpson 2000). These studies find that not only are symmetrical faces more attractive, but that humans have a specialized subconscious mechanism for detecting symmetry (Penton-Voak et al. 2003). Supporting this, people find faces more attractive when they have been digitally manipulated to be more symmetrical (Rhodes et al. 2001; Perrett et al. 1999).

It might be argued that this is not due to an innate process, but is instead the result of social conditioning—that symmetry is culturally esteemed and we thus learn to understand symmetry as beautiful. However, evidence supporting the evolutionary base finds that these studies are valid across cultures (Rhodes et al. 2001). Studies have also found a preference for symmetry in newborns (Slater et al. 1998). Here, babies spent longer looking at the more symmetrical faces, regardless of the gender, race, or age of the face they were shown. This suggests that notions of human beauty are somewhat based on innate traits, that are then likely augmented by culture. Beauty may not therefore just reside in the eye of the beholder, it lies in the human condition.

Facial attractiveness is not, of course, solely the result of facial symmetry or self-representation alone. A host of other factors are considered in those milliseconds of initial judgment, including facial characteristics such as a small nose and high forehead, prominent cheekbones, and arched eyebrows (Cunningham 1986; Cunningham et al. 1990). It is possible that some of these characteristics are the result of social processes. Markers of age are also visible on a face, and these might be culturally sexualized or not—not least depending on the gender of the person.

Smell also plays a role in the determination of attractiveness. Although stronger in women, both sexes report that body scent has a significant influence on sexual interest in a person (Herz and Cahill 1997; Lübke and Pause 2015; Martins et al. 2015). Thornhill and Gangestad (1999) demonstrate the power of smell in sexual attraction in their renowned T-shirt experiments. In one experiment, men wore T-shirts for several days, without using scented products or washing. After a few days of wearing the shirts, women were asked to smell the shirts blindfolded, ranking the odor from most desirable to least. There was general agreement in how women ranked the smell from the T-shirts. Significantly, when the women were then asked to rank the men in order of physical attractiveness by looking at photos of the men, those that were rated highest for smell were also *independently* ranked as more attractive visually. Potentially an evolutionary mechanism to motivate mating with males who possess genes that increase offspring viability or other components of offspring fitness (Møller and Alatalo 1999), it seems that attractive people smell good.

Bodies are important to sexual attraction as well. This explains how gay and bisexual men can find sexual partners on Grindr and other hook-up apps, being attracted to the physical body prior to meeting the person. The form this sexual attraction takes is likely a product of both biological and cultural conditioning (Frederick et al. 2005). For example, muscle definition, youthfulness, and hairless bodies are all esteemed in contemporary gay male culture, whereas muscles and a hairy chest have been socially valued in prior decades (Coad 2008). Yet evolutionary psychologists also suggest that the shoulder-to-hip ratio is important in men's sexual attractiveness, theorizing it to serve as a cue of genetic and social fitness and arguing that women have evolved preference for muscularity (see Frederick and Haselton 2007). It is argued that evolutionary processes attach increased importance to particular body types (e.g. muscularity) which are then reproduced and emphasized by social processes (Frederick et al. 2005).

Collectively, these components of sexual desire suggest that a significant amount of rapid automatic processing of physical characteristics occurs when two people meet and that this is important in determining sexual attraction. Before we begin social and psychological interactions with another person, we are first attracted or repelled by their biology. It is normally this immediate sense of attraction that gets one 'in the door' to a romantic relationship, not 'how nice' someone is. It is thus this sexual attraction—rooted in deep-seated biology—which attracts us to a person and makes us want to engage in sexual behaviors.

Sexual Repulsion

While sexual attraction is vital to understanding sexuality, it may be just one component of what is important in sexual desire. There is an argument that while sexuality tends to be about *attraction to*, it is also influenced by *aversion from* particular sexual acts or bodies. This idea is currently being studied by Michael Bailey, who theorizes that sexual aversion can also play a role in people's sexuality. Smell might be an important component in this (Herz and Inzlicht 2002; Thornhill and Gangestad 1999).

The thesis of combining attraction to and aversion from has particular importance for thinking about bisexuality. Traditionally, bisexuality is conceived as *attraction to* both males and females. However, it might also be the case that some bisexuals have an attraction to one sex but rather than having a strong attraction to the other sex, they just lack an aversion to it. There might, then, be two forms of bisexuality: one with strong sexual desires directed at males and females, and another which is the latent effect of an absence of repulsion for one sex (Bailey 2011). While not being averse to one sex may not in itself be a sexual orientation, it nonetheless complicates how we study sexuality.

Supporting the notion that sexuality is in part about repulsion or lack of it, Stief et al. (2014) use online survey data to suggest that while sexual orientation is normally independent of personality factors, it might nonetheless play a role for bisexuals. They find that certain personalities seek sex with both sexes, despite only being sexually responsive to one. This is because they are thought to maintain personalities which seek sexual sensations and sexual excitability. Compared to heterosexual and homosexual participants, bisexual participants had higher levels of both sexual sensation seeking and sexual curiosity, particularly among bisexual women (see Lippa 2007). Similarly, Rieger et al. (2014) found that bisexual-identified men were higher in "sexual curiosity" than other groups, and those high in sexual curiosity were more likely to show bisexual arousal patterns—likely attributable to a lack of repulsion. Together, these studies indicate that for some people bisexual behaviour might be a lack of repulsion alongside value placed in sexual novelty.

Sexual Behavior

Sexual behavior refers to the sexual acts one engages in. It is often framed as sexual contact, but this can be misleading as it does not have to include another person (e.g. masturbation). Similarly, we do not include non-consensual sex here as it is not sought by the victim involved. Sexual acts with another are complicated not just by whether that person consented but also by how those acts are interpreted. This is exemplified by kissing. Young straight male university students in the United Kingdom regularly kiss each other on the lips, and even use tongues on occasion (Anderson et al. 2012). While people normally understand prolonged kissing as a sexual act, these men interpret these behaviors as a form of nonsexual, humorus, social bonding. Thus, sexual behavior is not just about acts but about context, meaning and interpretation as well.

Definitional issues persist in many areas of sexual behavior. Everyone agrees that having intercourse with another person is a sexual behavior, yet what does intercourse entail? While it is generally accepted that penile-vaginal or penile-anal penetration is sexual intercourse, there is less consensus for other behaviors. In a study of 599 undergraduate students, Sanders and Reinisch (1999) reported that 60% of respondents would not class oral-genital contact as "having sex." Is it a sexual act if two men masturbate alongside each other without touching? What if they masturbate each other for a short period of time? Highlighting the diversity of definitions of "having sex," Pitts and Rahman (2001) found that 6% of their participants regarded touching breasts and nipples as having constituted sex.

These issues are made more complex in the digital world. In Anderson's (2012) study on monogamy, he found that young men had no clear agreement on what it meant to behave sexually because they disagreed over the relevance of online sexual activities. There was no agreement as to whether masturbating to porn counted as a sexual behavior, nor whether masturbating with another person on webcam did. There was just as much debate as to whether sexting is a sexual behavior. These digital forms of interaction make even this most basic label of sexual behavior a slippery definitional category. Digital technologies call the nature of reality into question (Waskul 2003), merging fantasy and behavior in ways that trouble the discrete categorization of these components of sexuality.

It is also important to recognize that consensual sexual behaviors are not necessarily indicative of sexual orientation, either. One need only consider porn stars to recognize that the doing of sexual acts does not necessarily connote the preferred sexual experiences of the actors. For example, it is well known that mainstream gay porn star, Jeff Striker, is heterosexual, and by having gay sex on camera he is doing what is commonly called "gay for pay." Levy (2006) calls this performative bisexuality, arguing that an increase in bisexuality in porn does not mean that bisexuality itself is becoming more socially acceptable.

Sexual Identity

Sexual identity refers to our personal conception of our sexual selves. It is a crucial component of sexuality because it is the way by which we make sense of our desires and behaviors. While many people develop an understanding of their sexual identity through the process of having sex (Herdt and Boxer 1993; Sears 1991), Dubé (2000) highlights that many sexual minority males arrive at a gay identity without engaging in sexual intercourse. Sexual identities are complex, and incorporate a range of feelings and behaviors related to sex, emotional attachments, and romance.

People have deep, emotional attachments to their sexual identity, as it helps people understand their personal, emotional, and erotic lives (Plummer 1995). While sexual identities are socially constructed and dependent on the historical period in which we live, most people do not feel that they choose their identity. Appiah (2005: 69) observes:

> ... if all there is to an identity is a conventional set of behaviours, and you are capable of them, then you can choose whether to adopt the identity. But when the criteria for ascribing a certain identity include things over which you have no control – as in the case with gender, race and sexual orientation – then whether you identify with that identity, whether, for example, you think of yourself as gay and act sometimes as a gay person, is not only up to you.

While we make behavioral choices, it is culture which determines the possible identity labels available to us; and it is culture which determines how we are perceived and thus treated for that identity. As Rust (1992: 366) argues, "the consequences of identity are both social and political."

The significance of identity is highlighted by its use in most research on sexual orientation, including routine monitoring forms and government and other social survey questions. In the UK, the Office for National Statistics (ONS 2009) defines sexual identity in the following way:

> Self-perceived sexual identity is a subjective view of oneself. Essentially, it is about what a person is, not what they do. It is about the inner sense of self, and perhaps sharing a collective social identity with a group of other people. The question on sexual identity is asked as an opinion question ... it is up to respondents to decide how they define themselves.

Identities can also change. A relatively recent example of this is the emergence of the notion of asexuality (Bogaert 2012). Today, many individuals identify with this label and are asexual not just through absence of sexual desire, but by identity.

However, before the cultural adoption of this label they were more likely to consider themselves heterosexual with a low (or non-existent) sex drive.

There is a central problem with identity labels in that they can easily consume all other aspects of a person's sexuality. We readily assume that if, for example, one identifies as heterosexual, it means that they only have sex with members of the opposite sex; that they only fall in love with members of the opposite sex; and that they relate to members of the opposite sex more intensely. How much this is attributable to living in a monosexist culture is debatable—what is key is that none of these assumptions necessarily follow a sexual identity label.

Romantic Love

While it is undoubtedly possible for sexual activity to occur without emotional attachment, modern understandings of sexuality are deeply entwined with love (Giddens 1992). Defining love, however, proves more challenging than defining all other aspects of sexuality.

Highlighting its complexity, the Ancient Greeks had four different types of love: *philía, éros, agápe,* and *storgē*. Although precise meanings are hard to interpret because these terms are contextualized according to our current culture, our understanding is that *philía* refers to the love of a friend; *éros* refers to sexual passion; *agápe* refers to the romantic love of one's partner; and *storgē* refers to the love of a child.

It is interesting to note that these do not map neatly onto a definition of emotional attraction. For some, the emotional attraction that is linked to sexuality will necessarily conflate *eros* and *agape*; yet for others, sexual passion soon dissipates while romantic love for a partner endures. Sexual attraction is likely to over-inflate notions of romantic love: sexual desires are likely to influence people to think they love someone, when they simply want to have sex with them (Anderson 2012). Engaging in sexual behavior may lead a "drug-like state," but it is not in-and-of itself a form of romantic love.

Whatever romantic love is, the importance and centrality of love in our social lives is clear. This is evidenced not only by the intensity of joy felt when 'falling' in love with a person, but also by the extreme emotional jealousy and pain felt when that attachment is threatened or taken from us. Indeed, research shows that when one's long-term love partner dies, the chances of the surviving partner dying dramatically rise (Martikainen and Valkonen 1996), something known as the widowhood effect. The worth of love is measured not just by the joy it provides, but also the intense sorrow experienced when romantic relationships are lost or taken away.

Sociologists of health describe loving relationships as vital to well-being. Kontula and Haavio-Manila (2004: 81) highlight the social necessity of these relationships, writing:

The implication of not having a long term romantic relationship is loneliness. The lack of alternative outlets for emotional expression and affective attachments has increased the personal stakes of not only finding a partner but also choosing one who will provide a continuing source of emotional fulfillment.

Overstating the importance of romantic relationships above other forms of intimacy, a clearer statement is that romantic love is a dynamic emotional state, constantly changing in type, intensity, and meaning. Love includes evolutionary, social and historical factors that compel people to be with one another in meaningful and semi-enduring ways. So, notwithstanding the complexity discussed above, our working definition of romantic love is that it is in general a relationship between consenting adults, in which goods, services, emotions and needs are exchanged and met. It is a form of relationship that is personally, socially and sometimes legally privileged above other equally valid types of love. It normally occurs with sexual activity, at least at the outset, but sexual activity is not required, and quite often, long-term romantic love lacks a sexual component after the initial few months or years. It also tends to be correlated with the person's sexual orientation.

Distinguishing Romance from Bromance

Whereas the concept of romance indicates both sexual and emotional attraction, emotional infatuations without any sexual desire have occurred across cultures and historical time periods (see Diamond 2003; Jensen 1999; Nardi 1999). Diamond (2003) argues persuasively that sexual intercourse and emotional attachment are "functionally independent"—just as it is possible to engage in sexual intercourse without developing feelings for a person, so too can love develop in the absence of sex. Diamond highlights that while emotional infatuation will manifest differently according to cultural context, it emerged as an evolutionary product of bonding:

> Research has demonstrated that the distinct behaviors and intense feelings associated with affectional bonds are governed not only by culture and socialization but also by evolved, neurochemically mediated processes that are a fundamental legacy of humans' mammalian heritage…Just as sexual desire is a species-typical phenomenon with both social and biological underpinnings, so too is emotional affection (Diamond 2003: 173).

Klein (1993) recognized the independence of emotional attraction from sexual attraction by providing a measure of "emotional preference" alongside "sexual preference" in his scale of sexuality (see Chap. 3). This recognizes that individuals will have their emotional attractions oriented toward either men, women or both. We call this an *emotional orientation*—defining it as the gendered-direction of one's desires for emotional intimacy (see also Savin-Williams 2014).

Whether emotional orientation is seen as an aspect of sexuality is a question of definition. If sexuality refers to sexual desires, than one's emotional orientation is excluded. But given that most people seek a partner that they are both emotionally and sexually attracted to, it might be reasonable to consider emotional orientation as an aspect of sexual orientation. Indeed, there is evidence that the one's romantic partner being one's primary attachment has evolutionary benefits (see Fisher 2000). From a sociological perspective, the value of emotional orientation will be heightened in contemporary culture where romantic partnerships are privileged as the ideal form of relationship; where one's sexual partner is also deemed to be one's primary attachment and "best friend" (Giddens 1992).

This association was reinforced by the social censure of close male friendships throughout the latter half of the 20th century. In this context, men were prevented from having open and honest emotional relationships with other men. As a consequence of fearing homosexualization or being socially perceived as unmasculine, American males have been discouraged from discussing love, fear and values with friends (Komarovsky 1974; Pleck 1975). Morin and Garfinkle (1978) suggested that the fear of being labeled homosexual—what we call homohysteria—interferes with the development of intimacy between men: that men have not known what it means to love and care for a friend without "the shadow of some guilt and fear of peer ridicule" (Lewis 1978: 108). Indeed, men have been so alienated from each other that Jourard (1971) showed that self-disclosure, a vital component of emotional intimacy, was utterly lacking between males. Instead, young men knew that they had a friendship with another male when they "did stuff" together. Conversely, women's friendships are defined by sharing emotions and secrets.

While these findings were true for the latter half of the twentieth century (e.g. Kimmel 1994), the transformation of intimacy in US and UK cultures means that this is no longer the case. Decreasing homophobia in the 21st century (Clements and Field 2014; Keleher and Smith 2012) has resulted in many men, particularly younger men, no longer caring if engaging in emotional conversations or other feminized activities render them gay in other people's eyes (McCormack and Anderson 2014). This has provided the intellectual space for men to develop profound emotional bonds with male friends, and the social dynamic to express their feelings. These feelings can include confusion about sexual desires, greater willingness to be open about sexually permissive attitudes, and the opportunity to discuss sexuality as a complex matrix rather than a simplistic binary (Anderson and Adams 2011).

The increasing importance of male bonds is also the result of other social changes. Contemporary society is currently witnessing the breakdown of long-term monogamy, with increasing numbers of people either living alone or marrying later in life (Arnett 2004). In this context, close friendship bonds become more important and people have more time to nurture these emotional connections. Without the responsibilities of early marriage and fatherhood in emerging adulthood, and the boundaries of men's friendships far less policed, men have the physical, social, and psychological space to develop profound friendships with other men.

The initial stages of friendship are relatively easy for millennial youth—doing "stuff" together, like sports, video games, drinking, exercising, shopping, and eating out, facilitates the possibilities of making new friends. However, they also have the opportunity to form strong, deep emotional relationships based on emotional disclosure with one another. This intimacy between heterosexual young men, documented extensively in our own research in the US and the UK, is often self-labeled a bromance (Anderson 2014). These relationships can be as emotionally deep as they are with their sexual partners – sometimes even deeper. It is this type of emotional intimacy that 16-year old Jake had with his best friend Tom, profiled in the introduction to this chapter. At the time of writing it is difficult to discuss prevalence of such behaviors as there is a dearth of research examining such friendships. There is evidence that these behaviors may be less pronounced in the US (see Way 2011), and we are aware of research currently under development that finds bromances increasingly embedded in the UK culture.

Naming these friendships as bromances permits one to step outside gendered boundaries (Anderson 2014). Young men in bromances say that they can express fear and other emotions as well as love, without worrying about social stigma. These relationships also enable physical tactility, often surpassing the physical closeness they engage in with women. Highlighting this, when we conducted forty interviews with heterosexual male undergraduate athletes at a British university about their homosocial practices, we found that these men could share beds, cuddle and even spoon—all without risking their socially perceived heterosexual identity (Anderson and McCormack 2014). This occurred in particular friendship circles, and tended to be a sign of group inclusion within a friendship network.

When we lecture on the topic we propose to our students that homosocial bromances frequently eclipse heterosexual romances. We ask the women in our classes how many of them find that they are often the second choice compared to their boyfriend's bromance—many women raise their hands. In one of these recent classes a female student was asked, "If he had to choose you or him, who do you think he'd choose?" "Him," she said, "without a doubt." In work not yet published, this topic is being examined by Stefan Robinson and Eric Anderson among heterosexual male athletes who unanimously report that the love they maintain for their bromance can be as strong and even eclipse the love they feel for their female romantic partners.

The love that young men show for one another today extends beyond their own private conversations, too. Social media, particularly Facebook, is bursting with florid expressions of emotions by young straight men (see Scoats 2015). It is common for these men to list themselves as "in a relationship" with their best male friend. Others show their love by listing their friends on Facebook as family members. Here, they either put down that their friends are "brothers" or they designate them with some other relationship label. Many more post hearts ("<3"), kisses ("xx") and touching emotional statements to each other. These messages are visible to all of their hundreds of Facebook friends. These men express intimacy for others in ways their forefathers were not permitted (Anderson 2014), resulting in open discussion and complex understanding of sexual behaviors and identities that were once erased or stigmatized.

The significance of bromances for our understandings of bisexuality can be seen by considering Klein's (1993) model of bisexuality. His model recognizes the importance of romantic relationships in any sexual identity, so heterosexual men's engagement in loving same-sex platonic relationships can impact upon the recognition of bisexual identities. Evidencing this, Anderson and Adams (2011) find that men who engage in these bromances discuss the legitimacy of bisexuality as a sexual identity, and even see some component of bisexuality in their own lives. Most of the men in this research understood bisexuality to encompass a spectrum of variables, and perhaps this is why nearly all of the men interviewed recognized some bisexuality in themselves. "I think we're all bisexual to some degree," Sean said. "I mean, I don't think it's purely a physical thing, I think it's an emotional thing, too." When asked to expand upon this idea of bisexuality being a universal sexuality, he said (p. 13), "All I'm saying is it's more complicated than just the physical."

These relationships are about love and desire, just not of a sexual kind. While it can be paired with sexual desires, some straight men feel jealousy that gay men are able to relate to each other with ease and perhaps more homogeneity than opposite-sex couples can. While this is likely one of the least important variables to describe as a constituent of one's sexuality, this may well relate to sexual drive—with those with lower sexual drives valuing emotional orientation more highly than those who have strong sexual desires. Even so, understanding the differences between romances and bromances needs further research, particularly regarding how they intersect with bisexuality. For example, little is known about whether bisexuals face difficulties in navigating such friendships, and how differences between the forms of relationship are experienced.

Types of Bisexuality

As the preceding section exemplifies, defining sexuality is a difficult and complex task. Because of these complexities, there are multiple types of bisexuality (see Yoshino 2000), where each variation is based on the aspects of sexuality discussed above, but with different components maintaining varying levels of importance across the definitions. Highlighting this, one study identified 34 different conceptualizations of bisexuality (Rullo 2010, cited in Rullo et al. 2014).

The most commonplace understanding of bisexuality is where someone maintains desires for men and women and publicly identifies as bisexual, yet people both call themselves and are called bisexual for reasons other than where their sexual attractions lie. For example, one form of bisexuality comes from gay men calling themselves bisexual in order to avoid the further stigma of being totally homosexual. This labeling of bisexuality privileges self-identity over attraction or behavior (Guittar 2013). Another comes from Latin American cultures which permit men to maintain a heterosexual label if they penetrate, but are not penetrated by other men (Lancaster 1986). These men could be labeled bisexual, but this would require the privileging of behavior over other components.

Bisexuality can also be seen in ritual behaviors of various cultures. Ritual bisexuality occurs with the Sambia of Papua-New Guinea (Herdt 1981), a pseudonym given by Herdt. Here, younger males fellate older men in order to ingest their "masculinizing" semen, where performing the act is the way to enter adulthood and achieve a position in the tribe. While Classical Greece and Rome are often cited for similar patterns, Trumbach (1998) argues that this also characterized pre-modern England. To label this behavior as bisexual would require only considering the behavior component, ignoring identity and attraction as well as the social context.

Situational bisexuality is another form that bisexuality can take. Here, individuals have sex with same-sex partners in prisons or other single-sex total-institutions (Kunzel 2002), like same-sex boarding schools. Situational bisexuality highlights the difference between actively desiring same-sex partners and seeking them out when opposite-sex partners are available, versus having sex with partners of the same-sex because opposite-sex partners are not available. To label situational bisexuality as plain bisexuality would be to privilege behavior over self-identity or attraction.

There are also those who engage in same-sex behavior because of financial need. These individuals are sometimes known as being "gay for pay." Then, there are labels which privilege self-identity over behaviors or attraction, one might consider the term bi-curious or questioning among these types of identity-privileging labels.

Yet there are also men who engage in the behaviors but reject identity labels. Savin-Williams (2005) contends that this is an increasingly common occurrence among sexual minority youth, and it has also been documented in other sexual minority populations. For example, Boykin (2005) discusses African-American men who have sex with same-sex partners while maintaining a heterosexual identify, describing themselves as "on the down low." These men clearly privilege their sexual identity over their sexual behaviors (see Carrillo in press).

Defining bisexuality is thus complex for a whole host of reasons. First, the complexity of sexuality more generally problematizes any simplistic understanding of bisexuality. Bisexuality is also difficult to define in relation to homo or heterosexuality, particularly as these relationships vary significantly according to the levels of homohysteria and the generational understandings of sexuality (Plummer 2010). Furthermore, any definition of bisexuality is dependent on what component of sexuality is given greater significance. This definitional slippage makes measuring bisexuality in the individual or population a rather difficult task.

Chapter 3
Measuring and Surveying Bisexuality

A fundamental component of studying any phenomenon is the ability to measure it, yet measuring sexuality, sexual identities and attitudes toward them is difficult (Matsuda et al. 2014). It is challenging not just because of the complex social and cultural patterns of how people identify, but also because people's identities sometimes change over time. It is further complicated by the fact that many people are not open about their sexual minority status. Matters are further complicated when one considers the complexity of sexuality and whether they are measuring behavior, identity, orientation, or any combination of those or any other variable. Furthermore, surveys are poor indicators of the type of experience that any given bisexual is having when it concerns his sexual identity as they rarely account for the complexity of human identity.

Even so, measures of sexuality are important for both political and scientific reasons. The scientific measures are obvious – in order to study a subject, we must be able to measure it. Related to the political, increasingly, and perhaps particularly in the UK, the government and academic institutions are recognizing that comprehensive information about LGB people is required in order to develop appropriate service provision, address inequalities and allocate resources fairly. Thus, whereas it once seemed inappropriate to ask someone about their sexuality, increasingly sexuality is viewed less as a 'personal' characteristic of one's total identity and more an important component of their lives. Similar to race, gender or class, it has become a variable of importance to assure equality. Highlighting this, sexual orientation is one of seven "protected characteristics" in UK law that people, organizations and employers are forbidden from using to discriminate against a person. This is not yet the case in the United States at the time of writing.

Given the importance of measuring bisexuality, this chapter examines the problems associated with these measures. We begin with the difficulties of surveying and discuss a range of measures used in research on bisexuality. We estimate the percent of the population that is bisexual, and then explore how bisexual by desire bisexuals are. Finally, we highlight how the fluidity of sexual identity that some people have complicated these measures still further.

© Springer International Publishing Switzerland 2016
E. Anderson and M. McCormack, *The Changing Dynamics of Bisexual Men's Lives*, Focus on Sexuality Research, DOI 10.1007/978-3-319-29412-4_3

Measures of Sexual Attraction

Measuring sexualities is an endeavor fraught with difficulties. The existence of the closet is the first, widely acknowledged, problem (Seidman 2002). Individuals afraid of the stigma associated with being a sexual minority are influenced to hide their sexual orientation, even from researchers. This means that the more homophobic a culture, the more error there will be in estimating the number of sexual minorities—and the greater likelihood that measuring sexual orientation and sexual identity will produce different results (Savin-Williams 2001b). The accuracy of estimates of the LGB population, even in a culture where same-sex and other-sex attractions are looked on with equal cultural esteem, will also be affected by the fact that some individuals do not know the 'truth' of their sexuality.

Given the issue of survey data and self-reporting, some researchers use physiological techniques to measure sexuality. This includes phallometric measures that assess changes in penile circumference to various stimuli (e.g. Rieger et al. 2014). One method of doing this involves a cylindrical tube being placed over the penis so that an erection pushes air out, and the expelled air is measured and expressed as degrees of arousal to stimuli; more recently, a metal strip is placed around the penis and changes in penile circumference are measured. Functional magnetic resonance imaging (fMRI) techniques are also used to measure sexuality. These look for distinct neural activity for sexual attraction to male or female stimuli.

More recently, pupil dilation has been used as a measure of sexual orientation because pupils dilate when a person views material that sexually arouses them (Rieger and Savin-Williams 2012). While less invasive than phallometric measures and brain scanning, all three methods are expensive and slow, making it hard to recruit large or generalizable samples for such studies. Rieger et al. (2014) find that while this method is powerful for gay and straight men, there is less correspondence between pupil dilation and genital arousal for bisexual men. They also report a larger disconnect between bisexual men's subjective answers and their physiological responses, meaning that pupil dilation may be less effective at measuring bisexuality.

A scientific measure that avoids the invasiveness of phallometry and brain scanning – and does not require the showing of pornography – might come from implicit measures of *attitudes* toward sexuality. The notion is that if a person has positive or negative attitudes toward a phenomenon, linking other words or images with that phenomenon will influence how they react to it. Implicit measures have been used successfully to show racist attitudes among people who state they are not racist (Fazio and Olson 2003). Two key measures have been used for doing this: an Implicit Association Task (IAT) and a Priming Task (PT).

The IAT is a task that requires participants to categorize two words that relate to the issue at hand. Snowden et al. (2007: 559) describe the process:

> The IAT requires the person to classify two sets of words (or pictures). One set relates to the target dimension (e.g., pictures of black or white faces) and the other to the evaluative dimension (e.g., pleasant or unpleasant words). In the crucial stages of the test, the person must classify these stimuli using only two buttons. In one block of trials one button should be pressed for either black faces or pleasant words (and therefore the other button for white faces or unpleasant words), while in another block the faces are switched so that one button represents white faces and pleasant words (and the other black faces and unpleasant words).

The idea is that a person with racist attitudes will find it far easier to click the button for black faces when it is the same button they have to click for unpleasant words. If a person has no bias, there will be no difference in the time it takes to click on black faces when the words are pleasant or unpleasant.

The Priming Task is similar in that a picture of a face (either black or white) is presented shortly before a person has to categorize a word as either "pleasant" or "unpleasant." The idea is that someone with bias against black people would take longer to categorize words as "pleasant" when they were primed with a black face.

In studying the usefulness of this procedure to measuring sexual orientation, Snowden et al. (2007) measured 50 heterosexual and 25 homosexual men and their responses related to sexual orientation. In the priming task, participants classified words as either sexually attractive or unattractive. Each word was preceded by a "prime" that was a picture of either a male or a female; the hypothesis being that people who were attracted to men would classify a word as sexually attractive quicker when they had been shown a picture of a man.

In the Implicit Attitude Test, participants were asked to classify pictures as "male" or "female" and then, separately, words as "sexually attractive" or "sexually unattractive." Then, both pictures and words were shown in the same test and, for half the participants, their response had a button which they had to click for "male or sexually attractive" while the others had a shared button for "male or sexually unattractive." The test was repeated with the assignment of gender and attraction switched.

The authors found that they could predict from the implicit measures whether the participants were heterosexual or homosexual to a high degree of accuracy. Thus, for determining heterosexuality and homosexuality, this might be a particularly strong way of measuring desire. Two key benefits are that implicit measures are less invasive than physiological techniques and they do not require the showing of pornographic material. The absence of porn is a benefit because people have a range of reactions to porn—not all people find porn arousing, people who find porn arousing often have particular tastes which mean they will not be aroused by certain types of porn, and the laboratory setting may also influence peoples' enjoyment differently. Another benefit of implicit tests is that they can determine the sexual orientation of participants without asking them questions which they may be embarrassed or ashamed to answer.

Implicit measures are relatively under-researched and a key issue is how effective such measures would be with bisexual men. Snowden et al. (2007) only studied exclusively heterosexual and homosexual men, and it is unclear whether bisexual men would show no difference, less difference or even heterosexual or homosexual bias. However, recent research suggests that it can be an effective measure of bisexual identity (Snowden et al. 2015). Similarly, matters are even less clear about what would happen if one accounted for people who were at other levels on, for example, the Kinsey scale. Implicit measures also only consider sexual attraction rather than the constellation of variables that account for sexual desire, as we discussed in the previous chapter.

Finally, a more direct measure of actual desire, but one that does not require cumbersome equipment is viewing time – Lippa (2013) uses an experimental paradigm developed by Lippa et al. (2010) in which participants are asked to rate swimsuit photos of models for attractiveness, unaware that they are being timed for length of duration that they look at each model before giving their answer. This is another form of measuring implicit attraction. Whereas heterosexuals tend to look longer at opposite-sex models, those describing as bisexual tended to look with more equal time. The problem with this technique, of course, is if one speculates that they are being timed for length of observation they can consciously influence the data.

Given the problems associated with all the measures discussed above, and as sociologists, we most therefore rely on the most widespread but also the most inaccurate method of measuring sexual attraction—self-report. For these reasons, and despite the problem with measuring bisexuals with survey methods, it is a longstanding sociological and sexological method.

Surveying Bisexuality

The first large-scale social scientific exercise in determining the percentage of the population who have had or currently experience same-sex sexual attractions came from the pioneering work of Alfred Kinsey (Kinsey et al. 1948). After analyzing responses obtained in over 12,000 face-to-face interviews using the Heterosexual-Homosexual Rating Scale (which is now called the Kinsey Scale), Kinsey and his colleagues suggested that sexuality lies on a continuum and thus cannot be easily categorized (Kinsey et al. 1948).

Focusing on the fact that desire for men and women is not a binary, they presented a scale that recognized different levels of attraction for men and women—where 0 is exclusively heterosexual, 3 equally heterosexual and homosexual, 6 exclusively homosexual and the other numbers a range in-between (Fig. 3.1).

The Kinsey scale was groundbreaking for its time, and instrumental in assessing and demonstrating to the American population that sexuality was more diverse and complex than the then-belief that everyone was heterosexual. This simple scale showed that bisexuality and homosexuality were existing variations of human sexuality.

Fig. 3.1 The Kinsey scale

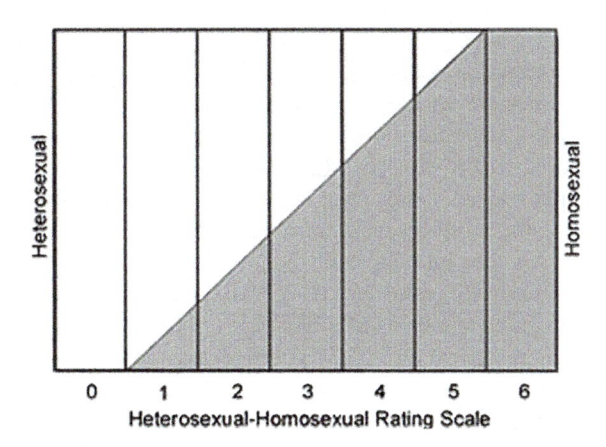

This scale provided a way of measuring sexuality that moved beyond a binary categorical model, to one that approximated a continuum. A recent internet study of 17,785 subjects in the United States and 47 other countries found strong support for Kinsey's hypothesis that sexual orientation lies on a continuum rather than discrete categories. It found a range of levels of attraction to men and women that mapped neatly onto a continuum, rather than being clustered around particular identity categories (Epstein et al. 2012). Supporting this, Savin-Williams (2014) found that when using both a 9-point scale and sexual orientation labels in the same study, there was significant overlap in the range of the scales for the sexual orientation labels (i.e. identity categories). He highlights that while the use of sexual identity labels was accurate to identify the sexual attraction of those who were exclusively gay or straight, they were far less accurate for those who recognized some level of desire for their non-preferred sex.

While Kinsey and his colleagues highlighted the complexity of sexuality, empirically documenting differences in identity, orientation and behavior, they did not incorporate this in how they measured sexuality. Thus, the first-ever wide-spread scale of human sexuality used just one dimension, conflating sexual attractions with behaviors and desires. For example, if one reads the 1948 book's "homosexual outlet" chapter, the focus is on behavior, but the legend says both psychologic and overt experience (p. 638). On pages 639–641 the classification (Kinsey 0's, 1's, etc.) seems to involve behavior and "psychic" reactions.

Masters and Johnson (1979) provide further methodological critiques concerning the arbitrary manner in which subjects were placed on Kinsey's scale. Kinsey's methodology made it possible to place people with radically different sexual histories into the same category: for example, a man with hundreds of same-sex partners, versus a man who had merely fantasized about same-sex attraction without acting on it could be allotted the same number. Others question whether the results are distorted because subjects were asked in-person about their Kinsey scale position (Gonsiorek et al. 1995).

There is also debate about the extent to which the Kinsey scale is a continuum or an expanded categorical design. Sell (1997) has noted that the seven discrete categories are an ordinal scale rather than a continuum. He also questioned whether these categories should be equally spaced. In other words, is a change from 0 to 1 equal to the change from 1 to 2? Similarly, Weinrich (2014c) highlights that intermediate values (e.g. 1–2) were permitted, and that Kinsey's use of the scale was not a self-measure from participants, but assigned by authors after interviews.

Another problem with Kinsey's scale is what we call the *zero-sum game of sexuality*. Shiveley and DeCecco (1984) argue that the Kinsey scale effectively measured homosexuality and heterosexuality against each other—where an increase in homosexual desire has a corresponding decrease in heterosexual desire, and vice versa (see also Sell 1997).

The problems of a zero-sum game approach to sexuality are apparent when one considers two people with differing attractions. For example, compare a man with a high sex drive, who is attracted to men and women equally, with a man of a low sex drive but attracted almost entirely to men. The former would likely be placed as Kinsey 3 and the latter as a Kinsey 6, despite the man with bisexual desires having more same-sex desire. These criticisms are magnified when considering bisexuality, given the increased definitional complexity when compared to heterosexuality and homosexuality.

Shiveley and DeCecco (1984) recognize this issue and argue for the measurement of homosexual and heterosexual desire independently from each other. They argue that when homosexuality and heterosexuality are measured independently, as opposed to on a continuum, the degree of homosexuality and heterosexuality can be determined.

In order to address these issues for understanding bisexuality, scholars have sought to examine sexual orientation as a construct that includes more than just sexual behavior, identity and desires wrapped up into one scale. It is also possible to account for temporal aspects of one's life. The most significant in bisexuality studies has been Klein's sexual orientation grid.

In 1985, Fritz Klein and colleagues developed the Klein Sexual Orientation Grid as a way to represent the multi-dimensional aspects of sexuality. The grid not only accounts for sexual attraction, behavior and identity, but it adds other dimensions as well. Specifically, the Klein Sexual Orientation Grid looks at seven categories of sexuality (Table 3.1).

Drawing on survey data of 200 people using Klein Sexual Orientation Grid, Lovelock (2014) suggests that the Grid offers a robust method for self-identification of respondents' sexuality. He argues that for sociological studies, self-identification should be the starting point for categorizing respondents, but that the Grid offers valuable additional insights into emotional and social behavior. Klein's Sexual Orientation Grid is therefore useful for answering the criticism that Kinsey's scale over-simplifies matters because it greatly expands upon the units measured.

Surveying Bisexuality

Table 3.1 Klein's sexual orientation grid

Variable	Past	Present	Ideal
A. Sexual Attraction			
B. Sexual Behavior			
C. Sexual Fantasies			
D. Emotional Preference			
E. Social Preference			
F. Self-Identification			
G. Straight/Gay Lifestyle			

1	2	3	4	5	6	7
Other sex only	Other sex mostly	Other sex somewhat more	Both sexes equally	Same sex somewhat more	Same sex mostly	Same sex only

Yet Klein's grid is not a resolution to all the problems related to how to assess human sexuality. Recent research highlights that many non-heterosexual people find that the scales do not account for multiple identities or for how gender identity intersects with sexual identity (Galupo et al. 2014). Galupo et al. also highlight how it fails to account for some sexual minorities lived experiences—their participants reported that they did not feel the grid provided a good account of how they experienced their sexual identities.

There are other issues with the Klein scale. For example, Weinrich et al. (1993) used factor analysis to determine that all 7 of the dimensions of sexual orientation measured by Klein's Sexual Orientation Grid seem to be measuring the same thing. In other words, the additional complexity provided by Klein did not seem to be producing a more nuanced understanding of the phenomenon. A further complicating factor is that we do not know what effect the cultural dynamics of the period of study have on the findings (McCormack and Anderson 2014; Plummer 2010). For us, the most important critique is that he still adopted a zero-sum game of sexuality.

Surveying Bisexuality in Our Research

Researchers desiring to measure sexual orientation have at their disposal a number of imperfect measurement vehicles. This is significant because it severely questions the reliability and generalizability of much quantitative research on sexual minorities (Savin-Williams 2001b). Simply put, if it is unclear what is being measured, data will be hard to interpret, and findings will only have so much value. This is one reason why there is such a strong place for qualitative research on sexualities within sociology.

Given our sociological approach to our data alongside our concern for interdisciplinary research, we sought to combine two approaches to studying the data. Our main interest was participants' lived experiences, so we asked them to explain their sexuality, personally, through in-depth interview. We then also asked them to fill out a modified Klein Grid, to give us an understanding of how they conceived of their sexuality and their sexual desires.

We were concerned about the complexity of the Klein Grid, however, particularly related to participants' ability to distinguish between multiple measures of sexuality (Galupo et al. 2014). We thus removed items C and G from Klein's Sexual Orientation Grid, as well as the 'ideal' category. This is because we assumed that items sexual fantasies and gay/straight lifestyle were already appropriately measured with other scale items and our interviews, and the 'ideal' category has little empirical necessity. We also reworded some of the questions to make it more accessible: we replaced 'desire' with a question about masturbatory fantasies.

Still, we found our participants' narratives to be more illuminating than their scales. In fact, they often contradicted their scales with their spoken narratives. Highlighting the problem of survey research over qualitative interviews, several participants found the scale difficult to fill out, asking for our assistance. We thus doubt the validity of some of their answers to the scale because they seemed not to comprehend some of it. We include our scale here (Table 3.2).

Thus, while we used the modified Klein Grid in our empirical research, we were left downtrodden by its difficulty. After the research project was over, and in the writing of this book, we consulted with multiple sexuality scholars about the

Table 3.2 Modified Klein Grid used in this research

	PAST up to a year ago	Present within last year	Future eventually
Who are you attracted to?			
Who do you have sex (any type) with?			
Who do you masturbate to?			
Who do you fall in love with?			
Who do you prefer to hang out with?			

1 = Women only
2 = Women mostly
3 = Women somewhat more
4 = Both sexes equally
5 = Men somewhat more
6 = Men mostly
7 = Men only

creation of our own measuring system. We finally devised a system that permits participants to, very simply, indicate what it is that we desire to know.

We principally sought to address the zero-sum game of sexual desire (measuring them on one scale) which does not accurately measure how many people feel about their sexual attractions. Most importantly, we wanted to take into account two related issues that others do not: asexuality and strength of desire. Asexuality is particularly hard to measure on these scales (Storms 1980), but the effect of the strength of sexual desire on identity and behavior is under-theorized in studies of sexuality. With the expansion of sexual identity categories in contemporary culture (Kuper et al. 2012; Vrangalova and Savin-Williams 2012), it is likely that asexuality will also rise in visibility and legitimacy, and it thus needs to be accounted for in studies of sexuality.

It is for this reason that we develop the sexuality thermometers. It moves us from one-dimensional models into a two-dimensional model by accounting for the strength of desire alongside the direction of desire (toward males or females). It also ameliorates the problem of the zero-sum game earlier described, and also allows for a continuum of sexual desire, rather than a discrete categorical scale like Kinsey's. Participants would be expected to put a mark measuring the strength of their desire for males and females separately, explaining it to them as measuring the heat or intensity of their desire. Importantly, we have not put a scale alongside the thermometer to avoid priming participants into trying to match percentages. A scale could be used after by the researchers to quantify the level of attraction.

The strength of our sexuality thermometers is that they enable participants to quickly and accurately describe the strength of their sexual desire in relation to each sex independently (no zero-sum game). It then also accounts for asexuality and the strength of one's sexual desires. The thermometers are simple, but yield complex data. To illustrate the use of the thermometers: If someone puts a mark at the bottom (freezing), it can reasonably be deduced that they are asexual. A mark near boiling for both men and women means that they are bisexual with a robust sex drive; while a mark in the midsection of both would indicate that they are bisexual, but with a lower sex drive.

A mark at the base of one sex and a mark anywhere up the thermometer of another would indicate monosexuality (i.e. gay or straight), but it also gives us an idea of the strength of their sexual desire: A heterosexual male might mark the base (freezing) for sexual desire for men, but only mark the sexual desire for women just above the base. Thus, he would be heterosexual but with a low sex drive. If quantification is necessary, one can simply lay over each a scale.

This model could be critiqued for the strength of sexual desire being estimates of sexual desire, and not necessarily reliable ones. This is, of course, true and is the result of adopting a continuum. We highlight that other scales have the same problem, without the benefits of the continuum approach: for example, the Kinsey scale is critiqued because there is no certainty that two people who place themselves as the same number actually have the same level of desire. Our sexuality thermometer is thus more open about its imprecision. We also highlight that while the

                    Boiling   Boiling

                    Freezing   Freezing

                Sexual Desire   Sexual Desire
                  for males   for females

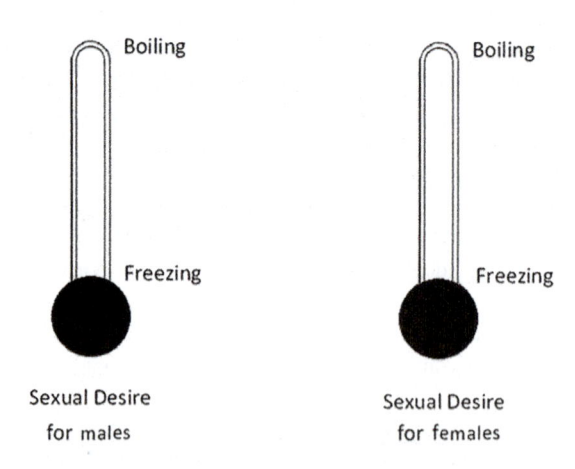

Draw a line on each thermometer to indicate the strength of your sexual desires for each sex

Fig. 3.2 Anderson McCormack sexuality thermometer

precise measures will not be accurate per se, the relationship between male and female desire for each participant will be.

Our thermometers can also be critiqued for not accounting for the age categories that one is attracted to (i.e. pedophilia (ages 10 and under), hebephilia (11–14), ephebophilia (ages 15–19), teleiophilia (sexual preference for full grown adults), gerontophilia (sexual preference for the elderly), and these are at least as culturally important as the strength of one's sexual drive or the direction(s) of their drive. However, this would be easily remedied by giving separate sets of thermometers with differing age categories assigned to them (Fig. 3.2).

Problems in Estimating the Bisexual Population

There is an understandable fascination with understanding the statistical size of the sexual minority population. In this section we first highlight the pitfalls of such statistics, before attempting an estimate ourselves. We began this chapter by explaining the difficulty of survey research, conceptually. Firstly, even if one can determine a measuring system that more accurately reflect the reality of peoples' senses of their own identities and experiences, there are other, linguistic, issues with surveys. These difficulties relate to the specific questions and how these are understood. For example, the use of "heterosexual" on a survey can be problematic as some respondents mis-read this as referring to gay people rather than straight. Furthermore, the term 'homosexual' is increasingly regarded as an imposed term of the homophobic religious right; it is therefore increasingly viewed as offensive and replaced by the more socially acceptable term of gay. Exemplifying this, The Gay and Lesbian Alliance Against Defamation (GLAAD) has put the term homosexual on its list of offensive terms, and in 2006 persuaded The Associated Press—whose stylebook is the widely used by many news organizations—to restrict use of the word. Similarly, the American Psychological Association now recommends that the term homosexual should not be used as a noun.

There is also concern about the use of the word sexual in identifying aspects of sexuality, as the word still connotes stigma for some. Labelling the question as "sexual orientation," "sexual identity," or "sexuality" might all cause concern or confusion among survey respondents. Savin-Williams and Joyner (2014) also highlight the problems of "mischievous" respondents, where group studies that consist of small numbers (such as bisexuals) can have the results significantly skewed by heterosexuals playing the role of a joker by answering as if they were a sexual minority.

Exemplifying this debate, in a March 21, 2014 Online New York Times Fashion and Style article titled "The Decline and Fall of the 'H' Word," the author, Jeremy Peters, quotes George Chauncey as saying, "'Homosexual' has the ring of 'colored' now, in the way your grandmother might have used that term, except that it hasn't been recuperated in the same way." In the same article, William Leap, a professor of anthropology at American University who studies the field of "lavender linguistics," said the offensiveness of the word stems from its medical history: "It already has all that clinical baggage heaped on it: that's the legacy of the term now."

Furthermore, there is no colloquial word to describe bisexual with cultural relevance. Whereas homosexuals can go by gay or lesbian, and heterosexuals can go by straight, there is no equivalent for bisexuals. Indeed, most of the alternative labels also end in sexual. Pansexual is often adopted, but it both ends in sexual and is sufficiently vague, while ambisexual and omnisexual are less recognized and also end with 'sexual.' Flexible implies the ability to willingly change desires, something that makes bisexuality seem less legitimate than homo or heterosexuality. Given these limitations, we settle upon the word bisexual for this book, accepting its limitations but recognizing that no widely held terminology is better and because it seems to carry little cultural baggage of medicalization and pathology.

Yet it is not just in what words are used that is important, but how they are used. Aspinal (2009) highlights that, in addressing this situation of measuring sexuality, the Office of National Standards (UK) has extensively tested survey measures (i.e. how questions are asked). This body of evidence led them to determine that the wording: "which of the options [...] best describes how you think of yourself?" is preferable to: "which of these [...] do you consider yourself to be?" as "How you think of yourself" recognizes that a process of "best fit" is involved and not one where categories are assumed to be exact descriptors of a person's sexual orientation. Other problems include using survey methods that are not representative of the population. Kinsey et al.'s (1948) research as well as that of Masters and

Johnson (1979) are criticized for failing to engage in probability sampling. Gorman et al. (2015) highlight that forthcoming data and analysis techniques that are part of the National Health Interview Survey will enable assessment of different data collection methods because it will include face-to-face data collection techniques.

Survey Results of Sexual Minority Populations

Using these measures of sexuality, various attempts have been made to measure the size of the LGB population. However, they have attempted this in diverse ways. Kinsey found that 25% of the male population had more than incidental homosexual experience or reactions in that they rated a 2–6 on his scale for a minimum of three years between the ages of 16 and 55. He found 10% of the males rated themselves at 5 or 6. In other words, under his time and age restrictions, Kinsey thus found that 15% of the male population fell within the bisexual range (Kinsey 2s, 3s, and 4s) while 10% of the male population fell within the homosexual range (Kinsey 5s and 6s).

Epstein et al. (2012) also did not use a population-based sampling method when surveying nearly 18,000 respondents with an 18-point scale (which included questions about the past and present, as well as questions about one-off fantasies). Their results also find high rates of bisexuality; only 6.2% of the respondents had a perfect straight score and only 1.2% of the respondents had a perfect gay score, leaving 92.6% of the sample with past or present attractions to both same and opposite sex individuals. Issues with sampling and definitions of bisexuality mean that it is likely that both surveys overstate the percentage of sexual minorities in the US.

Laumann et al. (1994) used a population-based survey, categorizing sexuality separately according to desire, conduct, and self-identification. Subjects were asked to complete the phrase, "In general are you sexually attracted to ..." with one of five responses: (1) only men; (2) mostly men; (3) both men and women; (4) mostly women; and (5) only women. For men 3.9% were attracted to both men and women. Like the Kinsey finding, this figure shows that bisexual men outnumber gay men, who were only reported at 2.4%.

Aspinal's (2009) population-based survey found that approximately 2% of the British population is bisexual by identity, but the figure drastically under-reports those who are bisexual by behavior. Mosher et al. (2005) found that 13% of women and 6% of men report attraction to more than one gender even though only 2.8% of women and 1.8% of men actually identified as bisexual.

Gorman et al. (2015) used the Behavioral Risk Factor Surveillance System (BRFSS) across multiple states in the U.S. to examine health disparities among sexual orientation groups. It is possible, however, to infer a percentage of the population who identify as bisexual from this data. While there 362,213 participants who identified as straight and 5,874 that identified as gay or lesbian, 3,263 identified as bisexual. Of the 412,068 participants in total (including those who refused to answer etc.), this leaves 0.8% of the survey population self-identifying as bisexual.

U.S. demographer Gary Gates at the William's Institute at the University of California, Los Angeles conducts high quality research on this topic (Gates 2011). He draws upon information from four recent national and two state-level population-based surveys. His analyses suggest among adults who identify as lesbian, gay, or bisexual, bisexuals comprise a slight majority (1.8% compared to 1.7% who identify as lesbian or gay); women are substantially more likely than men to identify as bisexual. Furthermore, estimates of those who report any lifetime same-sex sexual behavior and any same-sex sexual attraction are substantially higher than estimates of those who identify as lesbian, gay, or bisexual. An estimated 19 million Americans (8.2%) report that they have engaged in same-sex sexual behavior since turning 18 and nearly 25.6 million Americans (11%) acknowledge at least some same-sex sexual attraction. Many of these people might identify as "mostly heterosexual" (Savin-Williams and Vrangalova 2013).

In what is likely to be considered the gold standard for population-based survey research about bisexuality, Gallup Daily tracking conducted 206,186 interviews between June 1 and Dec. 30, 2012 (Gates and Newport 2013). This phenomenal number of participants makes the poll the largest single study of the distribution of the LGBT population in the U.S. It is a shame, though, that they did not use more distinct terminology in their survey. They asked, "Do you, personally, identify as lesbian, gay, bisexual, or transgender?" This, of course, makes it impossible to separate bisexuals from the other identity categories included in the question. A second limitation is that this approach measures broad self-identity, and does not measure sexual or other behavior, either past or present.

However, it is the first survey that has had large enough sample sizes to provide estimates of the LGBT population state by state. The results from this analysis counter some stereotypes that portray the LGBT community as heavily grouped in certain states. Ten percent of people in the District of Columbia identify as LGBT. Other than this state, the range in percentage of LGBT people in a State is 3.4 percentage points, from 1.7% in North Dakota to 5.1% in Hawaii. A state-by-state breakdown can be found at http://www.gallup.com/poll/160517/lgbt-percentage-highest-lowest-north-dakota.aspx.

The overall average for the United States was found to be 3.5% of the population. Given that the United States has approximately 320 million citizens that equates to a minimum of 11.2 million citizens who identified themselves as LGBT. The figure is a low estimate for a number of reasons: (1) it is impossible to survey the closet; (2) their wording could be improved; and also (3) because there exists a drop-off in LGBT identification with this poll: older people (as a cohort) maintained greater reluctance to admit to being non-heterosexual than younger cohorts. Here, the "yes" responses seem to be replaced by "don't know" responses and/or refusals to answers, rather than simply saying "no" in the older groups.

If the weights of the younger cohorts are carried into the older, the overall rate of LGBT population is nearer 6.4% than 3.4%. Thus, if sexual orientation is the product of innate biological determinants, and not the product of socialization, there should be no reason why there are fewer sexual minority 80 year olds than 18 year olds. That approximately 500,000 people died from AIDS related illnesses between

1980 and 2001 is unlikely to affect this contention because these deaths occurred across age cohorts at the time, and not all of these deaths will be for sexual minorities. Thus, any difference measured would be an effective measure of the closet.

Because of these exceptional difficulties, both of using the proper survey methods and choosing words which best elicit a response, there is a lack of reliable, current information on the size of the lesbian, gay or bisexual population. It seems safe to say that a minimum of 1.8% identify as bisexual, but that many, many more find themselves attracted to both sexes, and sometimes engage in same-sex behaviors.

How Bisexual Are Bisexuals?

Pew Research (2013) asked nearly 500 people who identify as bisexual questions about their sexual desires. Using a five point scale, with one being attracted only or mostly attracted to males and five being attracted only or mostly to females, only 10% and 3% of bisexuals were registered at the extremes in the study (1 and 5 respectively). Almost 30% suggested that they are equally attracted to both sexes (3), and 34% and 23% suggested that they are somewhat attracted more to men and women respectively (2 and 4). Regarding bisexual men specifically, near-equal numbers say they are more attracted to men 34% and more attracted to women 38%, leaving 28% are attracted to both equally.

Pew research identified people as bisexual by self-report. This means they are more likely to find bisexuals who had equal same-sex and opposite-sex attraction: We theorize that those who self-report are more likely to locate themselves somewhere in the middle of the scale and that this does not speak to the prevalence of maintaining both same-sex and opposite-sex desire more generally. When considering those who maintain some level of dual desire for men and women, the preponderance of these people will likely be those who identify as straight but maintain limited same-sex desires or behaviors.

Evidence for this comes from our own study. In recruiting men from the streets for interview, we were likely to select men who strongly identify as bisexual, not mostly gay or straight men with a small degree of other attraction. In the research on 90 bisexual men that we use for this book, we highlight that most participants said there desires on the Klein grid were 4. This was the case for all five of our measured scales. In other words, those in our study were halfway between both gay and straight, or equally attracted to men as women for sexual attraction, masturbation thoughts, sex, socialization and love.

Expanding Categories and Sexual Flexibility

Scientific research on sexuality began with the notion that there are just two types of sexual orientation: heterosexual and homosexual, with homosexuality considered deviant. Given this societal bias, research on bisexuality was stymied for many years (Diamond 2008). This is changing, however, and scholars are arguing that a marked expansion of labels is occurring to account for the greater complexity afforded to sexuality in contemporary culture (Epstein et al. 2012; Kuper et al. 2012).

The growing number of sexual identity categories is required to accommodate the range and variability of behaviors, feelings, and identities that people report. Other dimensions of human sexuality are also starting to be recognized, from asexuality to the age of person to whom one is attracted.

In addition to the diversity of sexual desire, another complicating factor related to sexuality is *flexibility*. While conflicting definitions exist in the literature, we refer to sexual flexibility as the openness of people to engage in sexual behaviors with people of the same sex that is not the one they are primarily attracted to. It would be possible to describe bisexuals as inherently flexible or non-flexible and this choice is rather arbitrary. The dominant usage is to refer to straight and gay/lesbian identified people. Here, heterosexual women have been thought to be more open to sexual experiences with both men and women than heterosexual men. One study found that women were three times more likely than men to have had both male and female partners in the past year (Mosher et al. 2005).

Fahs (2009) suggest that women are more flexible sexually because of heterosexist norms that expect heterosexual women to engage in same-sex sexual behaviors for men's pleasure. She argues that although Rich (1980) once posited that "compulsory heterosexuality" required women to identify as heterosexual to comply with implicit social norms, compulsory bisexuality is likely a more appropriate notion today. Fahs suggests that in the light of increasing reports of heterosexual-identified women engaging in homoerotic behavior with other women, usually in front of men and in social settings like fraternity parties and clubs, women's bisexual behavior is socially expected.

Supporting this contention to an extent, Esterline and Galupo (2013) show that women are asked to participate in bisexual behaviors more than men, and that they are less likely to ask men to do the same. However, women who complied with men's requests also reported significantly more positive attitudes toward lesbian women, bisexual women, and same-sex marriage than women who did not. While this may be evidence of unequal gender relations (women do not feel able to reciprocate men's request), it could also be explained by women being less homophobic than men and thus more willing to comply with men's desires.

Diamond (2003) suggests that bisexual behaviors might exist among people with heterosexual desires because of the relationship between sexual attraction and love. She develops a biobehavioral model of love and desire that contends that one can fall in love without experiencing sexual desire and as a result individuals can develop "novel sexual desires—even desires that contradict their sexual orientations—as a result of falling in love" (p. 173). She suggests that this is why teenage girls often consider themselves bisexual, when later they show not to have bisexual desire. Here, interpersonal relationships exert a greater influence on female adolescents' first experiences of sexual desire and behavior than on males' (see Hyde and Jaffee 2000). Women also place less emphasis on the sexual component of their lesbian or bisexual identification, both during and after a sexual identity questioning process (Whisman 1996), and are thus more likely to report that their sexuality is fluid and chosen versus fixed and biologically given (Rosenbluth 1997).

There are many other arguments as to why women may be more flexible in their sexual behaviors than men (see for example Peplau and Garnets 2000; Rust 2000). These include the proposition that women's sexual flexibility flows from lesser political and physical prowess paired with lower sex drives (Baumeister 2000) to the contention that media representations of bisexual women encourage more intimacy in same-sex friendships (Thompson 2006).

Others argue it is an effect of evolution. For example, Diamond and Wallen (2011) contend that differences in selective pressures on males and females in the human lineage have a significant effect in why women are more sexually flexible in the present. They argue that females' sensitivity to information about the sex of potential mates in sexual stimuli (known as proceptivity) has become unlinked from arousability—the factors by which people become sexually aroused. This means that arousability influences response to sexual stimuli in women to a proportionately greater degree than in men. Being "unoriented" allows for bisexual response in women, whereas men's sexual desires are still influenced by this proceptivity and that the sex of a person is thus of far greater importance for men.

Chivers and Bailey (2005) also show that sexual situations themselves can lead to women's arousal—evidenced by research showing that women are genitally aroused when witnessing chimpanzees having sex. They found that women showed small increases in vaginal blood flow to nonhuman stimulus and large increases to both human male and female stimuli. Men did not show any genital arousal (as measured through penile enlargement) to the nonhuman stimulus and demonstrated a category-specific pattern of arousal to the human stimuli that corresponded to their stated sexual orientation. This study showed that women's genital arousal appears to be an automatic response to sexual stimuli, whereas men's genital arousal is dependent on stimulus that is specific to their sexual interests—seemingly because it is more detrimental for women not to be physiologically ready for sex.

Of course, genital arousal is different from psychological arousal and these results also highlight that genital arousal measures only examine one component of sexual desire. Indeed, Gerritsen et al. (2009) have shown that when the clitoris is measured for stimulation, it is much more target specific. In other words, it is the clitoris and not vagina which is the equivalent of the penis. But taken in conjunction with Diamond's (2009) life-history work, evidence suggests that stimulus features necessary to evoke genital arousal are much less specific in women than in men.

In line with showing that women are more sexually flexible than men, Chivers et al. (2004) also found that most women studied showed vaginal arousal to both male and female pornography independent of whether they identified as lesbian or heterosexual. In contrast, they found men exhibit a bipolar arousal pattern, with men's arousal pattern tending to match their stated sexuality. Indeed, research suggests that women's sexual orientation is slightly more likely to change than men's (Baumeister 2000; Kinnish et al. 2005). The notion that sexual orientation can change over time is known as *sexual fluidity*.

Even if sexual fluidity exists for some women, it does not mean that the majority of women will change sexual orientations as they age – rather, sexuality is stable over time for the majority of people. Mock and Eibach (2012) examined reports of sexual orientation identity stability and change over a 10-year period, drawing on data from the National Survey of Midlife Development in the United States (MIDUS I and II), testing for three patterns: (1) heterosexual stability, (2) female sexual fluidity and (3) bisexual fluidity. The average age was approximately 47 years, and 54% of the 2,560 participants were female. At the time of the first study, 97.42% reported a heterosexual identity, 1.25% a homosexual identity, and 1.33% a bisexual identity. At wave 2 (ten years later), a little over 2% reported a different sexual orientation identity. Although some support for the latter hypotheses was found, sexuality was mostly stable.

More evidence for the lack of sexual fluidity among men compared to women comes from "conversion therapy." These "therapies" are historically, and still today, levied upon gay men through fundamentalist religious organizations. Those attending them are highly religious and strongly desire to rid themselves of their sexual desires. Although no reputable scientist has shown that such "treatments" are effective, it does not stop organized religion from postulating that, "through the Lord," anything is possible. People who attend these conversion therapies tend to be highly motivated to become heterosexual, yet even here; there is remarkably little success (LeVay 2011). Any shift to heterosexuality is likely exaggerated, with subjects submitting to the same societal pressures that keep many gays closeted in the first place. The failure of gay conversion therapies is evidence of the stable nature of sexual orientation.

Finally, evidence of the staying power of sexual orientation concerning age of attraction also shows resiliency. Whereas Müller et al. (2014) found that about half of pedophiles could lose their sexual attraction (as measured by penile arousal), several scholars immediately showed that they didn't find the pedophiles changed into non-pedophiles. Instead, they found that his phallometric test was spewing random results (see: Bailey 2015; Cantor 2015; Lalumière 2015).

Accordingly, all we can really say about sexual fluidity and flexibility is that (1) there are multiple types of bisexuality that will impact on men in different ways and will also be dependent on the homohysteria of the broader culture; (2) male homosexuality cannot be changed through therapy; (3) women are more flexible than men and perhaps more sexually fluid; (4) people can engage in sexual behaviors that are not representative of their primary sexual attraction for a range of reasons, and it is likely that such sexual flexibility (and exploration) will increase in cultures of inclusivity (with little or no homohysteria).

Chapter 4
Bisexuality as a Unique Social Problem

Academics have studied the nature and effects of prejudice and discrimination against sexual minorities for several decades (Flowers and Buston 2001; Page and Shapiro 1992). This research has shown that their lives have often been defined by social marginalization (Herek 2004). Minority stress theory is one way of understanding the damaging consequences of being a sexual minority (Meyer 2003). It contends that sexual minorities experience chronic stress that stems from stigmatization in the broader culture, including psychological burdens distinct from heterosexual populations (Hatzenbuehler 2009). This is supported by a body of research highlighting elevated psychosocial problems for sexual minorities compared to heterosexuals (e.g. D'Augelli et al. 2001).

The prejudice against sexual minorities has largely been conceptualized as *homophobia* (Weinberg 1972). Research on homophobia has tended to focus on: (1) the prevalence of homophobic attitudes and behaviors among individuals and within institutions; (2) its negative impact on sexual minorities; (3) the mechanisms by which it is reproduced; and (4) the impact on heterosexuals. While the term is not without its limitations, it has proven effective in analyzing a range of attitudes and behaviors that pertain to the negative treatment of sexual minorities (see McCormack and Anderson 2014a).

One of the key benefits of the term *homophobia* is that it refers to both attitudes and behaviors (Plummer 1999). Given that public attitudes play a key role in determining legislation, homophobia has historically been enshrined in public policy (Burstein 1998). Attitudes are thus vital, yet researching them is complex, as they can pertain to sexual acts, individuals and sexual identities, personal morality and civil rights (Avery et al. 2007; Loftus 2001).

Herek (2004) argues that the term *homophobia* helped change the framing of anti-gay prejudice by "locating the 'problem' of homosexuality not in homosexual people, but in heterosexuals who were intolerant of gay men and lesbians" (p. 8). While he also critiqued it for its psychological implications, alternative terminology encounters similar definitional problems. *Anti-gay* can be deemed to exclude other sexual minorities, and *anti-homosexual bias* additionally relies on the medicalized term homosexual (Plummer 1999). While *prejudice* and *stigma* account for attitudinal components, they do not incorporate behavioral ones (Rivers 2011). *Homonegativity* avoids the psychological implications, but there is definitional uncertainty and slippage in the accuracy of its usage (Lottes and Grollman 2010). Similarly, when *heterosexism* is used to understand behaviors that denigrate homosexuality, the power to understand the implicit and structural privileging of heterosexuality is weakened (McCormack 2012a). As we have argued elsewhere (McCormack and Anderson 2014b), literal interpretations of the etymology of a word are less important than the conceptual value that they maintain.

The use of homophobia as a broad category to understand discrimination against sexual minorities is in-line with much research on the topic. It is also supported by the fact that positive attitudes toward homosexuality are correlated with positive attitudes toward bisexuality (Mohr and Rochlen 1999)—meaning negative attitudes are likely to be related as well. Accordingly, we will continue to use the term homophobia when relating to matters of discrimination that apply to gays, lesbians and bisexuals together.

Even so, one problem with homophobia studies is that the experiences of bisexuals are frequently erased (Burleson 2005). Indeed, while individuals' experiences in such a culture will vary according to the category of one's minority status (Worthen 2013), research has regularly examined the experiences of sexual minorities as a homogenous group; often failing to recognize important differences both within and between them (Savin-Williams 1998). This is significant because research indicates that heterosexuals may have more negative attitudes toward bisexuals than gays or lesbians (Herek 2002), and that bisexuals suffer discrimination from gays and lesbians as well as from heterosexuals (McLean 2008). Bisexual youth have also been found to experience higher levels of harassment and suicide ideation than their lesbian and gay peers (Pompili et al. 2014; Robinson and Espelage 2011). Indeed, Savin-Williams (2001b) contends that quantitative research that groups bisexuals with gays and lesbians exaggerate negative findings related to gays and lesbians because bisexuals have significantly worse experiences. Exemplifying this, in the recent analysis of Behavioral Risk Factor Surveillance System (BRFSS) data from 2005 to 2010, across seven states, Gorman et al. (2015) found that bisexual men and women have worse rates of self-reported health compared to both heterosexual and gays and lesbians. In fact, gay men reported better rates of health than straight men.

It is thus important to study the ways in which bisexuals suffer discrimination that is independent from the stigma faced by gays and lesbians. We use the term *biphobia* (Eliason 1997) to understand this phenomenon, including antipathy directed toward bisexuals from other sexual minority communities. We will also use the term biphobia when discussing research that has focused on bisexual populations. However, we use the term homophobia to describe general antipathy toward same-sex sex, regardless of the sexual identity of the individual who engages in this.

Biphobia and Bisexual Burden

There is no single reason for biphobia. Much of it may be linked with anti-gay animus, although given the sexualized nature of stereotypes about bisexuality; biphobia is particularly focused on behaviors rather than identity. Another component may be that during the early stages of the AIDS epidemic, bisexual men were thought responsible for the spread of HIV to heterosexuals (Stokes et al. 1996). This is despite just 1% of annual HIV infections being transmitted by bisexual men to female partners at the time (Kahn et al. 1997). In this book we describe biphobia as the same as homophobia for gay men: it represents an antipathy toward them.

However, there is also increased social hardship for bisexuals, even in absence of antipathy toward them. These hardships are rooted in stereotypes (Zivony and Lobel 2014). Whereas minority stress theory says that sexual minorities maintain elevated problems above heterosexuals as a unified group, we conceptualize 'bisexual burden' to represent the myriad of problems that bisexuals face beyond those experienced by gays and lesbians. We document the specific burdens that manifest in the lives of bisexuals, and examine the evidence for their existence.

Types of bisexual burden are numerous, and we discuss 11 distinct kinds documented in the literature. Klein (1993) suggests bisexuals are stigmatized as being (1) neurotic, (2) unable to love, (3) sex crazed and (4) less capable of monogamy than those attracted to a single sex. In addition to these factors, bisexuals also suffer from (5) negative stereotypes about their identities from other sexual minorities, (6) being thought as confused about their sexual orientation, or (7) seen as being within a transitional phase (Diamond 2008). As a result, bisexuals are accused of (8) attention seeking, and (9) not being brave enough to fully come out (Eliason 1997).

Bisexual burden is particularly apparent in relationships. For example, when bisexuals are in a relationship with someone of a different sex, they are (10) frequently accused of holding on to heterosexual privilege (Burleson 2005); yet when they are in a relationship with the same sex, they are (11) perceived as gay (Yost and Thomas 2012) or accused of not being wholly out; again, being seen to cling to straight privilege (Firestein 2007). These forms of burden are not an exhaustive list, but highlight the existence of a set of practices and beliefs that set bisexuals apart from gays and lesbians in the social processes that esteem heterosexuality in society.

Supporting some of our 11 forms of burden, Zivony and Lobel (2014) recently demonstrated that heterosexuals maintain prejudicial beliefs about bisexual men in accordance with the stereotypes described above. Their quantitative research documented that heterosexual men thought bisexuals were confused, less inclined to monogamy, unable to maintain long-term relationships, un-trustworthy and open to new sexual experiences in ways gay or straight men were not thought to be.

These results are significant as they show that heterosexuals' stereotypes of bisexual men are similar to those reported by bisexual men (McLean 2007). Zivony and Lobel also found that heterosexual men rated bisexual men higher on these stereotypes if the bisexual man was currently dating a man rather than a woman. Indeed, Eliason (1997) shows that stereotypes about bisexuals are more focused on sexual acts than those about gays and lesbians. This supports the notion that prejudice against bisexuals is linked with a particular form of conservative sexual morality (Hemmings 2002); one situated within a monogamous norm that bisexuals are seen to transgress by nature of their desires (Paul 1984).

However, biphobia is exacerbated by social and political divisions that exist between sexual minorities, too. Indeed, bisexuals have been shown to be ostracized in gay communities (Mulick and Wright 2002; Welzer-Lang 2008). Some gay men questioned the legitimacy of bisexuality because they perceived bisexual men to be calling themselves bisexual in the gay community while simultaneously presenting themselves as heterosexual in the straight community (Weiss 2003). Rust (2009) argues that bisexuals are still perceived as enjoying the pleasures of same-sex sexuality while avoiding the burden of sexual oppression, and that some lesbian feminists have viewed bisexual women as traitors or cowards for not rejecting men entirely.

Bisexuals also face unique issues when coming out (Anderson et al. 2013). Primarily, bisexuals' experiences of disclosing their sexual identity have traditionally been characterized by a consistent expectation to defend the legitimacy of bisexuality (Page 2004), particularly against the stereotypes that bisexuals are confused, greedy or in denial about being gay (Klein 1993).

The issues encountered in coming out are particularly pertinent when considering relationships and deciding whether to come out to a partner's friends and family. Watson (2014: 120) suggests that the family is a contentious arena for bisexuals, because it sits at the juncture of, "intersecting spheres of the private and public, in which personal biographies are framed in and through a complex nexus of relations with intimate others and family members." Part of sexual minorities' "friendships we choose" (Weston 1994), friendship groups can also prove problematic for bisexuals. Highlighting this, research shows that lesbians are more likely than bisexuals to have their non-heterosexual relationships recognized within their friendship groups of heterosexual women (Galupo 2007).

McLean (2007) argues that some bisexuals decide against coming out to particular groups because of the pain and anguish this can cause to themselves and their partners. Accordingly, bisexuals are strategic in determining when, to whom, and how they come out (Brown 2002). They tend to tell their friends about their same-sex desires before their parents, and are more likely to tell their mothers before their fathers (Weinberg et al. 1994). Furthermore, Barker et al. (2011) suggest that bisexuals often have a dual coming out process to contend with: they must face stigma from both heterosexuals and the gay community, whereas gays and lesbians face stigma from one.

However, Baldwin et al. (2014) caution against automatically assuming that complex coming out processes are evidence of a social problem. In their research on sexual self-identification among men who were behaviorally bisexual, they find that participants maintained sophisticated and complex understandings of their sexual identities, not necessarily viewing them as a monolithic identity that was central to their lives, but as one component to an array of identities they experienced in different social contexts. They highlight that many people's identities do not fit the gay, straight or bi typology, and that non-disclosure can be a result of the inadequacy of thinking of sexuality in this categorical manner (see also Pallotta-Chiarolli in press).

Even so, the overwhelming social attitude toward bisexuality has been one of denial, erasure, and stigma. The prejudice and stigma associated with bisexuality is compounded by the lack of academic research into bisexuality as a unique sexual identity. Barker et al. (2007) highlight that bisexuality is not even indexed in Piontek's (2006) *Queering Gay and Lesbian Studies*. They add that two thirds of psychology undergraduate introductory textbooks did not mention bisexuality at all, discussing instead a binary of heterosexual and homosexual. This lack of academic research into bisexuality is why the *American Institute of Bisexuality* is committed to funding research into bisexuality, including the study presented in this book.

Characteristics of Bisexual Burden

Erasure Bisexuality is erased in US and UK cultures by heterosexist norms and monosexist attitudes. As Blumstein and Schwartz (1974) argue, this is partly attributable to the lack of a substantial bisexual community: whereas gays and lesbian receive validation within their minority communities, bisexuals are stigmatized within both the gay and straight world meaning that their identity does not receive social validation.

Yoshino (2000) contends that bisexuality is also erased as part of a broader political project of straight and gay communities. He writes that, "… erasure occurs because the two dominant sexual orientation groups – self-identified straights and self-identified gays – have shared investments in that erasure" (362–363). He adds, "It is as if these two groups, despite their other virulent disagreements, have agreed that bisexuals will be made invisible" (p. 363). While the politics of LGBT groups is fraught with internal struggles (see Rubin 2012), we find Yoshino's perspective less helpful for understanding the complexities of bisexuality in an age of decreasing homohysteria, where an organized plot against bisexuals seems rather unlikely.

Another form of bisexual erasure occurs as a result of the one-time rule of homosexuality (Anderson 2008, and see this chapter). Here, one same-sex experience is socially perceived as indicative of being "entirely" gay, erasing bisexuality as a possible identity (Yost and Thomas 2012). This perception is likely influenced by the use of derogatory words such as fag and queer to describe gay men in times of high homohysteria (Thurlow 2001). The use of *homophobic* epithets rather than biphobic ones serves to further consolidate the binary of sexuality—while it may mean that bisexuals are less overtly stigmatized, it also makes their identities less visible.

A further component of this erasure is the changing use of these words as cultural homophobia decreases. McCormack (2011) showed that derogatory labels are reclaimed by gay and straight men as ways to bond, with the stigma expunged by the implicit understandings in the group and the context and emphasis with which they are said. Given that this playful use of words is a way of further reducing homophobia, bisexuals are denied another way of challenging their stigma.

While there are social and structural processes that render bisexuality invisible, bisexuality is also erased because of human beings' cognitive processes. Namely, we tend to make sense of a complicated world through the creation of binaries. Structural anthropology posits that binary thinking is a spontaneous and necessary act of the human condition (Barnard 2000), necessary to simplify a complex world. Using this theory, bisexuality is erased in part because of blindness to intermediate categories—because of structural and cognitive problems with contesting a dominant binary way of thinking. While we see some merit to this argument, a sociological approach highlights the importance of social norms in binary categorizations—and specifically, the influence of heterosexism.

The Role of Heterosexism in Bisexual Erasure Heterosexism refers to the cultural processes by which heterosexuality is privileged in society. It focuses on those with power by analyzing the social processes of *heterosexuality*. Just as scholars of race have looked at whiteness in addition to ethnic minorities, and academics interested in gender have researched masculinities in addition to studying women's cultural experiences, so heterosexism turns the lens of analysis on heterosexuals rather than sexual minorities. Studying heterosexism helps understand how forms of prejudice that are not overt still impact powerfully on individuals.

Heterosexism is particularly relevant to bisexuals because of its relationship with monosexism. Privileging heterosexuality as the *ideal* sexuality and deeming other sexualities as inferior sets up a binary of sexualities. Just as the privilege of gender has seen a diversity of sexes categorized into "men" and "not-men" (see Brown 1997), so heterosexism reproduces sexuality as "straight" and "not-straight." The differences between bisexuals, homosexuals, pansexuals, omnisexuals and others are conflated because all that matters in a heterosexist, monosexist culture is whether you are straight or not. Thus, our predisposition to exclusive binary categories is exacerbated by a culture that privileges heterosexuality, meaning that despite maintaining numerical dominance compared to gays and lesbians, bisexuality is erased a distinct identity category.

Notwithstanding these issues, there is a counter-intuitive component to heterosexism that sees bisexuals *gain* from a culture that privileges heterosexuality compared to gays and lesbians. One of the processes of heterosexism is that people are assumed to be heterosexual unless they publicly identify otherwise—something called the "heterosexual presumption" (Epstein and Johnson 1994). In this context, anyone in a same-sex relationship cannot engage in any public displays of affection or intimacy with their partners without, in effect, coming out. Thus, the force of heterosexism for anyone in a same-sex relationship is to trap their lives into the private sphere unless they decide to actively declare their sexual identity. This places the social burden on the sexual minority to have their sexual identity properly understood, rather than on the prejudice of the broader society.

The impact for gays and lesbians in relationships is clear. They can only have their relationships, lovers and social lives recognized by coming out of the closet and facing whatever opprobrium awaits—which will be dependent on the homophobia of their local context. The relevance for bisexuals is that the heterosexual presumption erases just a portion of their desires and, as a group, their relationships. Bisexual men who are dating women do not need to come out to have their relationship publicly recognized in a way that gay men or bisexual men in a same-sex relationship do. While being mistaken as heterosexual is undoubtedly a component of bisexual burden – and while bisexuals in a relationship might feel stigmatized through having their identity erased – there is still the option to have sex, affection and a relationship without having to contest dominant social norms. In this regard, and for bisexuals who either want or are in a relationship with another sex, heterosexism serves to mask the condemned aspects of their desire and provides a level of shelter from forms of stigma. This is not to argue that heterosexism does not affect bisexuals, but that it can do so in less damaging ways than for gays and lesbians.

This means that bisexual men have less need to come out than gay men. For gay men, to avoid living a life of secrecy and fear, there is a need to come out of the closet—particularly if they want to have enjoyable sex, romantic relationships, and friendships with other gay men. While bisexuals would need to do so as well if they wished to participate in sexual minority communities, they can have sex, romance and friends without necessarily being dishonest about themselves. That bisexuals face less pressure to come out than gays and lesbians is not without social implications.

The first is that bisexual men come out later in life than gay men (Martos et al. 2015; Weinberg et al. 1994). This also means that bisexual men likely fear sexual stigma for a longer period of time than gay men. Indeed, bisexuals who retain heterosexual privilege may not accurately perceive the degree of social ostracism they would face if they came out. Illustrating these issues, Pew (2013) research on 1197 sexual minorities found that gay men and lesbians are much more likely than bisexuals to say there is a lot of social acceptance of the LGBT population in their city or town. 39% of gay men and 31% of lesbians say there is a lot of acceptance where they live, compared with 20% of bisexuals.

The decision to delay coming out negatively impacts upon public perceptions of bisexuality. The *fear* of discrimination becomes a vicious circle: Bisexuals are discriminated against and choose to remain closeted, which comes with fewer costs associated with it than for gays and lesbians. The longer they stay in the closet, the greater they perceive biphobia to be, and the harder it is for them to come out, keeping them in the closet; yet remaining closeted promotes the erasure of bisexuality more broadly. In other words, the privilege of choice contributes to the absence of a strong political voice of bisexuality in broader culture.

Self-erasure Something overlooked by the research on bisexuality is that bisexuals themselves contribute to the erasure of bisexuality. In the 2013 Pew Research poll, only 28% of bisexuals said most or all of the important people in their lives knew about their sexual orientation, compared to 71% of lesbians and 77% of gay men. Whereas 53% of gay men have told their father, only 24% of bisexuals have. When it comes to hiding sexuality, only 10% of gay men say that only a few or none of the important people in their life know they are gay, yet this figure is 39% for bisexuals. This is particularly significant given that LGBT people believe that contact with sexual minorities is the primary reason for decreasing cultural stigma against sexual minorities.

In addition to this, the Pew survey found that only 11% of bisexual people said most of their closest co-workers knew about their sexual orientation, compared to 48% of gay men and 50% of lesbians. It is perhaps unsurprising then that academic research shows that half of bisexuals surveyed maintained that both straight and gay/lesbian people misunderstand bisexuality (Green et al. 2011).

One reason for this disparity is that bisexuals are less entrenched in their bisexual identities than gays and lesbians. Pew (2013) found that while 68% of gay men and 58% of lesbians had refused to purchase a product or service because the company that provides it does not support LGBT rights, only 34% of bisexuals had done this. Gay men are over twice as likely (58%) to attend an LGBT rally than bisexuals (25%), and more than twice as likely to attend a pride event (72% compared to 33%). Gay men are also twice as likely to give money to a LGBT political organization, much more likely to have met fellow sexual minorities on line, and more likely to reveal their minority status on a social networking site (53% to 34%). Figures about lesbians are near comparable to gay men.

Bisexual men are also less likely to maintain social networks with other sexual minorities, thus contributing to the lack of community which can be used to promote psychological wellbeing for minorities. While 22% of gay men tell Pew (2013) that all or most of their close friends are LGBT, only 5% of bisexuals say the same. Bisexual men are much more likely than bisexual women (67% vs. 47%) to say only a few or none of their close friends are LGBT.

These statistics are even more divergent when gender is taken into account, with bisexual men being the most distant from LGBT communities and identities. 88% of the bisexual women said that they had told a close friend about their sexual identity, while 55% of bisexual men said that they had. Similarly, while one-third of bisexual women say most of the important people in their life know they are bisexual, only 12% of bisexual men say the same. Conversely, 65% of bisexual men say that only a few or none of the important people in their life know they are bisexual.

Pew's research found that the primary reason bisexuals didn't come out was fear for the lack of acceptance, which also explains why bisexuals are significantly more likely to date someone of the opposite sex than the same. This clearly indicates a strong element of self-censorship on the part of bisexual men. This was evidenced in the 1200 interviews conducted by Pew as part of the same study: Reasons that bisexuals gave for remaining closeted included the ability to remain silent, something that gay and lesbian men are less likely to be able to do. One 39 year-year old bisexual woman said:

> It's just never come up. I rarely discuss details of my love life with anyone since I am a deeply private person. If I were to make a serious commitment to another woman, I would tell my mother about it.

A 54 year-old bisexual male told Pew:

> This is not a subject to discuss or tell anyone about, ever, except those with whom I may enjoy having sex with. It's not my identity. It is an activity - like bowling, or gardening, or pick-up basketball games in the neighborhood, or joining the PTA - except that it's more intimate and personal, as a matter of discretion and respect for proper behavior in polite society.

We do not wish to contribute to bisexual burden by advocating that bisexuals date members of the same-sex; one should be free to date, love, and marry whomever and however many people one wants. Even so, the complicity with heterosexist notions of romance and monogamy that accompanies the silencing of bisexuality is problematic. If 77% of gay men say that most of the important people in their lives know that they are gay, and only 12% of bisexual men do (Pew 2013), the leading factor in the erasure of bisexual men are bisexual men themselves.

All of the above factors suggest that a gay identity is more important to gay men than a bisexual identity is to bisexual men. Thus, it is unsurprising that when Pew asked their participants about the importance of their identity specifically, only 25% of gay men said that it was not important to them, whereas 54% of bisexuals said this. While it might be progressive to argue that one's sexual minority status is unimportant (Savin-Williams 2005), there are political ramifications for this position in a culture in which power and privilege are distributed unequally to heterosexuals.

While we expect that there is a generational cohort effect in this data, and we discuss this in Chaps. 8 and 9, these are striking statistics that highlight the erasure of bisexuality from cultural perspective exists because of three reasons: (1) that bisexuals are intentionally erased as an indirect artifact of perceived heightened intolerance of bisexuals; (2) bisexuals are structurally erased by monosexist culture, exacerbated by cognitive processes; and (3) bisexuals themselves chose not to be public, visible, or political with their identities.

Erasure of Bisexuality among Men of Color When bisexuality is recognized, research shows that this is predominantly among white people. One reason for this is sampling effect: the majority of empirical research on sexual minorities has been conducted with overwhelmingly White, middle-class participants.

When researchers have examined men who have sex with men (MSM) who are non-white, they have done so under an umbrella of AIDS research. For example, Muòoz-Laboy (2004: 55) says that Latino male bisexuality has been studied for the most part "with a focus on men who have sex with men (MSM) and with little attention to sexual desire."

When research is carried out on sexual minority men of color, it tends to be done so on gay, not bisexual, men. Some research has been carried out on gay African American (Boykin 2005), Asian American (Chan 1995), Latino/Latina (Carrier 1992; Carrillo 2002), and Native American men (Brown 1997). Other research includes comparative analysis of Latino, Black, and Asian MSM and how the intersection of cultural background, race, and ethnicity influence comportment and identity formation over time (Manalansan 1996). This is all valuable research, but it confirms Muòoz-Laboy's (2004) point that that there exists very little research on bisexuality by identity rather than behavior among men of color (Carillo and Fontdevila 2011; D'Augelli and Patterson 1995). The situation of dual oppressions, and how they intersect, should not be overlooked.

Supporting the erasure of race, Collins (1999) argues that until recently most identity theories and models—which are generally housed within the discipline of psychology—have been based on single social identities, like being black or female. In other words, they have examined a specific social identity as if the group members were homogeneous, monolithic and lacking multiple identities. Interest in intersectionality largely grew from the critique of gender and race-based research which failed to account for the complexity of the lived experiences of people who have multiple identity categorizations (Collins 1999; McCall 2005). Accordingly, it is argued that ignoring one mode of oppression weakens an analysis because an integral stratifying force is overlooked.

While the origin of the term *intersectionality* is most frequently credited to Crenshaw (1991), its central tenet – that forms of oppression can intensify when combined – predates this (see Davis 1981; Loewenberg and Bogin 1976). The concept highlights that there are many modes of oppression that structure an individual's identity, and that these ordering principles are mutually reinforcing.

Importantly, these identities intersect in ways that produce new forms of oppression and it is not possible simply to add together the types of oppression for each identity and come up with the final experience. Collins (1999) and Crenshaw (1991) argue that this approach fails to address or even acknowledge that multiple and complex identities must be considered together. This is particularly important for bisexual people of color. Individuals who are both bisexual and members of a minoritized racial group must deal with at least minority statuses.

This can influence bisexual men in many ways. For example, the cultural bifurcation of black and gay/bisexual identities are complicated by cultural understandings of psychological models of homosexual development, which seem to maintain that homosexuality and bisexually are problems for whites only. Freudian and post-Freudian theories falsely attribute male homosexuality as a product of an overbearing mother and an absent father figure (Freud 1905; Spencer 1995). However, both in their theorizing, as well as in dominant cultural understandings, this only seems to apply to whites.

Highlighting the whiteness of homosexuality, when the Moynihan Congressional Report discussed the deterioration of the black American family in 1965, attributing this to the absence of the black American father, it was never assumed that these black children would "become" gay. Models of pathological homosexual genesis, whatever their etiology, appear only to work for white families. Even with this complexity, when sociologists examine the issue of intersectionality they mostly examine the intersections of gender, race and/or sexuality by holding women as the focal point of their analysis (Abes et al. 2007).

Authenticity A significant component of bisexual burden is the disavowal that bisexuality exists—that proclamations of bisexual identity are inauthentic. This is not new: Some 20th century sexologists doubted it, too. For example, Bergler (1956: 80–81) wrote:

> Bisexuality—a state that has no existence beyond the word itself is an out-and-out fraud... The theory claims that a man can be alternatively or concomitantly homo and heterosexual... Nobody can dance at two different weddings at the same time. These so-called bisexuals are really homosexuals with an occasional heterosexual excuse.

This belief that bisexual men today are tomorrow's gay men is exemplified by the media response to British Olympian Tom Daley. In 2013, he used YouTube to announce that while still being attracted to girls, he was currently in a relationship with a man. Doing so permitted him to craft his message the way he desired, without media interpretation. Daley refrained from using the words gay or bisexual, but he indicated bisexual desires when he said, "Of course I still fancy girls."

There was a great deal of skepticism to Daley's disclosure, as well as bisexual erasure. There was wide spread labeling of Daley as gay on Twitter. Furthermore, five months later in April 2014, Tom Daley was described by a member of the media as gay in a live television show. While Daley did not explicitly contest the new label, we interpreted his hesitant response not an endorsement of gay identity but rather embarrassment at being asked the question without any warning. Nonetheless, the media reported it as Daley "finally" identifying as gay, supporting the notion that bisexuality is a transitional phase rather than a separate identity.

Whether Daley is bisexual or gay, the perceived shift, widely covered in the press, from bisexual to gay is not unusual (Fox 1991). Coming out first as bisexual is a common tactic with gay men, particularly of older generations (see Chap. 7). This is precisely because of the zero-sum model of sexuality, where bisexuality is seen as "less gay" and thus "nearer" to heterosexuality; presumably neutralizing the sexual deviance. Then, once the individual has built up sufficient self-esteem as a gay man, and oftentimes with a community of support, the bisexual label is dropped for one that more accurately reflects their same-sex desires. This event was so common that it has accrued a cultural motto of "bi today, gay tomorrow."

Research also finds that some bisexual men had once said that they were gay (Weinberg et al. 1994). While some may do this to fit into the gay scene, always recognizing their bisexual identity, Udis-Kessler (1990) explains this reverse-transition by theorizing that these bisexuals first recognized the same-sex impulse, only later recognizing their bisexuality. This notion is particularly powerful in homohysteric times, when the one-time rule of homosexuality was in operation, and individuals may have internalized this rule and assumed their same-sex desires negated their heterosexual ones. In other words, bisexuality may involve coming to terms with a new identity for a second time.

There are other reasons why people question the authenticity of bisexuality. Some argue that bisexuals are simply trying to maintain heterosexual privilege. Other negative attitudes are based on the view that people who claim to be bisexual are confused about their sexuality; that they are unable to decide which of the two dichotomized sexual preferences is for them (Bronn 2001).

Indecision Another way in which bisexual identities are questioned is through the labeling of bisexuals as indecisive. In line with the zero-sum game of sexuality, Zivony and Lobel (2014) suggest that because men and women are perceived as "opposite sexes," attraction for men and women are seen as discrete forms of sexual desire. Thus, if bisexuality is perceived as a mixture of two separate attractions, bisexuals inhabit an ongoing dissonance. This can explain why bisexuals are stereotypically perceived as never being satisfied with a single partner and therefore unlikely to be monogamous.

The belief that bisexuals are simply confused or indecisive about their true heterosexuality or homosexuality is an aspect of bisexual burden that likely maintained more salience in previous decades than it does today. For example, in one study conducted over fifty years ago (Cory and Leroy 1963: 61), the authors wrote:

While appearing to encompass a wider choice of love objects… [the bisexual] actually becomes a product of abject confusion; his self-image is that of an overgrown young adolescent whose ability to differentiate one form of sexuality from another has never developed. He lacks above all a sense of identity…[He] cannot answer the question: What am I?

With the rise of bisexual scholarship, and greater cultural awareness of bisexuality, it is hard to imagine this kind of writing appearing in scholarly publications today.

Disloyalty to the Lesbian and Gay Community Another component of bisexual burden is the perception of some lesbian women and gay men that bisexual individuals are not entirely committed to sexual minority communities, or the lesbian and gay politics of equality (Mohr and Rochlen 1999; Udis-Kessler 1990). Some of these concerns are best understood within the context of the history of lesbian feminist communities that developed as resistance to sexism and patriarchy. This political aspect of lesbianism led to the view of relationships with men as "sleeping with the enemy" (Rust 2009).

Some gays and lesbians may also resent bisexual individuals because their own stereotypes of bisexuality see bisexual identity as an unwillingness to stand in solidarity with lesbian and gay communities (Israel and Mohr 2004). Similarly, bisexuals might be thought of as trying to benefit from the political gains won by the labor of the lesbian and gay rights movement without giving up their heterosexual privilege.

Tension between gay and bisexual men may not be as extreme as commonly reported, however. In their study of the relationship between gay and bisexual men in the AIDS era, Weinberg et al. (1994) found that shared fear of death improved relations between these two groups. We add that while we do not empirically examine the nature of the relationship between gay and bisexual men, it makes theoretical sense that tensions originating from a lack of dedication to gay political causes would diminish now that sexual minority rights have won so many civil liberties (Weeks 2007). It is interesting to note that many of those writing about antipathy from gays toward bisexuals did so in a time before modern gay rights were achieved.

We also note that there is a division in the bisexual community: some desire to be activists, like the organization of the Bisexual Convention and Bisexual Research Convention, while others simply desire to be part of a community, such as amBi, based in Los Angeles and with aims to build a community focused on social events and friendship networks.

Inability to be Monogamous Society has undergone significant change in the recent decades related to sexual behaviors and relationship types in the US and the UK. Linked with processes of sexualization (McNair 2013), 'hooking up' cultures have emerged that esteem one-off sexual encounters with other people at the same time as monogamy within relationships has maintained hegemonic dominance (Anderson 2012). This is despite increasing political activism and a burgeoning body of queer and feminist sociological research into non-monogamies (e.g. Klesse 2006; Yip 1997). Furthermore, anthropological literature highlights that a variety of polygamous marriage practices and culturally acceptable nonmonogamous behaviors for romantic relationships exist across many cultures (Sanderson 2001). Even so, when it comes to coupled relationships, there seems to be slow cultural progress toward the acceptance of any model other than monogamy (Anderson 2012). Instead, there remains just one esteemed script for romantic relationships, and it is a coupled (dyadic) form of sexual monogamy (Willey 2006).

The cultural valuing of monogamy occurs at the same time as a high percentage of couples of all sexual orientations cheat. Anderson (2012) calls this 'monogamism,' highlighting that the hegemonic perspective in society means that the costs of monogamy are not examined. He has shown that despite this cultural reverence for monogamy, there is a gap between what people want and what they do: multiple forms of non-monogamies exist as the covert norm for many, and even people more fantasize about cheating on their partner.

The values of a monogamist society intersect with a heterosexist one to marginalize sexual minorities. While people of all sexual orientations cheat, it is sexual minorities that are castigated for not living up to the standards of monogamy (Anderson 2012). This is because it is always those in power who determine what is acceptable behavior. Just as white people judge what is racist (Dyer 1997), it is heterosexuals who maintain the power to determine what is acceptable behavior related to sexuality. Heterosexuals can condemn sexual minorities for a lack of sexual fidelity, maintaining the illusion of personal monogamy whilst projecting their own dissonant feelings about sexual desire and relationships.

The stereotype about the inability to be monogamous is thus both a form of bisexual burden but also a narrative that privileges a monogamist view on relationships (Schmookler and Bursik 2007). Following from the misrepresentation of non-monogamy as infidelity, cultural understandings of bisexuality also imply that bisexuals will always cheat on their partner because it is assumed that one lover, male or female, cannot satiate a bisexual because they are attracted to both men and women (George 1993). Rarely is it acknowledged that there are other options for bisexuals in relationships other than deception or infidelity, and rarely is it recognized that just one sex partner for heterosexuals or homosexuals is rarely enough to sexually satisfy one for the duration of decades of coupledom (Anderson 2012).

Research suggests that when one or more of a couple is bisexual, these couples put more time and effort into negotiating their relationship type in order to come to a sexual arrangement that suits them (Hartman-Linck 2014; McLean 2011). Even with this honest and open sexual negotiation, McLean (2004) argues that bisexual people are ostracized for failing to conform to the expected monogamous relationship structure of couples. Defining intimacy this way means that even agreed-upon sexual activity outside the primary relationship is always constructed as a negative. She argues that bisexuals in open relationships may find themselves being accused of having affairs or otherwise implying some sort of secrecy of their relationship. She suggests that primary partners are even pitied for having to 'tolerate' acts of infidelity by their partners. Those who then defend their rights to have open partnerships are constructed as foolish or immature.

Research also shows the difficulties bisexuals have with monogamy. For example, Mark et al. (2014) show that bisexual men find monogamy more of a sacrifice than gays, lesbians and bisexual women. While these authors also found the majority were in monogamous relationship, McLean's (2004) study of 60 bisexual couples found that 60% of the bisexual men and 52.5% of the bisexual women indicated that their relationship could be broadly described as 'open.' She found that only 25% of the men and 35% of women were in what was defined as an exclusive relationship. Similarly, in their study of bisexuals in San Francisco in the 1980s, Weinberg et al. (1994) found that multiple relationships and non-monogamy were widely accepted within the San Francisco scene.

There are also problems beyond stigma with non-monogamies. Sheff (2010) shows that with the lack of legal recognition of such relationships, there can be problems such as partners not being recognized as family in medical contexts, additional parents in polyamorous families struggling to gain custody following a break-up, and problems over property rights when somebody dies. There are also multiple forms of marginalization for openly non-monogamous bisexual people who are even more likely to be stigmatized for supposed promiscuity or to be seen as sexual predators.

Sex-Crazed Sexual Permissiveness Even when bisexual men are not in a relationship, they are still associated with sexual stigma – namely because they are associated with sexual permissiveness. This refers to sexual attitudes toward recreational sex that are less conservative than in the broader context, be it local or cultural. Vrangalova et al. (2014: 2) define sexual permissiveness as "attitudes or behaviors that are more liberal or extensive than what is normative in a social group." It is characterized in general by a set of behaviors including, "actual or desired frequent, premarital, casual, group, or extradyadic sex, and sex with many partners, early sexual debut, or even nonverbal cues signaling availability (e.g., provocative clothing)." Sexual experience is rated as less desirable than sexual restraint (Coutinho et al. 2007). Vrangalova et al. (2014) even suggest that is among the least desirable traits one seeks in a friend. They suggest that there are both evolutionary and sociocultural reasons for the undesirability of permissiveness. These include not only the perception that sexually permissive people will be sexually unfaithful to a partner (Bailey et al. 2000), but also that they are more likely to have sex with someone else who is in a monogamous relationship (Schmitt 2004).

This policing of sexual permissiveness is known as sexual conservatism. In addition to serving as a mechanism of social control, sexual conservatism also has a self-promoting function of simultaneously preserving one's reputation and promoting one's status (McAndrew and Milenkovic 2002). Girls and women are particularly susceptible to being thought sexually permissive (Kreager and Staff 2009). Females who engage, or are perceived to engage, in permissive sex are thought to be less desirable as friends, dating partners, and spouses. Additionally, they are considered less moral, less likable, less intelligent, less trustworthy, and less socially adjusted (Vaillancourt and Sharma 2011). If bisexuals are thus seen as being more sexually permissive, they are simultaneously, and stereotypically, socially devalued as friends, lovers, and human beings.

The Psychological and Health Effects of Bisexual Burden

The multiple forms of cultural burden that bisexuals experience as a result of the overlapping and intersecting bias toward them may have a profound impact on their psychological wellbeing (e.g. Bostwick 2012). Dodge et al. (2007) find that bisexuals have higher rates of depression, anxiety, substance use, victimization by violence, suicidal ideation and sexual-health concerns than gays and lesbians. Similarly, Pompili et al. (2014) report that bisexuals have an increased risk of suicide attempts and suicide ideation compared to their homosexual and heterosexual peers. They found that risk factors included related victimization, peer judgments, and family rejection. Bisexual individuals also reported higher rates of mental illness and substance abuse.

Pew (2013) research also suggests that bisexual men and women were less at ease about their sexuality than lesbian and gay people. Bisexual men, in particular, were found to experience more psychological distress than gay men. They were also more likely to cite their sexuality as the reason for harming themselves. Barker et al. (2008) highlight a vicious cycle of those experiencing mental health difficulties: they were more likely to experience homelessness, abuse and violence, which, in turn, increase the risk of mental health problems.

Research has also found bisexual people have poor experiences with health professionals (King et al. 2007). For example, one US study found that over a quarter of therapists seen by bisexual clients erroneously assumed that sexual identity was relevant to the goal of therapy when the client didn't agree. About a sixth of the health care workers saw bisexuality as an illness, and 11% attempted conversion to either heterosexuality or homosexuality (Page 2007). In other words, many therapists displayed discomfort about bisexuality.

A recent analysis of data from the large scale Behavioral Risk Factor Surveillance System (BRFSS) survey across seven U.S. states found that bisexual men and women report significantly worse health outcomes than gays, lesbians and heterosexuals (Gorman et al. 2015). Using data collected between 2005 and 2010, and including an analytic sample of 10,128 sexual minority (gay, lesbian, and bisexual) and 405,145 heterosexual adults, they argue that these health disparities are tied to socio-economic status, with bisexuals reporting lower incomes and educational levels than gays, lesbians and heterosexuals. These results were significant not just because of the size and rigor of the survey, but also because they concurred with other research in the area (e.g. Conron et al. 2010).

It is possible to explain these health disparities through minority stress theory (Meyer 2003). Here, intersecting modes of oppression are likely to facilitate decreased health outcomes. While intuitively an attractive proposition, it seems unlikely that bisexuals would have such significantly worse health outcomes than gays and lesbians. Furthermore, Vrangalova and Savin-Williams (2014) found similar patterns regarding the health outcomes of those that are "mostly straight" remarkably similar to bisexuals. It is not persuasive that mostly straights experience a significant level of minority stress, which points to other issues related to bisexuals.

Instead of attributing these issues to minority stress, other options seem more persuasive. First, it is quite possible that people who are bisexual or mostly heterosexual have other factors that impact their health—such as sensation-seeking, higher sex drive, disagreeableness, shared genetic disorders and other forms of stigma, such as those that are promiscuity-related (Lippa 2008; Rieger et al. 2013; Stief et al. 2014; Zietsch et al. 2012). There are also questions related to the validity of some of the large-scale quantitative research on the problems faced by sexual minorities. The relative lack of engagement in sexual minority communities of bisexual men that skews participant recruitment in qualitative research (see Chap. 5) will also have an effect in quantitative research. Furthermore, Savin-Williams and Joyner (2014) show that heterosexual youth jokingly filling out surveys as gay or bisexual can significantly skew data, and that this is the mostly likely explanation of one recent high-profile study that found particularly negative experiences among sexual minorities.

Bisexual Privilege

Not all beliefs about bisexual men concern burden. In fact, some attitudes toward bisexuality are positive and affirming (Morris et al. 2014). This is likely to increase as generational changes contribute to the emergence of positive views as youth become more accepting of bisexuality in the wake of challenges to heteronormativity by the lesbian and gay rights movements (Herdt 2001; Pew 2013). Furthermore, in contrast to the dichotomous view of sexual orientation that underlies the denial of bisexuality; many people situate bisexuality on a continuum of sexual orientation (Bronn 2001). In some of our previous research on the attitudes of team sport athletes toward bisexual men (Anderson and Adams 2011), we showed that this led many of these young men to conceptualize bisexuality as the most natural or ideal state (Mohr and Rochlen 1999b).

Unfortunately, the academic literature on bisexuality almost unanimously focuses on the negative aspects and burdens of being bisexual in a monosexist culture. Reporting these may be necessary for political gain, but there are a number of structural privileges that bisexuals benefit from that often go unrecognized. Some of these relate to privilege over gay men, and others to privilege over both gay and straight; some to escaping persecution and others to finding sex.

Concerning privilege over gay men, the most striking finding from our research of men from the older cohort we studied is that the extreme homophobia of the 1980s and early 1990s did not seem to impact upon them to the extent that it did for gay men. It seems that their desires for men might have to remain private, but they still had their desires for women realized. Where studies have found particularly negative experiences of bisexuals this is likely due to sampling issues and the smaller percentage of bisexual men who have associations with LGBT activist communities from which participants are normally recruited (Pew 2013).

When it comes to sex, and particularly its acquisition, bisexual men have an advantage over both straight and gay men. Bisexuals can partake in heterosexual privilege, and yet still pursue sex with men. They not only have more opportunities for casual sex (i.e. they can go to a party and hit on everyone), they also have an easier time arranging threesomes in their coupled-relationships, should they desire. Whereas heterosexual couples have to negotiate how they will have a threesome, and whether it be with a male or female, a bisexual male is less concerned about the gender of the third person. This also makes it easier for a couple, where at least one member is bisexual, to progress into other forms of non-monogamies or polyamory.

There is also a greater possibility of aligning one's sexual behaviors to romantic and/or emotional preferences. As discussed in Chap. 1, there are a number of dimensions to human sexuality beyond sexual attraction, and romantic and social attractions and preferences are also important. If one is bisexual in their sexual attractions, it means that one has a better chance of finding a partner where romantic, social and sexual attractions align. From this perspective, bisexual individuals may be viewed as cognitively and interpersonally flexible, and may be admired for their attraction to personal qualities rather than simply to the gender of a partner (Zinik 1985).

Supporting this, Rostosky et al. (2010) interviewed bisexuals from multiple countries and found that bisexual people report that they feel freedom from the social binaries of sexuality and gender. This meant that they considered themselves more able to develop identities which felt right for them, and to form relationships without restrictions around who they could be attracted to. Many linked this to a sense of independence, self-awareness and authenticity. Participants also discussed their acceptance and appreciation of other people's differences, of diversity generally, and of their understanding of privilege and oppression more broadly. They felt that they were well-placed to see social biases and assumptions and to challenge these on issues beyond sexuality. So while we recognize the burden that contributes to negative effects of being bisexual, we also argue that there are benefits to being bisexual; that, when considering varying cultural zeitgeists, there can be significant variability in the bisexual experience. Thus, while the social study of bisexuality must examine the burdens bisexuals encounter, it should not discount privilege as well.

Chapter 5
The Gendering of Sexuality

In March of 2013, British Royal, Prince Harry, was reported by PinkNews.co.uk as having graciously accepted the phone number of a gay man in a nightclub. While details of the actual exchange are unknown, the gay man tweeted, "I gave Prince Harry my number tonight, he promised he'll call me if he changes his mind about women. Or men. #epicwin." If reported properly the exchange is indicative of the fact that this young, laddish, helicopter-flying, war-veteran Prince is not offended by being sexually propositioned by other men. The young Prince does not appear to be defensive about his heterosexuality. His expressed attitude, even if in jest, was one of acceptance for the legitimacy of same-sex intimacy. Backed by his support of gay charities, the Prince exemplifies the inclusivity of young men of his generation (McCormack 2012a).

This is particularly noteworthy because, historically, men would be considered gay if they engaged in or even, as in the case of Prince Harry, expressed tolerance of a same sex sexual act. Almaguer (1991: 253) suggested that American and Western European cultures historically carried "a blanket condemnation of all same sex behavior…because it is at odds with a rigid, compulsory heterosexual norm." Lancaster (1988: 116) similarly argued, "Even homosexual desires [in absence of behavior] stigmatize one as homosexual." This conflation between a single sexual act or stated desire and a sexual orientation and identity has been called the *one-time rule of homosexuality* (Anderson 2008).

Borrowing from theories of racial hypodescent in which anyone with a single "drop" of African ancestry was labeled as black (Harris 1964), the one-time rule of homosexuality describes the phenomenon where any same-sex sexual act or desire is perceived to make that person gay, regardless of other desires, identity or sexual history.

However, the inverse of this rule has never applied to gay men: a gay man who has sex with a woman is not perceived as heterosexual or bisexual. Schwartz (1995: 12) wrote:

> We have to rethink how we have demonized the power of homosexuality so that we assume it to be the greater truth of our sexual self—as if one drop of homosexuality tells the truth of self while one drop of heterosexuality in a homosexual life means nothing.

The one-time rule of homosexuality contributed to the erasure of bisexuality. Highlighting this, if a self-identifying straight man were to be caught having oral sex with another man in the 1980s, he would not have been socially perceived as bisexual, but rather he would have been cast as gay. The solitary drop of homosexuality in the life of an otherwise heterosexually identified male erased the entirety of heterosexuality. Likewise, a man being behaviorally bisexual was still viewed in society as gay.

There were some exceptions to the one-time rule: heterosexual men who financially profited from sex with men were less inclined to fear gay stigma (Klein 1993). Same-sex sex was also less threatening to heterosexual men in certain masculine institutions, like prisons and the military, where heterosexual relief was not available (Gear and Ngubeni 2002). More so, there might be cultural, iconic exceptions, like rock star David Bowie. Even so, the general rule for most heterosexual men in American and British culture was that a heterosexual identity was partially based upon exclusively opposite-sex sexual behaviors (Kimmel 1996).

The one-time rule of homosexuality existed because heterosexuality has traditionally maintained hegemonic dominance in North American and Western European cultures, where privilege is unequally distributed according to one's sexuality (Rubin 2012). What is crucial to understand about the one-time rule of homosexuality, however, is that it is not solely about policing sexuality—it also polices *gender* (Anderson 2008). This is because of a broader conflation of gender and sexuality in society. Here, the notion is that sexual orientation can be inferred from a person's gendered displays. Put simply, male homosexuality is equated with effeminacy, while women 'acting butch' is deemed synonymous with lesbianism (Griffin 1998; Pronger 1990). In this framework, gender is perceived as the window to ones sexuality.

This conflation of gender and sexuality means that it is vital to theorize the intersection of their sexual identities with their gendered identities in order to understand bisexual men's lives. This is because the experiences of bisexual men will be contingent not just on broader attitudes toward bisexuality and homosexuality, but how these intersect with dominant conceptions of masculinity as well (McLean 2007). In other words, social notions of what it means to be bisexual will alter depending on the cultural zeitgeist in relation to homophobia and the gendered practices it regulates. Accordingly, in this chapter we focus on the intersections of homophobia with masculinity and the recent developments in conceptualizing men's masculinities in periods of low homophobia. We analyze the relationship between masculinity and men's sexuality through the notion of homohysteria (Anderson 2009; McCormack and Anderson 2014a) to highlight the gendered policing that occurs in times of high homophobia. We finish the chapter by documenting the social trends that have emerged as homohysteria has decreased.

Homohysteria

Sociological research has demonstrated that masculinities in Western cultures have been closely related to personal and societal homophobia (e.g. Connell 1995; Epstein 1997; Plummer 1999). Our own research has demonstrated how decreasing homophobia has a positive influence on heterosexual young men (Anderson and McCormack 2014; McCormack and Anderson 2010a). However, levels of homophobia do not in-and-of themselves explain changes in masculinities. Homophobia is only part of the social equation of importance to masculinity and sexuality. The cultural awareness of homosexuality existing within one's culture is also important.

Anderson (2009) developed the concept *homohysteria* to explain the power dynamics of changing homophobia on the masculinities of heterosexual men. While earlier scholarship demonstrated that high levels of cultural homophobia influence individuals to distance themselves from social suspicion of homosexuality through the avoidance of gender atypical behaviors (Floyd 2000; Ibson 2002), there was less attention paid to how changing social norms would influence these behaviors. Anderson used the term homohysteria to situate this scholarship within specific social and historical conditions, arguing that homophobia only operates this way in *homohysteric* settings. In other words, homophobia only influences gendered behaviors in particular social and historical contexts.

There are three social conditions that must be met for a homohysteric culture to exist: (1) widespread awareness that homosexuality exists as an immutable sexual orientation within a significant portion of a culture's population; (2) high levels of homophobia in that culture; and (3) an association of gender atypicality with homosexuality. As each of these factors change, the level of homohysteria and the nature of gender dynamics in the culture will vary. Given that each of these factors can and do change, it is clear that there will be: temporal variation within any given culture; variation across cultures; and organizational variance within any given culture.

Homohysteria is particularly useful for understanding different attitudes to homosocial tactility in homophobic cultures. We ask why men can hold hands in Iran without being socially perceived as gay, but in America in the 1980s they would have been. Both of these cultures had high degrees of homophobia. The difference occurs because it is simply not accepted within Iran that homosexuality exists (Afary 2009)—the first condition of homohysteria mentioned earlier. Instead, homosexuality is claimed to be a Western, imperialist phenomenon (Frank et al. 2010). From this cultural perspective, homosexuality is considered an aberration (Zuhur 2005), and combined with extreme homophobia, homosexuality is effectively erased.

Iran, and other similar cultures in Africa and the Middle East are thus highly homophobic but they are not homohysteric. This is why homophobia does not regulate these men's gendered behaviors. Supporting this, news reports that document the persecution of gay men in these countries tend to report that the men were found engaging in same-sex sexual acts—they are not identified through their gendered behaviors. Thus, homohysteria provides an explanation for the differences between the intersections of homophobia, masculinity and men's tactility in differing contemporary cultures, explaining why homophobia retains the ability to regulate gender in one culture but not another.

Considering countries like Iran also highlights that attitudes toward homosexuality can become more intolerant as well as progressive (Plummer 2014). Homophobia is often used for political gain, and can also be seen as another form of the rejection of imperialism in particular contexts. Even so, Smith (2011) highlights that while trends in homophobia occur in both directions, the global trend is "towards greater approval of homosexual behavior with 87% of countries moving in that direction and with the gains in approval also being larger than the declines."

Homohysteria is also contingent upon the social dynamics of organizations within any macro culture. This recognizes that levels of homophobia vary greatly even within countries, and particularly one as diverse as the U.S. Anderson (2005b) demonstrates this in his ethnography of competing co-educational university cheerleading associations. Both of these cultures were aware that homosexuality existed as a sexual orientation, but homophobia was only stigmatized in one. The men of universities belonging to one cheerleading association adhered to orthodox notions of masculinity, while the men of universities belonging to an association which supported gay rights celebrated femininity among men. Males in the inclusive association would dance provocatively and be thrown in the air by women without censure, while the conservative teams perceived these behaviors as indicative of homosexuality and thus inconsistent with masculinity. Accordingly, within the same broader culture, and the same sport, one organizational culture was homohysteric while the other was not.

A Stage Model of Homohysteria

Based on the foundational arguments of homohysteria discussed above, we have developed a stage model of homohysteria that is rooted in research on masculinities in the U.S. since the late 1800s. This model has three stages: (a) homoerasure; (b) homohysteria; (c) inclusivity, and we suggest, particularly given similar developments in the UK and Australia, that it may prove useful for understanding homophobia, changing masculinities and the importance of sexual minority politics in other contexts.

While we devised our stage model in relation to homohysteria, other concepts have been used to highlight three significant cultural zeitgeists in the 20th century related to homosexuality (Dean 2014). For example, Ghaziani (2014: p. 9) discusses the "closet, coming out, and post-gay eras." He argues that the closet era was defined by concealment, isolation and shame, and lasted until the mid-1940s. He defines the period between 1945 and 1997 as the coming out era, as a period when 'gayborhoods' flourished and people increasingly lived as openly gay (although not necessarily without stigma). The third era emerged in 1997 and is known as

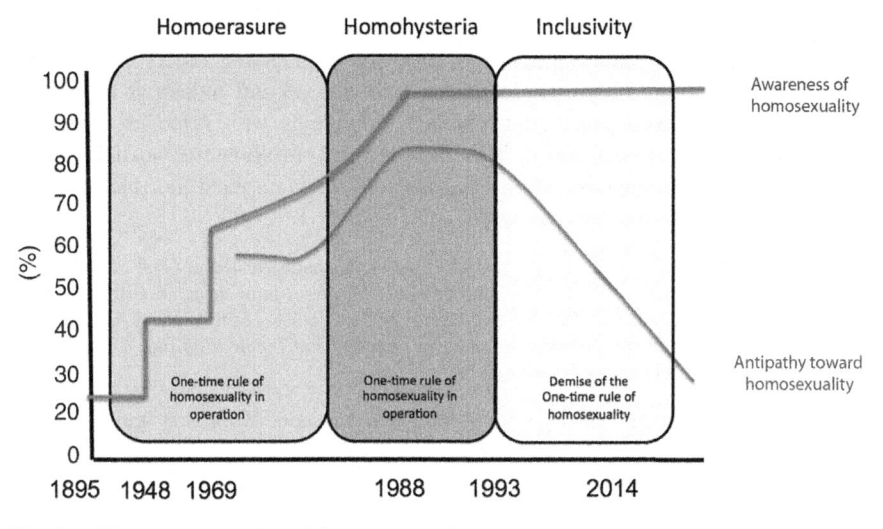

Fig. 5.1 Visual representation of the stage model

"post-gay," characterized by a "dramatic acceptance of homosexuality and a corresponding assimilation of gays and lesbians into the mainstream" (p. 9). There is significant similarity between Ghaziani's characterization of the 20th century and our own, with the differences in time explained by his focus on the influence of homophobia on urban sociology and the organization of local gay neighborhoods and our focus on the influence of homophobia on gendered behaviors. We now explicate our stage model as a way of demonstrating the emergence and contemporary decline of homohysteria in American culture.

Figure 5.1 provides a visual representation of this stage model. The levels of homophobia are drawn from GSS data (see Anderson 2009; Loftus 2001).

Homoerasure

Anderson (2009) argued that homohysteria is a product of modernity, and that the conditions for a culture to be homohysteric are the result of the discourses of gender and sexuality that emerged from the second industrial revolution in the west (see Cancian 1987). Recognizing that contemporary taxonomies of sexual identity are the result of specific historical, social and intellectual circumstances (Giddens 1992; Greenberg 1988), the modern understanding of gay identity is pivotal to the emergence of homohysteric cultures. There is only evidence supporting homohysteria in modern cultures, and homohysteria does not apply to cultures that have no understanding of sexual identities, such as pre-modern Western civilizations (Spencer 1995).

Prior to urbanization, the majority of the population lived in rural areas and males with same-sex sexual desire were unlikely to encounter others with similar desires. However, the migration to the cities of the second industrial revolution provided a population density that enabled individuals with same-sex desire to organize socially (Spencer 1995). This included the emergence of sexual subcultures of gay men (Chauncey 1994). D'Emilio (1998: 11) argued the role of social identity grew during this time as well:

> The interlocking processes of urbanization and industrialization created a social context in which an autonomous personal life could develop. Affection, intimate relationships, and sexuality moved increasingly into the realm of individual choice…in this setting, men and women who felt a strong erotic attraction to their own sex could begin to fashion from their feeling a personal identity and a way of life.

Related to the censure of these identities, new forms of labor that included long working hours structured men away from their families (Cancian 1987), influencing Freud's (1905) theorizing of same-sex sexual desires as a form of gender inversion. Near contemporaneously, Westphal, Ulrichs and Krafft-Ebing sought to classify homosexual acts as belonging to a *type* of person—a gender invert.

The emergence of sexual identities was supported by developments in the public and political sphere. The 1895 conviction of Oscar Wilde for "gross indecency" was particularly important: So extensive was the media coverage around the trial of Britain's celebrated playwright, it became emblematic of the gay male identity. The case consolidated the conflation of gender a-typicality with same-sex attraction; the image of the male homosexual as effeminate. It was reported that many men fled to France after Wilde's conviction (Norton 1992). Thus, the first wide-scale social recognition and awareness of same-sex sexuality as a static and relatively immutable sexual identity was accompanied by social and legal oppression of same-sex sexual acts. Ibson (2002) provides evidence that this British phenomenon influenced American men's behaviors, too.

This stigmatization of same-sex sexual identities was also consolidated through the medicalization of homosexuality (Greenberg 1988). Corresponding with an increasing criminalization of male same-sex sex, doctors sought to define these acts within a medical framework as a way of consolidating their own emerging respectability as a profession. As a result, homosexuals were considered mentally ill or morally depraved (Greenberg 1988).

While sub-cultures organized around same-sex desires existed in the early 20th Century (Beisel 1998; Chauncey 1994), threat of social and legal censure kept these cultures mostly underground and the general population was unaware that such cultures existed. Where there was knowledge of same-sex desire, it was greatly stigmatized and the general population rejected the notion that same-sex sexual identities were legitimate (Johnson 2004). These were thus cultures of *erasure*, where homophobia was so extreme that social and legal persecution forced sexual minorities to conceal their sexual desires and identities, preventing identity politics from occurring.

In this stage of erasure, gendered behaviors are not regulated by homophobia and men did not find their behaviors policed in the way we often think of today. In the latter decades of the 19th century and early part of the 20th, men exhibited a great deal of physical intimacy, posed for photos while sat on each other's laps and gently hugging, and expressed themselves emotionally in letters (see Deitcher 2001; Ibson 2002). These cultures were homophobic, but not homohysteric.

A key development in the emergence of homohysteria in American culture was the publication of Kinsey's (1948) study of males' sexual practice (Anderson 2011a). Occurring during the dawn of the political context of McCarthyism, Kinsey presented homosexuality as a "normal" variation of human sexuality (Weeks 1985), claiming that 10% of the population was homosexual and that far more had engaged in same-sex sexual acts (see Introduction). Partially because Kinsey's research raised awareness of the existence of homosexuality in the US, sexual minorities were purged from public office and homosexual men were labeled "sex deviates" (Johnson 2004). The oppression of homosexuality was near-total: it was culturally stigmatized, classified as a mental illness, and criminalized with harsh sentencing (Nardi et al. 1994). Thus, most same-sex attracted males remained silent about their desires. While this "Lavender Scare" could be conceived as evidence of a homohysteric culture, we do not classify it as such because homosexuality was effectively erased.

However, the sexual conservatism of the 1950s was contested by increasingly liberal attitudes toward sexuality in the 1960s and 1970s (Spencer 1995). Political activism regarding sexuality split into assimilationists that supported a politics of sameness alongside a more revolutionary politics that parodied masculinity and embraced gender a-typicality to contest homophobia and heterosexual privilege (Shepard 2009). Even though a growing proportion of the heterosexual population was aware of homosexuality as a static sexual identity and, while societal attitudes were still largely negative, there was less overt oppression even as legal discrimination persisted (Greenberg 1988): This was because people did not readily believe or suspect that a friend or family member could be gay. During this time, sexual minorities were still perceived as belonging to sexual subcultures in particular metropolitan cities. It was only in the 1980s that American culture entered a phase of *homohysteria*.

Homohysteria

Despite the liberalizing trend in the 1960s and 1970s, a combination of social factors led to an upsurge in homophobic attitudes in the 1980s in the West. In the mid-1980s, high levels of homophobia (Loftus 2001) combined with a closing-down of inclusivity that had resulted from the feminist movements and beat neck politicking of the 1960s and 1970s (Hall 2013). This occurred for three reasons:

1. HIV/AIDS

HIV/AIDS made visible the notion that homosexuals were present in the population in large numbers (Shilts 1987), giving cultural credibility to Kinsey's figure of 10%. Iconic figures dying of AIDS-related illnesses, like Robert Reed (Mr. Brady of the Brady Bunch) and Rock Hudson, also highlighted that homosexuality existed in men who seemed to embody masculinity and heterosexuality. In this culture, homosexuality was pathologized as a danger to physical health (Weeks 1991) and AIDS-phobia was exacerbated by a media panic. Rumors persisted that AIDS could be caught by a handshake or sneeze. Health care professionals, schools, and even airlines denied service to those with HIV/AIDs; some undertakers refused to bury those who had died from illnesses related to the disease (Weinberg et al. 1994). The image of the effeminate homosexual was replaced by that of the emaciated one (Weeks 1991).

2. Fundamentalist Christianity

Fundamentalist Christianity grew increasingly concerned with and opposed to homosexuality and bisexuality, positioning them as threats to the nuclear family while conveniently using this fear to increase donations to the church in an age in which church attendance began to decline (Chaves 1989). This corresponded with an increasingly conservative moral outlook more broadly. As Loftus (2001: 765) describes, "From the 1970s through the mid-1980s, Americans held increasingly traditional religious beliefs, with more people supporting prayer in school, and believing the Bible was the literal word of God."

3. The Grand Old Party (Republicans)

Republican politicians adopted the religious right's culture war against homosexuality, realizing that elections could be won through inspiring socially conservative Christians to vote (see Sherkat et al. 2011). These conservative politicians drew on fears of homosexuality and bisexuality and HIV to foster a moral panic about sexuality, social change and so-called traditional family values (Lugg 1998).

It was in this epoch that awareness of homosexuality as a static identity in America was near-total and attitudinal homophobia reached its apex. Evidencing this, data from the 1987 General Social Survey (GSS) documented 77% of Americans stating that homosexual sex was *always wrong*, a rise from the previous decade. Following from the emergence of modern sexual identities and the conflation of gender and sexuality, these conditions proved to be a perfect storm for homohysteria. In this homohysteric culture, where femininity in males was conflated with homosexuality, men had to distance themselves socially and attitudinally from homosexuality (Floyd 2000; McCreary 1994). They aligned their gendered behaviors with idealized and narrowing definitions of masculinity.

Men used culturally-endorsed sports to consolidate their masculine standing (Burton-Nelson 1994), and demonstrated masculinity through anger and violence, while denying fear and weakness (Kimmel 1996). They also stopped engaging in homosocial intimacy (Pollack 1999). Derlega et al. (1989) found undergraduate heterosexual males rated photos of men hugging as significantly more "abnormal" than photos of men standing alongside each other; conversely, they did not rate mixed-sex couples or women hugging as abnormal. It is understandable that in such a culture many bisexual men would be more likely to pair up with women, removing themselves from this cultural war.

However, while HIV/AIDS led to the hysteria of the 1980s, it also served as a catalyst for identity politics and more inclusive attitudes. Given the power of social contact in improving social attitudes (Smith et al. 2009), the increased numbers of openly gay and bisexual males that resulted from the visibility of HIV/AIDS began to improve cultural attitudes among heterosexual communities in the early 1990s, particularly with Bill Clinton's advocating for gays to serve in the military in 1992. This is a trend that continues today (Anderson 2014; Kangasvuo 2011). As homophobia decreased, so did the hysteria and homophobia gradually became less effective in policing gendered behaviors—something McCormack (2012: 63) describes as a "virtuous circle of decreasing homophobia."

Inclusivity

The decrease of homophobia in British and American cultures accelerated in the 21st century (e.g. Baunach 2012; Clement and Field 2014). We describe a culture where people with positive attitudes toward homosexuality are in the majority, and where there is widespread recognition of homosexuality as a sexual identity, as one of *inclusivity*. This does not mean that these cultures are inclusive in general, as there may well be issues related to class, ethnicity, and disability among other forms of discrimination. *Inclusivity* refers to attitudes toward gay men and lesbians, and even here heteronormativity may persist.

This cultural condition is also distinct from that of erasure for two reasons. First, the history of the UK and US is such that there are cultural signs and reminders of the previous homohysteric culture; and second, because of the awareness of homosexuality in the culture—near total today where it was almost completely erased a century earlier. It is hard to claim that the cultures of masculinity in the early 1900s were inclusive of homosexuality (Ibson 2002), and there is significant evidence to say they were homophobic (Spencer 1995).

The key driver of decreasing homohysteria during this stage has been the improving attitudes toward homosexuality. The late 1990s and first decade of the new millennium saw the political labor of feminist and LGBT identity politics come to fruition. During this period, in which homohysteria decreased but homophobia was still used as a political tool (Harris 2006), men started to lose some of the hypermasculinity of the 1980s. One of the most visible elements of this was the emergence of the metrosexual (Coad 2008).

In the late 1990s, metrosexuality emerged as a counter-cultural trend among young men who cared about their appearance and had a sexualized image of themselves. McNair (2002, p. 157) described metrosexuality as "a homosexualized vision of masculinity, in the sense that this studied narcissism and attention to self-grooming are traditionally associated with gayness." The metrosexual was interpreted as a conscious rejection of more traditional male norms where such expressionism was strictly censured. The metrosexual is such an important figure in understanding decreasing homohysteria because metrosexuality was used by heterosexual men as a way to engage in a softer form of masculinity without being socially perceived as gay.

At the time, scholars queried whether the metrosexual was anything more than a surface level change, positing that men were seeking to keep their privilege in a changing social context (Demetriou 2001). It was during this time – in the 1990s and until the early 2000s – where changes were occurring but any confidence about decreasing homophobia would have had to be tempered by recognition that sufficient time had not passed for these changing attitudes and behaviors to become consolidated. While we characterize the 1990s as inclusive, their dynamic was distinct from the decade either side of it—no longer homohysteric like the 1980s, but not the relaxed inclusivity of the new millennium (Anderson 2014; McCormack 2012).

However, research has since shown that these shifts were in masculinities were the early stages of something profound. Anderson (2002, 2005a) found that openly gay men were being accepted on their sporting teams, challenging dominant forms of masculinity by being the *best* on their teams. Furthermore, he found other sporting teams where *competing* versions of masculinity held equal sway. A style of masculinity that was inclusive of gay men and valued the voice of women was valued by as many people as the once-dominant misogynistic and homophobic version (Anderson 2005b). At a similar time, metrosexuality moved from the counter-culture to be embraced in sports that were considered highly masculine (Harris and Clayton 2007) and among men who use make-up but perceive themselves to be part of mainstream culture (Adams 2011; Gough et al. 2014). These findings where supported by research showing the increasing inclusion of sexual minorities in a range of contexts (Jones and Clarke 2007; Savin-Williams 2005).

These shifts in masculinity corresponded with the sustained decrease in homophobia that continues to the present day. General Social Survey (GSS) data show the proportion of the US population condemning homosexuality has steadily declined since 1987. In a statistical analysis of this data, Keleher and Smith (2012: 1232) contend that "willingness to accept lesbians and gays has grown enormously since 1990." While more progressive attitudes toward homosexuality are partly due to generational replacement (Loftus 2001), Keleher and Smith show that all demographic groups analyzed became more tolerant, and, importantly, that all age cohorts became more tolerant at the same rate; arguing that "we are witnessing a sweeping change in attitudes toward lesbians and gay men" (p. 1324).

Recent Pew (June 13, 2013 available online) research found that 70% of those born after 1980 support same-sex marriage, and 74% of these Americans believe that "homosexuality should be accepted by society" and a May, 2014 Pew poll found 66% of Americans say it wouldn't matter if a presidential candidate is gay or lesbian; 27% say they would be less likely to support a gay or lesbian candidate while 5% would be more likely. Highlighting the speed of social acceptance, when the same questions were asked just seven years earlier, 46% said they would be less likely to vote for a homosexual candidate" (see also Baunach 2012). Supporting this, Smith et al. (2014) find that there is between 20.1 and 23.4 percentage point difference in people's attitudes toward homosexuality and gay rights for those under 30 compared to those over 65. They argue this is due to their cohort – their generation – and not the result of processes of ageing.

Data from other sources also provide evidence of this shift among young people. For example, a survey of over 200,000 undergraduates finds that 65% of U.S. freshman support same-sex marriage (Pryor et al. 2011). More recently, an ABC News/Washington Post opinion poll (Langer 2013) shows support for gay marriage across America is now at 58%. They highlight a shift of 26 percentage points since 2004, and that the number of people who think homosexuality is a choice has decreased from 40 to 24%, while those who think it is "just the way they are" (p. 3) has increased from 49 to 62%. Pew (2013) research also found that 70% of millennials (those born after 1990) support same-sex marriage in the US, and 74% of these Americans believe that "homosexuality should be accepted by society." The following year they found more striking results: that 85% of American Catholics aged under 29 support gay equality, and 75% gay marriage (Pew 2014). These figures are sure to rise because in June of 2015 the United States Supreme Court recently made gay marriage available to all American citizens, in all states.

Recent research in the *American Sociological Review* also highlights the dramatic change in attitudes toward homosexuality. In a national survey of just over 1000 people, Doan et al. (2014) found that almost 100% of heterosexuals supported legal equality for gays and lesbians. However, they also found a level of disconnect in this broader support when asked about particular laws such as marriage for same-sex couples—here 55% of heterosexuals supported the law. Similarly, 55% of heterosexuals approved of gay men kissing on the cheek in public. This is something Ghaziani (2014: 252) calls "performative progressiveness," where some heterosexuals proclaim values of equality without practicing them in their lives. It is an important corrective to any argument that no inequality exists for gays and lesbians, but it is still evidence of profound change—a clear majority of heterosexuals (55%) support gay marriage *and* public displays of affection among gay male couples. Given this does not take differences in age cohort into account, it is reasonable to assume that young people will be even more progressive in their interactions with gays and lesbians.

Evidence for the impact of decreasing homophobia is present in qualitative research, and helps understand the dissonance between attitudes and experience; showing positive effects on the lives of sexual minorities (Cohler and Hammack 2007; Ghaziani 2014; Savin-Williams 2005). This includes better representation of gay people in the media (Netzley 2010), an improving environment for gay students in schools and universities (Robinson and Espelage 2011), and more positive experiences for gay males within sports compared to a decade ago (Anderson 2011a). Highlighting the speed of change among young people, Savin-Williams (2005) argues that many gay youth are no longer defined by their sexuality, rejecting a victimhood framework of sexual minority development.

These changes have both been impacted by and helped bring about improved legal equality for same-sex couples. A 2003 Supreme Court of the United States decision found unconstitutional the few remaining states with sodomy laws on their books, and in 2013 it also ruled that Section 3 of the Defense of Marriage Act was unconstitutional. Numerous local, state and national measures next introduced to promote civil and legal equality for sexual minorities, including (at the time of writing) 37 states that recognize gay marriage before the US Supreme Court ruled that no state could deny gays the right to marry. Similarly, the first same-sex marriages occurred in the UK in 2014, and there are no anti-gay laws in the UK.

The development of positive attitudes toward homosexuality is influenced by a range of other factors, too: Positive attitudes have seen shown to be correlated to contact with sexual minorities (Smith et al. 2009), the existence of 'ally groups' within organizational or institutional communities (Szalacha 2003), early childhood experiences that normalize homosexuality (Stotzer 2009), and the role of the internet and improving media discourses of sexual minorities (McCormack 2014b; Netzley 2010). Smith et al. (2014: 13) argue that "positive attitudes towards homosexuality and gay rights are generally greater among younger adults, the better educated, those attending religious services less frequently, and women."

It is also important to stress that decreasing homophobia is an uneven social process. The visibility of gay and bisexual men is, for example, still restricted in professional sports, among senior politicians, within organized religions, and among elementary and high school teachers (Anderson 2011a). Notwithstanding this variance, considerable evidence documents a markedly improved environment for sexual minorities. Weeks (2007) provides an overview of this improved social, political and legal context in the U.S. and the U.K., arguing that:

> The momentum is positive, and largely due to one essential feature of this new world: grass-roots agency is central to the direction we are moving in. Increasingly the contemporary world is a world we are making for ourselves, part of the long process of the democratisation of everyday life (p. x).

The masculinities of men in this stage of inclusivity have changed dramatically (McCormack 2012). In general, adolescent males no longer police their gendered behaviors to avoid being socially perceived as gay; or do so to a much lesser extent. Because the stage of inclusivity is the contemporary zeitgeist, we discuss the effects of inclusivity in further detail below.

The Effects of Inclusivity

An Expansion of Gendered Boundaries

The erosion of homohysteria has led to a significant expansion of the set of acceptable gendered behaviors for heterosexual males. Researchers find adolescent males eschewing the heteromasculinity of the 1980s, and altering once-strong codes of gender and sexuality (McCormack 2012a). In settings of inclusivity, heterosexual men are not afraid to associate with homosexuals: research documents heterosexual men maintaining friendships with openly gay male peers (e.g. Adams and Anderson 2012; Stotzer 2009). Gay-Straight Alliances are an increasingly common and positive phenomenon in American high schools (Walls et al. 2013).

The erosion of homophobia has similar effects on the ways in which males embrace artifacts once coded as feminine and thus homosexual (Hall 2014). Adams (2011) documents adolescent males wearing pink soccer boots, and an Adweek report finds 45% of young heterosexual men engage in hair removal and 32% have facials (Moses 2013)—a figure that has been as high as 63.6% in academic research (Boroughs et al. 2005). Men are able to perform ballet and even play in gay football leagues without having their masculinity questioned (Haltom and Worthen 2014; Jarvis 2013). While some are skeptical of the gender politics of such trends (e.g. Frank 2014), men's increasing use of grooming products, including make-up, is a positive if consumerist trend that speaks to more inclusive masculine behaviors (Gough et al. 2014).

Whereas Pollack (1999) described heterosexual boys as unable to provide emotional support to each other, a growing body of work documents the ability of heterosexual males to openly value emotional intimacy (e.g. Anderson 2009). Luttrell (2012) documents ethnic minority boys esteeming love, care and solidarity in their friendships, while Baker and Hotek (2011) demonstrate that heterosexual high school wrestlers frequently provide emotional support to their teammates in caring and intimate ways.

Gentle touch and homosocial intimacy between men is another defining characteristic of heterosexual males in cultures of inclusivity. Hugging and soft touch is prevalent among American high school students (Anderson 2014), and there are significant levels of bodily touch in friendships between straight and gay men (Barrett 2013). We have documented how young straight men cuddle and spoon with their friends, explaining that such behaviors are ways of expressing love and support for friends and are regular, everyday occurrences in their social lives (Anderson and McCormack 2014).

Heterosexual males are also less likely to fight in a culture of inclusivity. Gottzén and Kremer-Sadlik (2012) show that while maintaining orthodox versions of masculinity in some domestic capacities, the fathers they researched in Los Angeles condemn violence in youth sport or around their children more generally.

Further evidence for these whole-sale changes to Western notions of masculinities comes from 2013 data from one of the world's largest advertising agencies, JWT (formerly known as J. Walter Thompson Company). In a survey of 500 American and 500 British men aged 18 and over, it shows that men are rapidly losing orthodox notions of masculinity, in multiple arenas (JWT 2013). The report summarizes:

> Conventional ideals about male and female domains, activities, behaviors and styles are evolving: we are moving toward a more nuanced concept of gender that questions some stereotypes and revises old assumptions. Millennials are leading the way, less confined to traditional gender roles and more willing to break long-standing norms to express their individuality. And…[this generation]…is poised to hold the least rigidly defined views of gender as they reach adulthood.

The report shows that 75% of men agreed with the statement "Men and women don't need to conform to traditional roles and behaviors anymore;" 72% agreed that it was okay for boys to wear pink and for girls to play with trucks; and 78% thought there was as much pressure on men to take care of their bodies as women. Most striking, however, is the evidence of a generational shift, with stark differences between men of two age cohorts.

	Aged 18–34	Aged 48–67
Approval of using skin care products	60%	50%
Approval of body hair removal	45%	22%
Wearing foundation	18%	4%
Wearing eyeliner	12%	1%
Wearing pink	39%	26%
Wearing a "man bag"	51%	28%

So what do these 1,000 men suggest makes a man in contemporary society? The most frequent response at 70% is being a "gentleman" with good manners, and the second and third most frequent are keeping his word, at 65%, and his personal values, at 64%. The next most frequent was intelligence, at 57%. A man's ability to "bond over sports," at 21%, was ranked lower than 15 other answers. Men ranked emotional support for family, parenting, and attractiveness higher. At the bottom of the list was number of sexual conquests, at just 8%. Without homohysteria, men care less about proving their heterosexual masculinity.

Data from dozens of other ethnographic studies of heterosexual men in both feminized and masculinized spaces supports this research on both sides of the Atlantic (Hall 2014; Magrath et al. 2013; Roberts 2013). The evidence suggests that inclusive masculinities are increasingly prevalent among adolescent and that the homophobia, misogyny, violence, and homosocial separation associated with orthodox masculinity is increasingly stigmatized (McCormack and Anderson 2014a; Roberts 2014).

Many of the long-held codes, behaviors, and other symbols of what separates masculine men from feminized men are blurring in this culture of inclusivity, making behaviors and attitudes increasingly problematic to describe as masculine or feminine, and also gay or straight. Yesterday's rules no longer seem to apply. The codes of gay are increasingly adopted by heterosexuals, and therefore become meaningless as symbols of sexuality division. This has a profound impact not just with their gender, but also on their sexual behaviors.

Erosion of the One-Time Rule of Homosexuality

The one-time rule of homosexuality that policed men's sexual behaviors so effectively in the 1980s has been losing its power in the 21st century. When men can identify as "mostly straight" because they engage in same-sex sex only occasionally

(Savin-Williams and Vrangalova 2013), the requirement of opposite-sex "purity" can no longer be seen as necessary for a heterosexual identity.

The rule started to lose its power in the 2000s. Anderson (2008a) found 40% of the athletes in one of his studies had engaged in some form of genital-sexual practice with another man, yet none were made gay or bisexual for it. The figure of the metrosexual also played with notions of homosexuality, as the desire to be objectified included welcoming gay men's desire for their bodies (Coad 2008).

The one-time rule has even less relevance in the second decade of this millennium: when self-identified heterosexual men kiss other men on the cheeks and lips in the UK, US, and Australia (Anderson 2014). Anderson and his colleagues used extensive survey, ethnographic and interview data in all three countries to demonstrate that self-identified heterosexual men are kissing other men. The UK has the greatest prevalence, with 89% of heterosexual male undergraduate men interviewed having at some point kissed another male friend on the lips (or having been kissed) and the United States trailing with 10% of American heterosexual undergraduate males kissing. Esterline and Galupo (2013) also find 12% of American heterosexual undergraduate men have kissed another male, normally framed as a form of joking.

Picture A

Men of the University of Chichester Hockey Club exemplifying that a kiss between men no longer is equated with homosexuality.

Although most of these informants maintain that the kisses have been stripped of all sexual connotations, this is not always the case with sustained kissing. While the British students who kissed for a sustained period said it was not a form of sexual pleasure, they were nonetheless aware that it could be perceived as a "gay act" by others in the shared public space.

Perhaps it is because of this awareness that these men played up their kissing, *performing* it in the context of homosocial bonding. Homoerotic behaviors sometimes serve as an ironic proclamation of one's heteromasculinity (McCormack and Anderson 2010a), and through kissing these men simultaneously trouble the one-time rule of homosexuality as they consolidate their own heterosexual standing. Still, there are limits to the extent to which dominant ideals about heterosexuality stretch. There is no indication that the heterosexual men studied in Anderson's work desired to engage in or accept as heterosexual extended kissing that has the intent of deriving sexual pleasure.

The influence of the one-time rule persists in other ways. Flanders and Hatfield (2012) gave 216 undergraduates a questionnaire to answer which presented participants with a one-paragraph vignette describing an individual that either desired or engaged in sexual behavior with another person. The different conditions of the vignette included an individual with a history of heterosexual dating and a current same-sex interest. Half of the vignettes described the target as desiring to kiss or perform oral sex on her or his same-sex interest, while the other half described the target as actually kissing or performing oral sex. 76% of participants said that performing oral sex classified men and women as something other than straight, while significantly fewer thought this was the case for desiring to do the act.

However, Flanders and Hatfield's (2012) research also shows the lessening of the rule. 25% of the participants classified those they read about as heterosexual, and of those who did not, more classified the individual as bisexual than homosexual. In other words, when presented with the unique perspective of the sexual history of an individual with both opposite-sex and same-sex desires or experiences, the majority of participants categorized both the female and male targets as bisexual, with significantly fewer participants classifying the targets as heterosexual or homosexual. Hatfield and Flanders thus illustrate that today's youth do not polarize sexuality.

Decreasing Biphobia

There have been very few investigations of heterosexuals' attitudes toward bisexuality specifically (e.g. Zivony and Lobel 2014). Although Matsuda et al. (2014) have recently created and validated an instrument to measure it—the Attitudes Regarding Bisexuality Scale—it has not yet been implemented. However, in June 2013, Pew Research released the results of a survey of LGBT Americans in which 92% of bisexuals said that society had become more accepting of them in the past decade; 92% also said that they expected matters to continue to improve in the forthcoming decade.

Yost and Thomas (2012) surveyed young heterosexuals about their attitudes toward bisexuality by asking participants what came to mind when they were presented with scenarios of different forms of bisexual desire. While the majority thought of definitions of bisexuality, some questioned whether bisexuality existed.

While showing elements of bisexual burden, these results highlight the low levels of such stereotyping among young people. Just 18% thought on first impressions that a bisexual man might be gay or straight is low, and only 8% thought this about bisexual women.

We do not wish to minimize the damage of homophobia or biphobia on lived experiences, but these findings might surprise some people, particularly those who maintain that matters of homophobia have not significantly improved. The most frequently reported form of homophobia came in the form of slurs or jokes, and here just 16% of those surveyed indicated that this had happened to them in the previous year. Regarding more serious issues, only 6% stated that they had been rejected by a family member or friend, only 5% had been treated unfairly by an employer, and only 4% had been threatened or physically attacked because of their bisexuality (unfortunately, the data does not say what percent were physical attacked). 77% of bisexuals have never been threatened or physically attacked.

Further evidence for the rise of positive experiences of bisexuality comes from comparing 2002 National Survey of Family Growth data on 17 year-old girls against 2006–2008 data. It showed that there was a significant increase in the number of girls engaging in same-sex sex, pointing to a decrease in sexual stigma toward these acts. This interpretation of the increase from 5 to 11% in the number of girls engaging in some form of sexual contact with other girls is supported by the fact that opposite-sex sexual contact decreased from 63 to 46% in the same time period (Gartrell et al. 2011). Taken together, these studies suggest that the operations of homophobia and biphobia are eroding, particularly among youth.

With quantitative research showing that bisexual youths maintain elevated social and emotional difficulties compared to gay or lesbian youth (Robinson and Espelage 2011), but in a context where overall cultural discrimination against sexual minorities is declining (Doan et al. 2014), we set out to explore how these sociological phenomena affect the experiences of openly bisexual youth in British sixth form colleges (Anderson et al. 2014; Morris et al. 2014).

This research is independent to our empirical work in this book, and is based on in-depth interviews with bisexual youth in schools in the UK. We found that, while there were some issues with their bisexuality at secondary school, once reaching 16 and attending what is known as 'college' in the UK, those problems were replaced by total support from their peers. The time during which they experienced bisexual burden also reduced, generally lasting a few days or weeks rather than years.

Highlighting the growing presence of sexual minorities coming out of the closet, the Pew (2013) findings on LGBT Americans found a greater preponderance of out sexual minorities at younger ages. In a statistically representative sample of Americans, 38% of those who publically identified as bisexual were aged 18–29. The first category of ages surveyed, spanning just 11 years, captured 38% of those that openly identified as bisexual. Compare that to those aged 50–64, a larger age bracket, which captured just 14% of the total population of bisexuals.

Pew is not alone in finding this. Results from the Gallup (2012) survey on LGBT Americans, as well as data from multiple General Social Surveys, also indicate that LGBT respondents are generally younger than the overall adult population. This means that more have come out of the closet in the previous decade than in decades prior. Importantly, this is not an artifact of survey methods. Pew, for example, used probability sampling methods and include both those with internet access and those without. They recruit panel participants through a combination of random digit dialing and address-based sampling. All of this shows that—concerning sex and sexuality—something profound is occurring with young people.

Changing Sexual Identities Among Youth

In this zeitgeist of inclusivity, significant shifts are evident regarding the recognition of sexual identity among both heterosexual and LGBT youth. Savin-Williams (2005) argues that sexual minority youth are entering a "postidentity" phase in which they no longer find solace or resonance with sexual-identity categories. Cohler and Hammack (2009) urge caution to these changes, but still recognize that identity is changing in the ways it is important. We argue that whatever the precise nature of this shift, it is the result of decreasing homohysteria, and whereas Cohler, Hammack, and Savin-Williams were discussing gay identities, the shift is actually most apparent in research when examining heterosexual students.

A substantive shift has occurred in how straight young men implicitly understand and define their sexual identities (McCormack 2012a). In the homohysteric 1980s and 1990s, there were two simplistic ways of determining sexuality for men — one for gay people and one for straight. If you said that you were gay, this was accepted without any interrogation: This is because the stigma attached to homosexuality meant that such a proclamation was accepted. It was perceived as a statement against one's own interests because of the social stigma that gay identity held. For gay men, sexuality was determined through self-identification.

Matters were not the same for straight men. Here, the one-time rule of homosexuality was heavily in operation. Given the heterosexual presumption, everyone was presumed to be claiming a heterosexual identity unless explicitly disclosed otherwise. And here, boys and men were examined for any potential same-sex desire, or any behavior that could be coded as gay. The claim to a heterosexual identity was unimportant because heterosexuality was determined by actions. The gulf between straight identity and behavior became a chasm into which the vast majority of straight men fell.

This difference between sexuality-as-identity for gay men and sexuality-as-behavior for straight men has become considerably less noticeable in contemporary culture; where a person self-identification is seen as key in determining socially perceived sexuality (McCormack 2012a). Related to this, there has also been a growing trend of people eschewing traditional sexual identity labels for terms that they feel better describe their sexuality. One focus of research has been on the 'Kinsey 1s'—men and women who identify as "predominantly heterosexual, only incidentally homosexual" (Kinsey et al. 1948). Savin-Williams and Vrangalova (2013) argue that this group of "mostly heterosexuals" form a sexual orientation group that is distinct from both heterosexuality and bisexuality (for other terminology, see Thompson and Morgan 2008).

We argue that the emergence of mostly heterosexuals as a discrete sexual category in contemporary times, despite being identified in Kinsey's research back in the 1940s, is attributable to decreasing homohysteria. The reduction in homophobia and the one-time rule of homosexuality provides the space for people to recognize their own desires without being stigmatized. Accordingly, while sexuality has traditionally been measured by three discrete categories (heterosexual, bisexual, and homosexual), there is growing evidence that this typology has outgrown its usefulness, and that more groups are necessary to accurately describe the sexuality of current cohorts of adolescents and young adults (Savin-Williams 2014). Specifically, both qualitative and quantitative data suggest the importance of considering a group that is located between heterosexuality and bisexuality, designating a heterosexual core with a slight amount of same-sex sexuality (Diamond 2009; Savin-Williams 2014; Savin-Williams and McCormack in press).

The changing and expanding understanding of sexual categories bring into relief the need for new ways to study sexualities and, crucially, recruit participants. In our empirical research on bisexuality that we document in this book, we seek to understand how decreasing homohysteria of the current era related to bisexuals' experiences—and we wanted to ensure we spoke to participants who have often not been included in academic research. We were keen to recruit bisexual men in new ways, and really understand how bisexual men's experiences have changed in the past 30 years—focusing on the shift from homohysteria to inclusivity, and explore how age and generation influenced these experiences. To do this required methodological innovation, energy and stepping beyond academic convention in recruiting participants.

Chapter 6
Taking Bisexual Research to the Streets

Conducting research on marginalized communities is never an easy endeavor. Given the double discrimination from gay and straight communities (Weiss 2011), it has often been difficult to recruit bisexuals for qualitative research. Hartman (2011) equates this task with finding a needle in a haystack, highlighting the difficulties of locating a large sample of what is a marginalized group within an already-marginalized group. Because of this, researchers have tended to rely on snowball sampling and other forms of non-probability sampling (Meyer and Wilson 2009), often from LGBT activist groups. Thus, rather than recruit a group of bisexuals from a diversity of ethnic, class and geographical backgrounds, academics have had to rely on existing networks of bisexuals, and those within particular social milieus. Highlighting this, the most substantial empirical research on bisexual men to date recruited participants through bisexual resource centers in San Francisco (Weinberg et al. 1994). Yet, even this significant piece of high quality research is restricted by its sampling procedures.

While recruiting from existing networks of bisexuals can still produce meaningful and significant research, this approach also restricts generalizability (McCormack 2014a). Traditionally, the existing networks come in the form of: (1) self-help groups; (2) counseling services; or (3) LGBT activist organizations. All of these organizations are designed to help sexual minorities in the face of discrimination. These recruitment locations have thus resulted in a privileging of narratives of people who have experienced discrimination and have, as a result, sought therapy or community support (Hartman 2011; Savin-Williams 2001b).

Highlighting how these groups are not representative of the broader bisexual population, recent Pew (2013) research finds that while 48% of gay men and 49% of lesbians have belonged to an LGBT group, only 28% of bisexuals have. This means that bisexual men recruited from these groups represent a significantly smaller percentage of the bisexual population than their gay and lesbian equivalents. Supporting this, Burleson (2005: 67) writes that:

> The motives bringing people to the bi community set them apart from the majority of bi's who don't share these motives; therefore, members of the bi community are probably not representative of bisexuals in general… It must always be kept in mind the bi community is a unique subset of all bisexuals with their own issues and concerns.

This selection factor therefore promotes an exaggeration of the negative aspects of bisexual narratives. This is exacerbated by the common practice of citing several qualitative studies as evidence for a broader social trend. Thus, if qualitative researchers, as a group, use similar recruitment methods, the net result is that the body of literature privileges particular narratives or experiences, excluding those from people that are harder to reach. Multiple research projects using the same recruitment methods, even from a diverse range of social demographics, will thus present a skewed version of bisexuals' experiences (see McCormack 2014a). In this instance, it is narratives of victimization that are privileged. This makes Barker et al. (2012, p. 385) warning apposite:

> Be mindful of the multiplicity of experience amongst bisexuals and bisexual communities. Do not assume that what is true for one individual, group or community will be true for all. Do not write about bisexuality or 'the bisexual' as if there was only one way of being bisexual or one bisexual experience.

In designing this research, we sought to avoid recruiting bisexual men through traditional routes, and we believe this is the first large-scale qualitative research on bisexual men that does not use snowball sampling to recruit participants. This is particularly important for research on bisexual men, as research has found that while 22% of gay men say most or all of their friends are LGBT, this is only true for 5% of bisexuals (Pew 2013).

In addition to eschewing snowball sampling, we also decided that we would *not* recruit men from counseling services and LGBT organizations. In order to achieve this, we had to change both how and from where participants were recruited. Fortunately, the cultural trend of improving attitudes toward homosexuality enabled us to undertake a method of participant recruitment that had not been available to prior generations of researchers—we took our recruitment to public streets.

We determined that if we wanted to find "average" bisexual men, we would need to recruit them directly from the broader population. While these men might be part of a bisexual activist or social community group, visit gay clubs or even see a counselor, we were not *selecting* men immersed in counseling services or existing sexuality networks. This would mean that if there was a trend of our participants seeing counselors, or we failed to recruit men with a diversity of ethnic, racial and geographic backgrounds, this would tell us something important about bisexuality in contemporary metropolitan cities and would not be a fault of our methods.

For this book, we therefore took to the streets of three metropolitan cities in order to recruit bisexual pedestrians. Standing on the busy city streets of Los Angeles, New York and London, we called for bisexual men to be interviewed for academic research, and we interviewed those who were eligible on the spot. Using this innovative approach, we recruited 90 bisexual men who came from a range of ethnic and classed backgrounds, and who were not necessarily part of gay social networks, therapy, or bisexual organizations—as it turned out, few were.

Situating Our Study

In order to frame our study within the broader methodological and sexualities literature, and to enable evaluation of our method, it is appropriate to provide more detail about our data collection procedures. We adopted a qualitative methodology in the form of in-depth interviews as we wanted to understand the meanings and emotional realities of bisexual men in contemporary Anglo-American cultures. While large-scale surveys tells us that social attitudes have changed in general (see Chap. 4), the power of interviewing men about their lives is that it enables individuals' experiences to both humanize and contextualize these broader social trends, and highlight subtle contradictions that may exist in our participants lives (Cancian 1992; Cook and Fonow 1986).

Interviews permitted us to move from descriptive accounts to a conceptual analysis which informs and augments the survey research showing positive cultural change. Loosely speaking, quantitative research tells us something has happened, qualitative research informs us as to the reasons why. Thus, we are concerned with exploring not just the extent that decreasing homophobia has influenced and potentially transformed individual bisexual men's lives, but also the mechanisms by which this change occurred, and how these changes manifest in these men's lives.

Interview research is not overly concerned with statistical generalizability. We are not trying to claim that the experiences documented in our 90 interviews apply to all bisexual men. Rather, our study provides a picture of what the lives of some bisexual men look like today in New York, Los Angeles and London, and they enable us to theorize how changing attitudes toward homosexuals are experienced by a different sexual minority.

In order to understand the complexities of how decreasing homophobia affects bisexual men's lives in these cities, we decided to examine for both generational and geographical differences. Accordingly, we recruited bisexual men from three age cohorts within three of the most cosmopolitan Western cities: Los Angeles, New York and London. We examined for differences between age cohorts by strategically selecting men whose adolescence occurred during a period of high homohysteria, declining homohysteria and low homohysteria. We did this by designing and then interviewing men from three different age brackets (18–23, 24–35, 36–42), ensuring that we had interviews with 10 men from each age bracket in each city; paying $40 per interview.

Given the metropolitan nature of these cities, and their popularity as tourist destinations, we were able to recruit bisexual men who lived in the cities as well as those visiting the area. This fulfilled our participants-per-cell design for analysis—their pseudonyms, age and race can be found listed in Appendix 1.

As stated in the introduction, it is important to note that we did not just interview the first 30 men that we found in each city. We had a systematic approach to recruiting participants to facilitate our generational cohort analysis. Crucially, we stopped recruiting men in each age cohort once we achieved the relevant number. This meant that when, for example, we had recruited 10 men aged 18–24 and 10 men aged 25–35 in Los Angeles, we turned men away from these age groups. We continued to recruit men aged between 36 and 42, until we filled this cell with 10 and then moved to the next city. Thus, the categorical neatness of our sample was the result of a carefully designed and executed process.

Also crucial to our analysis and the theoretical framing of the book, our age brackets for analysis are not divided into equal numbers of years—they are not, for example, brackets of 10 years; instead, they reflect a cultural period in which each group had their adolescence (which we position at 17). Accordingly, each group of men was divided into an age cohort reflecting a unique cultural zeitgeist concerning homohysteria (see Chap. 4) and their adolescence.

Older cohort	Middle cohort	Younger cohort
Aged 36–42	Aged 24–35	Aged 18–23
Mean age 39	Mean age 29	Mean age 20
Born 1968–1974	Born 1975–1986	Born 1987–1992
Aged 17 in 1985–1991	Aged 17 in 1992–2003	Aged 17 in 2004–2009
Aged 17 in an era of extreme homohysteria	Aged 17 in an era of decreasing homohysteria	Aged 17 in an era of inclusivity
10 from Los Angeles	10 from Los Angeles	10 from Los Angeles
10 from New York	10 from New York	10 from New York
10 from London	10 from London	10 from London
30 men in total	30 men in total	30 men in total

Our oldest cohort consists of men whose adolescence was in the late 1980s—the most homohysteric time in the US and the UK. Data from the 1987 General Social Survey document 77% of Americans stating that homosexual sex was *always wrong*, the highest it has ever been. Thus, we classified the first cohort as men who were born within dates that would make one's adolescence during this epoch (1968–1974), and participants' descriptions of their adolescents verified our categorical methods.

Homophobia remained steady until 1993, when it began to decline rapidly. Accordingly, men in the second group were selected for being 17 during the years 1992–2003—this is also the time in which metrosexuality emerged as an identifiable style of masculinity. Finally, the third group had their adolescence in a time of greatly reduced homophobia, and the era we describe as one of inclusivity. These men had their adolescence in the year we conducted this research (2010) or the five years prior to this (2005–2010).

We also decided that in order to understand the influence of decreasing homophobia and homohysteria on bisexual men, it was necessary to interview solely those that were open about their bisexuality; as closeted men would not have experience of how heterosexual people engaged with them as bisexual.

We defined "outness" as being open to at least one other person because this seemed to be the most inclusive definition, and because there is no universally accepted definition of being out that could be used. It also fits with our belief that people should be able to define whether they are out themselves as much as possible. It is worth noting that while our initial criteria on level of outness was low, all but two of our participants had come out to many more people than just one individual (see Baldwin et al. 2014).

It is of course likely that openly bisexual men will have different experiences from those in the closet, and we limit generalizations accordingly. There is even a sampling bias here as some bisexuals will remain closeted because of perceived hostile attitudes of their social groups, and these men will be excluded from our study. But this is why the generational cohort design is so important—it provides internal consistency across age cohorts meaning that the differences we find between groups are the result of social changes and not sampling issues. Furthermore, taking to the streets in a very public manner aligns our participant recruitment with the aims of our research—to understand the lived experiences of bisexuals who are open about their sexual identities.

While recruiting men directly from public spaces was exciting and innovative within the body of research on bisexuality, it also raised some issues. Given that bisexual men make up a small percentage of the overall population, alongside the additional limitations of our age cohort design, it was necessary to recruit men not only from public places, but from busy areas with thousands of people passing by. Accordingly, we stood in the most populated areas of Los Angeles, New York and London, announcing that we were looking to interview bisexual men for academic research.

These cities were strategically chosen because of the high density of people, which was needed to find the non-affiliated participants we sought. Given the diversity of race and class in these cities, our method also enabled us to recruit bisexual men from across these social demographics. By soliciting pedestrians in commercial and tourist parts of town, we increased our chances of finding men who had a free hour in which to be interviewed.

Researching men in cities has several other important implications. It is common knowledge that the experiences of sexual minorities within cities are different from those who live in rural areas (Gray 2009), not least because of the vibrant social spaces for sexual minorities that exist within cities, as well as the panoply of sexual activities that are available in places with high population densities (Ghaziani 2014). However, researching men in cities is about more than recognizing that experiences may differ from those in rural areas: as Houlbrook (2005, p. 4) argues, "male sexual practices and identities do not just take place *in* the city; they are shaped and sustained *by* the physical and cultural forms of modern urban life." While sexual minorities have traditionally lived in close geographical proximity in particular metropolitan cities, recent research suggests that decreasing homophobia may have contributed to a dissipation of the "gayborhood," and sexual minorities are now more integrated in these cities with profound consequences for the sexual organization of the city (Ghaziani 2014).

We decided the first location would be Venice Beach, Los Angeles. This was an ideal location as it is known as a bohemian area with offbeat activities, street performances, and large crowds of visiting tourists and locals out for weekend entertainment. Given this diversity of street activity, it provided us training in recruiting participants so publicly.

We found our method immediately successful. With three (all white male) researchers in the field, we recruited fourteen interviews in just six hours. During this recruitment, two of us would stand, clipboards and flyers in hand, in the middle of the passing crowed, calling out "bisexual men, we are paying forty dollars for academic research." When a pedestrian stopped to inquire about the research, we informed him of its nature, and vetted him for eligibility.

Once the participant was recruited, they were immediately interviewed. If this member of the team was already interviewing, one of the two "recruiters" would interview them instead. There were three times in total when all three researchers were interviewing at the same time. At Venice Beach, these recorded interviews took place on park benches, which permitted each member of our team to be visible to the others at all times while also providing privacy for the participants. Following this success, we selected a diverse range of other public spaces with high numbers of pedestrians in Los Angeles. We collected data on the Third Street Promenade in Santa Monica, as well as the Grove on Fairfax. Interviews were audio-recorded and transcribed at a later date.

We maintained our formula in New York, conducting research on St Marks Street, Washington Square, and on 6th Avenue and 19th Street, uptown. In London we recruited participants near a university campus in central London and just off Leicester Square. In order to improve the range of people we interviewed, we repeated this procedure at different times of the day, including late at night, as well as at weekends in all three settings.

While our research is deeply rooted in the city, it became clear in the early stages of data collection that that the processes of globalization meant that a taxonomic understanding of geography was not possible. Choosing metropolitan areas with a density of people enabled us to recruit our desired number of bisexual men within the time-constraints of the study, and promoted a racially diverse demographic of participants. However, finding busy areas in each city required going to locations where tourists and visitors were found among natives. In the US, we included participants from any of the US states (but from no other country, including the UK) and in the UK we included men from throughout the UK (but from no other country). Thus, our research is not just about being bisexual in a city, let alone a specific city. Perhaps for this reason, while we found differences between rural and metropolitan areas, analysis by city did not produce meaningful results. Accordingly, we do not routinely detail where our participants are from in the results chapters unless it has particular meaning to their narrative.

Evaluating the Method

This method of participant recruitment has many advantages. First, it made our research more visible to members of the public. While many looked amused, others were interested and stopped to speak to us about the research. We took these conversations seriously, often writing down references, websites, or other information. Others took fliers to find out about our research, or to pass on to bisexual friends. Several gay men wanted to discuss their coming out experience, and one student wanted to know how he could start a gay-straight alliance at his school (we referred him to the Gay, Lesbian and Straight Education Network). We believe that these conversations had positive social effects, and many people expressed their appreciation. In a time in which the social sciences are required to demonstrate their worth, this form of public dissemination is a constructive and valuable endeavor (see Nussbaum 2010).

This methodological innovation had a positive effect on our sampling procedures (see also Thomas et al. 2007). The first way this occurred was through making the research more accessible to people who were not sure whether they fit the criteria. A large number of people inquired about participating in the study, for example by asking if they could be interviewed given that they did not identify as bisexual. There were several other questions about whether people were suitable to be participants, including if having sex with a woman once 'counted' as being bisexual. Importantly, many of the men we interviewed initially spoke to us with doubt that they would be eligible to participate or be able to organize a time for interview. The implication was that they would not have responded to an advert or travel for an interview, but they were willing to spend an hour with a researcher on the spot.

The most significant benefit of this recruitment method is that it succeeded in locating a diversity of bisexual men. They ranged from those who had been out for 30 years to an 18 year old who had just come out. We interviewed those who frequented the gay scene, and those who had never been; single men, those in relationships with men and those in relationships with women, both monogamous and open. We interviewed men who were very pleased to accept the research money, and two men declined it, saying they did not need it. It also provided us with a racially diverse sample. The fact that we were not reliant on snowball sampling was an additional benefit, as this can have the effect of restricting participants to a small number of social networks (Pahl 1995). Accordingly, we believe our method enabled us to recruit a diverse section of society, and reach a number of bisexual men who would not normally respond to more traditional adverts about academic research.

Collecting data in this manner also strengthens the methodological logic of our research, establishing an alignment between our methods and the goals of the project. It can be argued that qualitative researchers have an obligation to ensure that their methodology should, in some manner, reflect the social realities of their participants (Ramazanoglu 2002). This can be a challenge for researchers (who are part of a privileged group) yet need in some way to 'represent' others, often from marginalized communities. In this regard, recruiting bisexual men from crowds recognizes the diversity of experiences of bisexuality and goes beyond the restricted sampling procedures of LGBT groups and counselors that have limited much of the research with LGBT populations (Hartman 2011). As our findings document, the experiences of bisexual men are diverse and more positive than older research suggests.

A Controversial Method?

It is our experience that some people view these recruitment methods as controversial. Certain academics have questioned us about it, and we even had one academic approach us on the streets of New York to give his unfavorable opinion. He suggested that our method could result in fraudulent narratives—that passers-by would pretend to be bisexual for the payment of forty dollars. While this critique might seem persuasive, it fails to understand that this is true of almost all research—it simply is not possible to provide a cast-iron guarantee that participants are being truthful (Johnson 2002).

We are skeptical that a heterosexual or gay man would be able to improvise a life history over the duration of forty-five minutes to an hour that would convince the experienced interviewer that his story was genuine. And even if someone did manage to lie about being bisexual for the money, those who respond to traditional methods of recruitment have *more* time to fabricate a story around their make-believe sexual orientation.

Another criticism is that some bisexuals might be deterred from approaching us; that there are certain types of people, including those we were specifically targeting, who would decide not to approach us in such public settings. We recognize that there is potentially some validity to this argument and it is possible that only more self-confident bisexuals approached us. However, given that our research aim was to see how openly bisexual men are treated by friends, family, colleagues and the general public, recruiting bisexual men in such a public manner helped select precisely the type of informant that was best suited to describe the experiences of being openly bisexual in urban settings today. Our method ensured we interviewed the type of men who are not ashamed to be thought bisexual, and this reflects a certain degree of "outness." It should also be recognized that this critique does not apply to the inter-cohort analysis, as participants of all age groups were recruited in the same manner.

Interview Procedure

After confirming that a potential participant had met our criteria, and finding a private space to interview him, we talked through what to expect from our research. We informed the participant that all data would be confidential, and anonymity provided in all publications that come from the study. Participants were then told that this included changing their names and institutional/occupational affiliations in the writing of the research, as well as potentially identifying information on their dating or sexual partners. They were also told that any other potentially identifying information would be changed or not included. We provided them with a research information sheet so they could contact us if they had further questions or wanted to amend their answers. We also provided paperwork to the participants showing that our project had been ethically approved by the university at which we were based at that time. Participants provided written informed consent, and they were told participation was voluntary and that they could quit at any time.

Participants were first asked to fill out the modified Klein Grid (see Chap. 2) before being interviewed. A small number of these grids were not usable, primarily as a result of poor handwriting or multiple answers—and we also noticed that some participants struggled to understand the form even with explanations from the researchers.

The interviews were designed to foster a non-judgmental exchange between researcher and participant (Johnson 2002) and the two gay researchers were open with the participants about their sexual identities (Kong et al. 2002). Our interviews were designed to reflect a conversation more than a structured inquiry. Most of these lasted approximately 45 minutes, although many lasted significantly longer and some were shorter. The order in which topics were discussed and the exact wording of questions depended upon the flow of each conversation.

Questions explored multiple facets of bisexual men's experiences, based on an initial review of the existing literature and interests in broader changes in cultural attitudes toward homosexuality. The interview schedule consisted of questions exploring how and when participants knew they were bisexual; their experiences of coming out to various groups of people; their experiences at school or work; their experiences in different towns and cities (if they had moved); who they dated and had sex with and (if the relationship had ended) why they broke up; their identification with the label "bisexual;" and their experiences with heterosexual and gay people more generally.

Participants were also asked to describe their treatment as bisexual by family, friends, colleagues and peers, and older men were asked how this treatment might have changed over the years or decades since coming out. We asked them to elaborate on their circumstances and to provide us not only with significant events in their lives but also on their everyday experience as bisexual. Participants were also asked to describe how they felt emotionally toward their partners and how their partners handled their bisexuality. We asked about monogamy, cheating, and open relationships, too. Interviews were also guided by participant responses, and we followed the flow of the interview rather than strictly adhering to the interview schedule.

Qualitative Analysis

This research was approached through an inductive framework, with themes "emerging" through on-going analysis (Charmaz 2014; Glaser and Strauss 1967). Each researcher inductively developed their own themes as they gathered interviews and at the end of each day, interviews were discussed alongside the emerging data and our initial thoughts on prospective themes. This coding in the field fed into successive data collection as the interview schedule was revised to account for themes that were developing during the course of research.

Upon returning from our fieldwork, coding and analysis continued in combination with intensified search for literature pertinent to bisexual men's experiences. We undertook further coding and identified patterns in the transcribed narratives (Urquhart 2013), first individually and then collectively. It was at this stage that we undertook a cohort analysis, searching for similarities and differences in the themes between cohorts. This was an inductive and iterative process, with themes grounded in and emerging from the data. We then used axial coding (the disaggregation of core themes), scrutinizing the codes to ensure that they were pertinent, accurate and distinct from each other. Through selective coding, we then incorporated the respective axial codes into a broad, overarching narrative of what is happening to these bisexual men's lives (Charmaz 2014).

The rigor of our analysis has been improved through inter-rater reliability, with both authors reviewing all the transcripts and initially coding the interviews separately before meeting to discuss themes. Three other academics who have also published on bisexuality also reviewed transcripts and contributed to our discussions on the developing codes.

It is the richness of content that enables us to get to the heart of the issue that makes qualitative research so powerful. In this research, we use excerpts from participants for each point, but it is a general rule that we explicitly comment when experiences are outliers or unusual in comparison to the rest of the data. In the following chapters discussing our findings, for ease of reading, we provide information about age and ethnicity for each participant the first time they are mentioned in a chapter and not again after that. We do not explicitly highlight the location participants were recruited from because location was not a significant issue in terms of experience. We draw out some of the small differences related to location in Chaps. 8 and 9.

However, our claims are still limited to particular groups and in particular circumstances. Despite interviewing men from other states than California, or New York, and apart from having interviewed men from outside London, we can only say that the lives of bisexual men are good and improving in these locales. We do not have the data to comment on the experiences of bisexual men who live in rural areas, or in other countries. Similarly, it is possible that the experiences of bisexual men who attend counseling and LGBT groups are still quite negative; although it is likely that this group is decreasing in size and that their experiences are on average improving as well. This research is designed to illuminate the lives of non-institutionalized bisexual men; it is not without its limitations, but it is the most thorough to date.

The Importance of Generations

While we adopt a generational analysis in this book, the complexity and diversity of social life means that one cannot talk simplistically of generations (White 2013). Highlighting this, the experiences of a rich, professional male in New York will bear little resemblance to those of a poor, unemployed woman in Texas, even if they were born on the same day of the same year. Yet the social zeitgeist into which we are born will have a fundamental effect on how we see ourselves and interpret the world around us—not just related to sexuality and gender but also technological and economic trends. In a wide-ranging discussion of the power of generations in thinking about sexualities, Plummer (2010) writes that, "Human sexualities are deeply generational and need analysis and study" (p. 170), arguing that our sexual selves are structured by generational narratives. This recognizes that the "stories we tell and the standpoints we take are deeply connected to how we organize and structure our memory worlds and our visual worlds" (p. 171). He identifies seven gay and lesbian cohorts forming in the twentieth century, and argues that these cohorts represent generational sexualities with respect to how they understand their sexual identities and their place within the social world.

The importance of generations to sexualities is gaining increasing recognition in sociological research (Dean 2014; Ghaziani 2014). Hammack (2014) highlights the centrality of generations to sexualities, while King (in press) demonstrates that older LGB people experience their sexualities in ways that while heterogeneous are still deeply influenced by their age and generational experience. It is something we have discussed related to homophobic and homosexually themed language as well (McCormack and Anderson 2010b). Thus, while we need to think carefully about the ways in which generational cohorts operate, there is great value in thinking generationally about sexuality and gender.

A Note on Women

We recognize that by focusing on the experiences of bisexual men, we are excluding the narratives and experiences of bisexual women—a point that some passers-by made to us as we recruited participants. It is our view that this is a necessary limitation of our research given the complexity of sexuality and gender, and the gendered lens we wish to bring to the study of bisexuality.

Russell and Seif (2002) highlight the unique experiences of bisexual girls, and rightly call for further research on them, while Worthen (2013) powerfully argues for separate analyses of bisexual men and women. It is for this reason that we have conducted separate research into the lives of young bisexual women (Anderson et al. 2014), and also why we focus solely on men in this book. Given that we have authored multiple other books about masculinities, and the lack of integration between studies of masculinity and femininity of all sexualities (Hargreaves and Anderson 2014), we decided to restrict this project to bisexual men.

Chapter 7
Challenging Identities, Changing Identifications

In their study of bisexuals in San Francisco in the 1980s, Weinberg et al. (1994) created a stage model concerning how individuals adopt a bisexual identity. They argued that the processes of becoming bisexual begins with a state of identity confusion—feeling different from others and 'struggling' with same-sex attractions. Weinberg et al. then argued that there were then two paths that bisexuals followed: one involved individuals who thought that they might be gay and one for those who thought they might be heterosexual. Bisexuality did not emerge as an option for these men.

Those that explored homosexuality began to associate with the gay community and have same-sex sex. These men attempted to integrate their sexual attractions with that of a gay identity, including public disclosure of a gay identity for some. However, those that explored heterosexuality socialized themselves in the dominant culture, and maintained a heterosexual identity. This group often displayed homophobia themselves, causing yet further psychological distress. For this group, long-term denial was ordinary.

The key element of Weinberg, Williams and Pryor's model, though, is that both groups of men seemed to initially eschew a bisexual identity; not because they wished to avoid one, but because they did not know one even existed. Surprisingly, few men with dual attraction in the early 1980s knew that bisexuality existed. Once they heard the word, it brought relief that they did not have to be one way or the other.

This generational ignorance of bisexuality does not apply to the bisexual men we interviewed, however. While sexual confusion still occurs in early adolescence, it had dissipated – particularly with the youngest cohort – by the time they reached their later teenage years. We show that these identifications have changed in two key ways; (1) the ability to recognize to oneself that both same-sex and different-sex desires are indicative of bisexuality occurs earlier and (2) coming out and maintaining a bisexual identity frequently occurs without first publically maintaining a gay or straight identity (beyond that which is presumed by others in a heterosexist society). It seems that bisexuality, as a concept, is now thoroughly embedded in western culture so that bisexual men no longer have to 'struggle' much with trying to push themselves into exclusive hetero or homosexuality.

Across all three cohorts, there was diversity in recognition of bisexuality. 26 participants realized their bisexuality in pre-adolescence (aged under 13), with 49 realizing during adolescence (13–17) and just 15 realizing in adulthood (18 and over). It is hard to know if this corresponds with the average age of awareness for male homosexuality, however prior research on the awareness of bisexual or homosexual desires, using a national survey of 1,752 college students, the Sexuality and Information Council of the United States, found it does. That research (www.siecus.org) found 48% of self-identified gay and bisexual college students became aware of their sexual preference in high school while 26% found their true sexuality in college. 20% of self-identified gay and bisexual men knew that they were gay or bisexual in junior high school, and 17% said they knew in grade school. Women were later to know. Only, 6% of self-identified gay or bisexual women knew that they were gay or bisexual in junior high school, and 11% knew in grade school. Still, this study does not break out bisexuals from homosexuals and some research suggests gay males might know earlier. Herdt and McClintock (2000) argue for a 'magical age of 10' writing (p. 597):

> Accumulating studies from the United States over the past decade suggest that the development of sexual attraction may commence in middle childhood and achieve individual subjective recognition sometime around the age of 10. As these studies have shown, first same-sex attraction for males and females typically occurs at the mean age of 9.6 for boys and between the ages of 10 and 10.5 for girls.

However, it is necessary to complicate the idea of awareness of bisexuality somewhat. Our findings are dependent on the participants' understandings of realizing they were bisexual—some may understand when they first remember desiring males and females, while others may refer to when they first identified as bisexual. While we probed this difference within interviews, it is possible that some imprecision still exists. We also highlight that it is possible that closeted men aged 18–23 at the time of data collection might come out in the future, meaning we cannot make definitive claims about changing coming out ages. However, analysis of timing of first recognizing bisexual desire did not yield any palpable social trends. Comparison of age cohort in relation to developing a sexual identity was a far more fruitful analysis of the data.

Confusion and Denial Among Men in the 20th Century

Thirteen of the 60 men of the oldest two cohorts only realized their same-sex desires post-adolescence. For Andy, white and aged 39, the realization of his bisexuality occurred when he was 18. He said, "I was freaked out. I had spent much of my youth being homophobic, calling everybody fags. And when I started to realize that I was one, it really freaked me out." He attributed his lack of understanding to a homophobic culture and the invisibility of bisexuality. "I was attracted to girls, no question. So I didn't even think about men, not in my area—everyone said gays were disgusting and wrong, so I just concentrated on fucking girls. The desire just grew when I was 18, and I couldn't ignore it anymore."

There were years of denial for some participants before they recognized their dual desires. Marcus, white and aged 35, said, "The feelings were there at 9 or 10, but I only really took notice of them around 16. I'm not sure I knew what the term bisexual was back then, it was pretty confusing, but I look back now and recall the feelings." Growing up in a Christian household in England, he said, "Sex wasn't discussed round the dinner table. We watched Coronation Street [a long-running British soap] after dinner. Bisexuality just wasn't on my radar."

Similarly, Phil, aged 31 and white, said:

> It was a weird feeling at first. I was 19, and finding myself looking more at the guy while jerking off to porn. I tried not to, by watching lesbian porn instead. But it just didn't do it for me. I fought it for a few years, but eventually I just had to admit to myself that I liked guys, too.

JP, Hispanic and aged 31, said:

> I played a lot of sports back at high school. But I didn't tell anybody about being bisexual. It was weird. I felt weird. You know, I thought 'these guys are cute' but I also didn't really realize at that time. I never did anything about it, and it was only afterwards, when I started going to college, started talking about it more, when I was a little more open that I came out to some of my friends. I was 23 when I did, although I hadn't planned it out or anything like that.

Fourteen men from the oldest cohort recognized their bisexuality during adolescence. Diego, aged 39 and Hispanic, talked about his desire for men gradually occurring during adolescence. He said, "About 10 or 11, I started to get crushes on girls. Really want them. It was about seventh grade when I realized I had the same feelings for my friend, Tom, as well." Initially ignoring these desires, he spoke about "fooling around" with Tom on sleepovers: "We'd stay over at each others' houses, and chat and sometimes we'd just sleep really close. Not in the same bed, but I could hear his breathing when he was sleeping, and it turned me on." It was after increasing erotic attraction for Tom that Diego started to process his bisexuality: "I couldn't not think about it. Here was this guy I was into. And I realized that while I really liked him, it wasn't *just* him. It took me a while, but I starting to think 'maybe I'm bi.'"

Robin, aged 42 and mixed race, spoke about recognizing his bisexuality during his adolescence: "I wasn't a horny teenager. Like at 15, I was dating girls and enjoying it, but I was more interested in the friendship than the sex." He added that he did not have strong desires for men, either, saying:

> I had great friendships with guys, and one guy in particular I really cared for. It was that guy, who I realized I wanted to date more than the girl I was seeing, that started me thinking about bisexuality. I really enjoy sex now, it's an important part of my life, but back then it was the emotional thing that made me think about my sexuality.

Darryn, aged 42 and black, said he was 15 years old when he first acknowledged his bisexuality. "It was a little weird at first, and I was in denial," Darryn explained, "Because I didn't know if how I felt was right or wrong, but as I matured I found out it wasn't just me who felt like that." He added that "it took time though," and his experience was evidence that early recognition did not necessarily lead to positive experiences.

Self-realization occurred in pre-adolescence for some of the older men, too. For example, John, 38 and white, realized his bisexuality at the age of 12. He said, "At that age I already had a sense of what excited me." He added, "It was men that really turned me on. I was attracted to women, but I couldn't ignore that real desire for men."

Interestingly, while men spoke of denial in this cohort, they did not mention being confused as much as in Weinberg et al.'s (1994) model. While John mentioned the strength of his sexual desire in adolescence, one reason for the lack of confusion in pre-adolescence might be attributed to a lack of strong sexual desires that occur during puberty. Louis's experiences support this thesis. Aged 24 and white, he said:

> I was 12 when I first had those feelings. But I wasn't bothered by them, not until around 14 when I started masturbating and would, you know, sometimes think of guys. This is also when my Church and my parents mentioned homosexuality, or at least when I began to notice them mentioning it. I started telling myself it was wrong because that's what they said.

Likewise, Bill, black and aged 33, recognized bisexual desires throughout his life, but only identified these as bisexual at college. He said:

> I think I've always been sexually attracted to women, and yet I've always felt a strong attraction, whether it's emotional or physical to men at the same time. But I never really entertained the idea that I was bisexual until college, when I realized that it wasn't just a question of being attracted to men on an emotional and physical level, but it was more a question of identity politics. It was more a question of how strictly we should be categorizing ourselves as belonging to one sexual orientation or another.

Nonetheless, these men had difficulty dealing with these feelings (see also Weinberg et al. 1994). For example, Bernie, white and aged 37, realized his bisexuality at the age of 16 and said that these feelings "didn't sit easy...I wanted to suppress them." He added, "I was like, 'this isn't normal,' and I didn't know what was happening." Jake, white and aged 24, said, "I was 12 and I didn't want anyone to know." He added that those initial feelings marked a difficult time in his life: "I felt bad, like I was different from everyone else and that I was weird."

AJ, felt similarly, saying, "At 16, if I got turned on by a guy I would tell myself to cool down, think about something else, try and think about some girls." This was a process of detachment that AJ has used throughout his life to his social detriment, as we discuss in later chapters. Thus, while age cohort did not appear to influence first age of recognition of bisexual desire, it did influence how the person dealt with these feelings.

Young Bisexual Men and Clarity of Desire

While the age cohort did not significantly influence the age of recognizing bisexual desire, there is evidence to suggest that men in the 18–23 age cohort had a more positive understanding of what it meant to be attracted to males at that age (see also Savin-Williams 2005). For example, Joseph, aged 20 and Hispanic, recalled a moment in his childhood, aged 8 or 9, where he was attracted to a boy. "I was watching TV with my friend… he was lying on the floor in front of the TV and I was on the couch. I realized I was looking at him, not the TV." The way he described this realization showed no evidence of confusion or shame: "I looked at boys that way, I looked at girls that way. I can't remember precisely when I connected this to being bisexual, but it wasn't something I had to think a great deal about."

Marco, an 18 year old Hispanic man was 15 when he first realized. "Even though I was dating this girl who I was really into," he said, "I still knew I was bi." He described the process of realizing he was bisexual as "a bit of a burden," adding "but I realized who I really was and that made me happy, you know?" Despite this worry about social stigma and what this may mean for their future lives, these men did not discuss confusion about their desires which may be attributable to greater discussion of sexual diversity in broader culture (Netzley 2010), and the growing number of sexual minorities coming out at earlier ages (Riley 2010).

The benefit of knowing other sexual minorities was a key difference from the older cohorts, and was regularly mentioned as a positive experience. For example, Mike, aged 18 and white, said:

> I knew what was up by 10 or 11. I just found myself drawn to guys as well as girls. But I wasn't too bothered by it. I wasn't going to tell anyone just yet, but I knew what gay was, and I knew there were gay kids in my neighborhood, so it wasn't really a big deal.

Tyler, a 19 year old Hispanic man, recollected being attracted to both boys and girls from the age of 7. He said, "I realized what 'being gay' was early on, my aunts had gay friends so that helped me come to terms with it. I knew some people frowned upon it, but I was pretty much always able to accept that about myself." Similarly, Jared, white and aged 21, said, "there was this openly bi guy at my school and, you know, girls were kissing guys and kissing each other. I had attraction for men and women, so it was pretty clear to me what I was." Importantly, these men's narratives did not include negative feelings about these desires, unlike men from the older two cohorts.

While most of these men discussed not being particularly troubled by their feelings at this age, some of men from this cohort still experienced feelings of guilt, confusion and embarrassment. Jeremy, aged 23 and white, said that he was confused during his adolescence:

> I wanted to call myself gay for a while, because I was really into men. I just assumed my attraction to women was just what society was telling me to do, and that it was a hang up I had with being gay. It took me a while to work through that you know, because the gay-straight alliance spoke about gay issues, but not so much bisexuality.

Even so, Jeremy's confusion was less difficult to overcome than for men of the older cohorts—he came out as bisexual aged 17 and had his first boyfriend the same year. "That was fine actually. He didn't care I was attracted to girls, though he did tease me about it. But it was a joke, nothing serious."

Kevin, black and aged 19, said that he only realized he was bisexual at age 17, and that "It was weird I just started to realize I liked men. It wasn't a switch coming on, but it was like 'oh, why didn't I realize this before.'" Similarly, Adam, black and aged 23, said he was only attracted to women until the age of 18, adding, "I didn't tell people immediately, as I needed to process what was going on. I came out about a year later." While both of these participants are black, there was no clear evidence of a racial component within our findings—with realization of bisexuality similar across racial groups.

We cannot make claims about there being a reduction in the number of people who realize their identities post-adolescence, because it is possible that there are men aged 18–23 at the time of data collection who will only realize their desires later in life—that is, the reduction could possibly be the result of the age of participants. What is clear, however, is that the stage model of adopting a bisexual identity proposed by Weinberg et al. in 1994 is not valid for bisexual men who experienced their adolescence in the 21st century. Given the rationale of our cohort design, we contend that this is the result of increasingly liberal attitudes toward homosexuality alongside a greater awareness of bisexuality as a legitimate sexual identity (see Anderson and Adams 2011).

Generational Differences in the Value of Identity Categories

There is no empirically-validated theory that explains why people find labels comforting for their sexuality. It might be attributable to the phenomenon that people welcome a label given to medical symptoms that they have. Perhaps it is because our culture is forged through science, and science often begins with taxonomies; helping us understand the world more easily. Or, perhaps the human mind thinks categorically to ease the information overload of social reality.

A sociological perspective highlights that identities are essentially narratives that enable social experiences to be integrated into a coherent account that makes sense of significant events and provides a purpose to life (Hammack and Cohler 2009; Plummer 1995). Whatever the reason – and it is important to recognize that labeling of sexuality is almost certainly present in all civilizations (Norton 2010) – sexual identities remain an important way of understanding personal experiences of sexual desire, and mediating these in the broader culture (Coleman-Fountain 2014).

Although the men in our study had to identify with the term bisexual enough to respond to our calls for participants, participants ranged from affinity to ambivalence in their identifications. Men in the older cohort tended to speak about the value of identity categories. Barry, aged 39 and black, highlighted the power of identity categories in coming out to potential partners. He said, "I bring that up right at the beginning and I say, 'look and understand that I'm not going to change my ways,'" adding, "But you know I say that because I *am* bisexual – it's who I am." Similarly, Alejandro, aged 36 and Hispanic, said:

> You see some guys nowadays not calling themselves gay or bi or whatever, but you need to identify what you are. You need to be open to society about who you are. Calling yourself by that identity is the way you have to do that.

There was little ambivalence in the oldest cohort's perceptions of identity categories. However, this was not the same in the younger cohort, where there was more resistance to identity categories (Savin-Williams 2005). William, white and 22, said:

> I don't use it [the term bisexual]. I don't talk about it. I just say that I'm attracted to men and women. I only use the word bi when I have to. A lot of times I just call myself gay. But then I take it back as I feel I need to remind people that I'm also attracted to women. But bisexual, it really doesn't work for me...It's trying to force me into a category when there's no need. What's the point?

Max also distanced himself from the utility of identity categories, adding, "It may be possible to label me as pansexual, but I don't know. As soon as you start wondering if things are right for you, you create pressure that wasn't there. Other's opinions start getting wedged onto you. I just prefer to leave it alone."

Jackson's perspective that sexuality was a spectrum influenced his understanding of the use of labels. White and aged 21, he said, "I believe all people are bisexual by nature, and it all depends on the context of the situation, the personality, everything. So yeah, bisexuality works as a label to capture that, sure." He added, "It's tough. If you don't have the categories then how do you talk about sexuality, but when you have categories you put people into them, and that doesn't suit everyone."

David, aged 19 and Hispanic, said that he was "not a big fan of labels. I just prefer to be myself I suppose. I'd rather say, 'I kinda like guys also.'" He attributed this in part to the focus on sex, saying "I like fit-looking dudes and pretty women. I don't see why we have to label that."

This fits with a broader trend where sexual minority youth eschew identity labels, defined by Savin-Williams (2005) as a "post-identity" phase, where an assimilationist politics has triumphed over deconstructionist and queer forms of protest (Coleman-Fountain 2014; Ghaziani 2014). There was a similar generational divide about how participants felt the label *bisexual* explained their sexuality.

Critiquing Bisexuality as an Identity Label

Many of the participants spoke about valuing the bisexual label at an inter-personal level, because it helped them discuss their sexual desires with others. This view was strongest amongst the older two cohorts, and particularly among men over 30. For example, Riccardo, aged 38 and Hispanic, said, "Being bisexual is important to me because it's about *recognizing* yourself, about working out who you are."

He added, "When you're hot for men and women, how do you understand that unless you call yourself bisexual?" Similarly, Anthony, aged 34 and white, identified as bisexual, but "leaned more towards men." Another man in this cohort said, "Bisexuality as a label works for me. Otherwise how do you explain to people that you like both when they don't understand that?" Similarly, Drew, 30 and black, said, "Yeah I use it, it just works. I use it if I'm in a relationship to make it known, you know. You need the language to explain who you're attracted to." Likewise, Vernon, aged 40 and white, said, "Being bisexual is who you are. How can you get treated right if people don't understand that?" Vernon talked about attending bisexual community groups as well as LGBT groups, saying "It's about your community. How can you live your life if you don't have your community. And how can I, as a bisexual man, do that without recognizing my bisexuality."

Others, particularly among the older cohorts, linked identifying as bisexual as having pride in their desires. Arthur, aged 42 and white, said, "I think bisexual is a good label. It's a different way of looking at the world... I think it's all about taking pride in what you do in your life." Ricky, Hispanic and aged 33, said, "I don't mind the label bisexual, I'm proud of what I am. I'm comfortable with it." Interestingly, both of these men had negative experiences when disclosing their bisexual identities, and encountered bisexual burden in multiple aspects of their lives—as we discuss in Chaps. 9 and 10.

While many participants located importance in bisexuality as a label, some found the word did not fit their identities well, or questioned whether a label was necessary. For example, Shane, aged 28 and black, had a positive coming out experience but did not place much value in the label: "I don't really care for the label but it works well enough. Nobody takes the label too seriously." Richie, aged 32 and Hispanic, said that, "Labels are useful, but I really don't care if they're used or not." He added, "I mean, if I say I'm into men and women, or I say I'm bi, what's the difference?"

Alongside Richie, Tyrone was the one other man over 30 to have a similarly ambivalent view related to the label. Aged 34 and Black, he said: "I don't really like labels to begin with. I feel like, whoever I'm in a relationship with at that point, that's what matters. Not what label I have." This generational divide in the value placed in identifying as bisexual is even more apparent in the way that the younger men critique the notion of identity categories altogether.

While a range of views about the label bisexual existed across the cohorts, there was a significant strand in the youngest cohort that de-emphasized the importance of sexual identity labels. Frank, Hispanic and aged 20, said:

> Bisexual is a little ambiguous for me, because it's hard to know what it means. The bisexual label seems too rigid...And you know that's why when I talk about my desires, with people I'm dating, or with friends, I find it easier not to use the terminology all the time. I prefer discussing it, and talking about my desires instead.

Ray's ambivalence to the label came from his experiences in talking with other people who doubted the existence of bisexuality. Aged 25 and Hispanic, Ray said that he used the label "when referring to other people, but not so much for myself.

What I say about myself depends on the situation because I may or may not be attracted to that man or woman." He explained that this was partly due to bisexual burden.

> The label bisexual doesn't work for me, and I don't think it always works for most people. There is always worry behind what you label yourself as – whether you'll get accepted by other people.

In contrast to the oldest cohort, while most of the participants in the younger two cohorts did not reject identity categories, they had little attachment to sexual identity labels. For example, Max, white and aged 27, said, "I find myself equally attracted to males and females so if I fit the criteria to be labeled as bisexual, then sure, why not." This approach was similar to Neil's. Aged 18 and white, he said that he uses the bisexual label because "…it implies evenly split desires. That's what I have, so I'm happy with that." Asked how he would feel if someone thought he was gay rather than bisexual, he said, "Well, if I was dating a guy, and being monogamous with him, then who cares – my desire for women would be private really. If I was out there dating men and women, then I'd think it a bit weird." These participants were happy to use the labels but their narratives were absent of any component that would suggest a deep-rooted emotional attachment to a bisexual identity.

Some of these young men even used their ambivalence toward identity categories and the label 'bisexual' to explicitly argue against its importance. George, white and 28, said that pronouncing a gay identity was sometimes easier and did not find this a negative thing. He said, "It depends who I'm with. I find it easier to call myself gay. But I went to a gay pride festival once and ended up going home with a woman, so I don't feel that it stops me doing what I want."

It was significant that those in the youngest cohort also in long-term relationships actively rejected using the bisexual label. For example, Sam, aged 23 and Hispanic, often said that he was gay because he was currently in a long-term monogamous relationship with a man. Rather than this being a form of bisexual erasure, however, Sam argued that it was about describing his sexuality most appropriately:

> The term bisexual, I don't associate with sex any more than it needs to be. Yes, I'm attracted to men and women. But the fact is I'm doing monogamy with my boyfriend, and I don't think of women that much at the moment. Technically, I might be 'bisexual' if you were to do scientific tests, but I'm happy saying I'm gay at the moment.

Similarly, Cooper, white and 22, said:

> When I was with a woman, I identified more as straight, and when I'm with guys I identify more as gay. I like the label bi, as it's good for explaining my desires. But I've always described myself as sexually open, and I don't see the point of identifying as bisexual when I'm in a gay relationship.

Rather than being a form of bisexual erasure, as with the older generation, this willingness to forgo a bisexual identity in a relationship seems to speak to how these men view the identity as a useful label, rather than a fundamental part of their identities (Baldwin et al. 2014).

Similarly, Saul, black and 19, said that "The term bisexual is a cop out term. It's more about what you feel about a person at the time. I'm all about the intimacy." The two themes of diminishing importance or outright rejection show a marked shift in attitudes toward sexual identity among participants in the youngest cohort.

These examples do not show a rejection of identity categories more broadly, but a diminution in their importance of bisexuality as a label to explain these men's desires—seemingly happy to switch between bisexual, gay and other labels as appropriate.

Conclusion

Confusion has often been seen as an inherent component of bisexuality. In addition to the accusation of being confused about their sexual identity as part of bisexual burden, the first stages of developing a bisexual identity were seen to emerge from confusion around desires for both men and women (Weinberg et al. 1994). This idea found support for men in the oldest cohort. Yet the younger the men, the less confusion played a role in understanding their desires. While some still feared discrimination or social stigma, none expressed being confused about their same-sex desires. We attribute this to the greater awareness of bisexuality as a sexual identity in the 21st century, at least within these three cities.

In addition to these changing ways of identifying as bisexual, we also found significant change in the nature of these identifications among young bisexual men. Savin-Williams (2005) argues that sexual minority youth are entering a "post-identity" phase in which they no longer find solace or resonance with sexual identity categories. Cohler and Hammack (2009) suggest that rather than identity ceasing to be of importance, it becomes important in different ways. They say that "shifting master narratives of queer identity in the twenty-first century… [necessitate] adequate sensitivity to and appreciation for the contextual basis of human development" (p. 456). Our research finds support for both positions, with identifications continuing to have significance for our participants but in different ways than for the older generations.

The youngest cohort still place importance on their sexual identity. Most, when coming out, used the word bisexual – some because this was the easiest way to explain their desires, but most used it because it is how they identify. While their experiences were significantly more positive than the older generations, the idea that they needed to come out – and that they had previously been in the closet – accurately described their experiences and feelings (Plummer 1995). The notion of a sexual identity resonated with them, and the positive receptions they received had a beneficial impact in their lives.

However, this chapter shows that the nature of these identifications is fundamentally different. Many of the youngest cohort simply do not have a strong emotional engagement with their sexual identity. Some were happy to "lose" their bisexuality in a relationship, while others felt the label was the best option for describing their sexual desires without stating any particular affiliation with it. The ease of coming out, described in Chap. 8, has quite possibly altered the value they place in their sexual identities. Were it not for the strategic value still placed in these sexual identities, they could almost be described as having a "sexual affinity" rather than identity (Guittar 2014: 71).

In his book *The New Gay Teenager*, Savin-Williams (2005, p. 222) hoped that he would "see the elimination of same-sex sexuality as *a* defining characteristic" in his lifetime. For many of the men in the younger two cohorts, particularly those under 30, this appears to be precisely what has happened. Bisexuality is still a useful label and identity that these men inhabit and use, but it is not the characteristic that defines their lives.

Chapter 8
Coming Out with 20th Century Baggage

In this chapter, we examine the coming out experiences of those participants whose adolescence was in the 20th century. The majority of our participants – those in the oldest two cohorts – first came out in the conservative 1980s and the somewhat more liberal 1990s. This means that the men of these cohorts had their formative years in cultures where people generally maintained homophobic attitudes (Loftus 2001), where laws discriminated against LGB people (Weeks 2007) and where the stigma associated with HIV/AIDS meant that people went to great lengths to maintain a heterosexual identity (McCormack and Anderson 2014). Society was not just homophobic during this period, it was also homohysteric: homophobia was used to police the gendered identities and sexual lives of men.

In these homohysteric times, the closet was deemed the defining feature of gay and bisexual men's lives (Dean 2014; Seidman 2002). Heterosexuality was presumed, particularly among young people (Epstein and Johnson 1994), meaning that to maintain a gay or bisexual social identity one had to announce their sexuality and disavow heterosexuality in the process. Disclosing one's self-identity was seen as an important step in ensuring that one's sense of self was in harmony with a public identity. As Plummer (1995: 86) argued, coming out was a way to "develop a consistent, integrated sense of a self" and form friendships and communities with similar people (Nardi 1999). However, McLean (2007) highlights that this process was more complicated for bisexuals than for gays and lesbians because they had to disclose an attraction for the same sex while also maintaining attraction for people of the "opposite" sex.

This complexity was particularly the case prior to the 1990s, when bisexuality was not considered a legitimate sexual identity (Weinberg et al. 1994). We argue that much of this is attributable to the "one-time rule of homosexuality" (Anderson 2008, and see Chap. 5). Here, any same-sex sexual behavior in men was interpreted as proof of a hidden gay identity—polarizing sexual identity into a gay-straight binary and erasing bisexuality in the process. It is in this context that bisexuals have faced particular stigma when coming out; not least that bisexuality is often seen as a transitional phase before adopting an identity of gay or straight (Diamond 2008), or bisexuals are accused of attention seeking when they come out, or not being brave enough to "fully" come out as gay (Eliason 1997).

We also examine how growing up during this time influenced their gendered and sexual identities. We find that the experiences of stigma, marginalization and even oppression documented in the literature were common, but we also highlight that they were not universally present among these men. We have conceptualized their difficulties as bisexual burden (see Chap. 3), an umbrella category that recognizes the diverse ways in which bisexuals are marginalized within society beyond that which gays and lesbians experience. While bisexual burden was an issue for these men, they also encountered more overt forms of discrimination. We discuss these experiences by examining the reactions of friends, family and work colleagues, and also highlight how some of these men have internalized heterosexist and misogynistic discourse of this period in ways that impact negatively upon them.

Coming Out to Friends

Research has documented that bisexuals face greater social stigma and marginalization when disclosing their sexual identity than is experienced by gays and lesbians (Burleson 2005). These burdens are exacerbated during the coming out process because the stereotypes of bisexuality directly contest the notion that bisexuality is a legitimate sexual identity. Most bisexuals opt to come out to friends before family as an attempt to ameliorate this (Weinberg et al. 1994), yet many experience discrimination here as well (Harbeck 1992). This is something we also found. For example, Simon, white and aged 39, discussed the impact of his coming out to his neighborhood friends when he was 22: "It was hard and I was so depressed." He recalled:

> It's really one of the reasons why I left that place. I told my friend, Jake, and he told everybody else. I got a lot of disgust from them after…I still miss them to this day but I don't think they miss me.

When asked about whether he tried to explain his sexuality to his friends, Simon answered:

> No. About as far as it got was one of them saying, 'I heard you're gay.' I told him I was bi, but he replied, 'same difference.' That's really the only time I talked with them about it. When I did see them after, we just pretended I hadn't said anything. But it didn't matter, they saw less and less of me.

Arthur, white and aged 42, first came out when he was 26. While his friends did not reject him, he said they "labeled me as gay…Looking back, I can see I was being made fun of, but I just told them I wasn't gay, that I was bisexual." This did not change his friends' behavior though; they continued to refer to him as gay, and in a manner he felt was "judgmental."

Similarly, AJ, Black and aged 38, said that all his friends who know he is bisexual tell him that he is confused and "going through a phase." He added, "It's the same with the guys I date, and I've been rejected by a bunch of gay men who are just like, 'I don't wanna deal with bisexual stuff.'" Explaining what this meant, AJ said, "they thought I'd be needy or high maintenance." The heterosexual men were also skeptical, with some telling him that he was "confused" because he "hadn't found the right woman yet," while others thought he was gay. AJ added, "You could see some of them thinking 'yeah right' when I told them I was bisexual, even when they didn't say anything."

It was common for men who came out in the 1980s and 1990s to be repeatedly told that they were confused. Ricky, who is Hispanic and aged 33, said that it "happened all the time." He expressed frustration at this, saying: "It really does confuse me. They'll also say 'you're bisexual now, but in the end you'll be gay.'"

Ricky recalled one heated conversation with someone he described as "not a real friend" asking, "If I like both guys and girls, then I like both guys and girls. How can I be confused?" He continued, "Wouldn't 'confused' mean I didn't know if I like men or women?" After the interviewer laughed, and remarked, "Good point. What did he say?" Ricky answered, "He said, 'You just are.' He wasn't my smartest friend."

Anthony, white and aged 34, described his experiences of coming out in positive terms, yet he also encountered stereotypical notions related to bisexuality. He said, "No-one has confronted me and said I'm sick or anything, but I did have a few friends who said, that it was the cowardly way, a way of being safe." He added, "I had one friend who said 'I don't believe in bisexuality' and she then said, 'I think it's just an excuse to make it easier on yourself before coming out as gay.'" Anthony was upset by this denial from his female friend, asking, "What's the point of being honest, working up that courage, if your friends don't trust you when you do anyhow?"

Anthony was particularly upset by the actions of one of his lesbian friends, who he said "ought to know better." Highlighting the double discrimination bisexuals encounter (Weiss 2003), Anthony reported that she "told me I was confused." Highlighting her hypocrisy, he added, "The funny thing is she was my best friend, and a full blown lesbian who got engaged to a man. At the time she was very passionate about being a lesbian, and that was the reason [he was so upset by it]."

Not all of our participants found themselves rejected or their sexuality denied. Robert, aged 42 and white, said that he had positive experiences among friends when he came out. But he was also fortunate to be "hanging out with people who were cool with that lifestyle, so it wasn't a strange thing to them." Robert informed us that he was artistic, and most of his friends were "artistic types." Despite this, Robert said that his military family upbringing meant that he was a "masculine guy." He said, "I think those two elements bought me some immunity." While his friends accepted that he was bisexual, he felt his desires were marginalized. "The bi thing wasn't talked about much. They knew I was, but we didn't really discuss it much," he said.

Bernie, white and aged 37, said, "I only told my closest friends, and that wasn't until I was 24." His friends' reactions were mixed:

> A couple of them didn't want to admit it. They were like "we've seen you in [straight] bars and seen you hook up with girls." One of them bitched me out, saying, 'bisexuality isn't possible.' I was like, 'well, I like men, too.'

Bernie also suggested that his younger friends had more positive reactions to his bisexuality: "They don't seem to have a problem with it." When asked about whether it made a difference whether those friends were gay or straight, he said, "No, my straight friends were just as cool with it as my gay friends."

John, white and 38, described the positive reaction of his friends when he came out aged 20: "I just came right out and said 'Hey, I got a date tonight with a guy' and no-one raised an eyebrow. I think they knew me well enough and I was pretty comfortable with myself." However, John remained closeted in the broader community. He said, "It wasn't easy, at that time and where I was living. It was ok if you wanted to keep it within your circle of friends or family, but my town was still working class and pretty conservative." Indeed, the majority of participants came out to their friends privately, eschewing broader discussion of their sexuality and remaining closeted either at school or in the workplace.

John's narrative highlights that many of the participants were strategic in their coming out, in an attempt to improve experiences of this event (see Brown 2002). Men of these cohorts tended not to come out to those who they thought would be hostile. Yet even with this strategic plan, the aspects of bisexual burden was the norm. For example, John also highlighted some of the more subtle forms of bisexual burden he experienced with his friends, who treated his male dates differently from his female ones:

> The first time I showed up at a party with a guy, I'm not sure they quite knew how much to be open to him, because they weren't sure if it was a fling, a fuck buddy, a date, whatever. I think the assumption is if she's a woman you can open up to her because she's a potential mate, right, but with another guy I think they might have been thinking that with gay men it's all about sex. It was as if my friends thought, there's really no sense in getting to know him, 'cause he might be gone next week.

While most of the participants had come out to increasing numbers of people as they got older, there was still deeply segmented identities for many participants. For example, AJ maintained a strict divide in terms of who he disclosed his sexuality to, stating that he had "two separate lives." The only people who know he is bisexual were gay or bisexual themselves.

Others came out to friends that they had not intended to because they "got caught." JP, Hispanic and aged 31, said:

> I was at the bar with some guy, and my friend saw me and he said 'what's up with that,' so I responded that I wanted to try both men and women. We didn't talk for a couple of weeks after that but then he called me and we talked and hung out. He said that when he thinks about gays, he thinks feminine, so I said 'I'm not like that, but I don't flaunt to everybody.

My business is my business so you don't have to worry about it.' I told him, 'If we're hanging out with friends, I'm not gonna be trying to grab ass or hit on anyone.' He said he was ok with that.

When asked about their experiences coming out to friends, two participants spoke about "traumatic" events. Ramone, 42 and Hispanic, said that he lost his best friend. "Yeah, I lost my best friend after coming out to him. He was actually the first person I came out to as well. It wasn't a great way to start my new life." He described what happened:

We grew up together, we went to the same school together, we lived down the street from each other. Then, when we were teenagers he got a job at a movie theatre and once I turned 16 he got me hired there too. We used to go to movies together all the time. I mean, we did everything together. But once I told him I was bisexual, he stopped talking to me.

When asked if he ever found out why this was, Ramone responded:

No. I never did. Part of me wonders if it maybe wasn't his parents. Perhaps he told his parents and they forbade him from speaking to me. I don't know. I know he didn't tell others, maybe because he was afraid that because we were so close that others would think he was my boyfriend. But nobody else at school found out, or at least said anything. I'd see him at school, and he'd do his best to avoid me. If he had to pass me by, he'd say, 'hey' or something, but that's about it.

Similarly, Lloyd, aged 38 and white, said, "I told my best friend. You know, we'd often talked about fucking girls and getting laid, but I had never spoke about wanting to fuck guys. This night we were drinking and I just told him. It wasn't good." Lloyd described how his friend jumped up in disgust, spilling their drinks. "He said 'fucking faggot, left the bar, and then we didn't see each other for weeks. Next time we met…well, it was obvious we weren't friends anymore."

In examining the experiences of participants whose adolescence was in the 20th century, there was also a marked improvement for some of the men in the middle cohort compared with the oldest cohort (see also Evans and Broido 1999). For example, Louis, white and 24, first came out as bisexual at 18 after graduating high school. He told us that, among his friends, it "wasn't an issue." He attributed this to his belief that most of his friends "already knew." When asked how that was, he said, "Well, I wasn't the most masculine guy. I didn't date much in high school, so I think they thought I was gay because of that." Not only were Louis's friends accepting of his sexuality, he said, "I think they would have liked me to have come out sooner. They didn't feel able to ask, but were maybe upset that I didn't feel able to tell them."

Similarly, Anthony, white and aged 34, said, "I had a lot of friends who were girls, they were really happy to know that I was, and a lot of my guy friends were also understanding." Eager to find out more about bisexuality, Anthony said that they "asked me lots of questions…it felt good to be able to share that with them." While Anthony was confident that his female friends would be accepting, he was less confident about his male friends: "You know girls were so much better with these issues—at least back then. So the guys' questions were a bit more ignorant, but I didn't get any shit."

Carl, white and aged 32, exemplified the mixed reactions for men of the middle cohort. He said, "Most people were confused, and I'd say 50% dropped me as their friend, and 50% stuck by me." Similar to Anthony, Carl found that telling his male friends was harder than telling his female ones. "It was more taboo for them," he recalled, "but they made an attempt to learn and to adapt to it." Even so, these experiences were more positive than those of several of the men in the oldest cohort. Many of Carl's friends asked him questions about his sexual life, which he enjoyed:

> I felt like I was teaching them something about myself. It felt good to be able to share that with them. It was something they didn't know and couldn't relate to before. So, for them to be curious about me and who I am. It felt good.

However, Carl also experienced rejection from other friends. He said, "They wanted nothing to do with me."

This was also true of Jose, aged 24 and Hispanic, whose coming out experience was unique among our participants. Having sexual experiences with girls and boys his own age from the age of 9, he was forced out at school when he was 13:

> One of my friends saw me giving head to a fellow class mate. It was all over the school.... The whole school knew, then the whole town. I was a 'known person' because of it. But because of that, everyone kind of got used to it. It started off bad – I got called fag or gayboy, but I got physical with guys as a way of showing them not to give me shit. After a while it was fine, and my friends were fine, and it wasn't too bad.

Six participants discussed the role of religion in their coming out experiences, and these were evenly divided across racial groups. For example, Tiago, aged 33 and Hispanic, had not come out to his parents, saying, "My family is very religious. If they found out that I was bisexual then they'd probably kick me out or at least be really angry with me." Similarly, Clark, aged 40 and white, was brought up Mormon. He said, "People's general reaction was that of being scared – in Mormon religion, being gay was the second biggest sin so it wasn't great."

George, white and 28, also attributed religion as having a negative influence on his experiences. He said, "My church and parents started talking about homosexuality and how it was a sin, and how you are supposed to like a girl. That was the first time I had ever thought anything bad about it." While those who mentioned religion did so because of the negative effect it had, their experiences were broadly fitted with the cohort in which they had their adolescence.

Accordingly, the dominant theme for men of these cohorts was that bisexual burden played a significant role in their first experiences of disclosing their bisexuality. Men of the older generation experienced the most rejection and denial, while men of the middle cohort found significant forms of prejudice interspersed with elements of acceptance or acceptance from particular groups. Similar to existing research on bisexual men's coming out experiences (Klein 1993), participants were strategic in coming out to their friends. While this was not always possible or effective, it was evident that this strategic thinking was the result of fear about biphobia and bisexual burden in society.

The Difficulty of Coming Out to Family

Most participants in the older two cohorts came out to their friends before their family (see also Weinberg et al. 1994). A key reason for this is that coming out to family poses greater risks. It is not possible to strategically select your family to be less homophobic and whereas lost friends can be replaced, this is not the same with close family (Savin-Williams 1998). Just as research has tended to find that bisexual men experience biphobia and bisexual burden when coming out to their families (D'Augelli et al. 2010; Klein 1993), the experiences of participants we interviewed whose adolescence was in the twentieth century followed a similar trajectory.

Andy, white and aged 39, came out to his parents and brother at 22. Hopeful that his family would understand, he told them because he could not "keep it in any longer." He described their initial reaction to the news as "not good." When asked for details he said, "They weren't very cool with it. You know, they were – disappointed – I guess is a good word for it." When asked how they expressed that disappointment, Andy recalled his brother's response: "He said to me, 'Why the fuck would you wanna be like that?'" When Andy told him that he did not want to be like that but that he "just was," his brother called him a faggot. Visibly shaken by the retelling of this story, Andy paused before adding, "He told me he didn't want a faggot as a brother." Moving off the topic because of Andy's discomfort, he later returned to the subject saying that his brother gradually became "accustomed" to his bisexuality, commenting that he is now closer (but still not close) to him.

A significant majority of participants waited until adulthood before coming out to family members. Many of the men from the older cohort explained that they stayed closeted a significant period into their adulthood, when they had some independence from their families (see also Weinberg et al. 1994). Regardless of the age that our participants first came out to someone, hiding their sexuality from their family was the normal experience.

Darryn, who realized he was bisexual at 15, did not disclose his identity to his family or anyone else until he was 28. He said, "I didn't feel like I could tell anyone. The men in my family were real masculine, you know? It was fear." He added:

> My parents were, well they still are, extremely religious. They think sex with men is wrong because it's in the Bible. And they had that idea of a man being real masculine. You know, hardworking, protect their woman, that sort of thing. Telling them I liked dudes? Nah, fuck that.

Robert also linked the masculinity of his male relatives and fear, saying:

> The men in my family are masculine, military. It's fear. Fear of what my father would think of me; what my cousins would think of me. Worried about what they would think of me instead of worrying about my own happiness.

Robert highlighted that his concerns were not related solely to his father's personal beliefs, but his reputation in his hometown. He said, "If I did tell him, his primary concern would have been keeping it from his friends. You know, especially back then, that sort of thing wasn't accepted in the military."

In addition to fear, Darryn, whose parents were extremely religious, also described feeling "a lot of guilt" growing up. This guilt was related to his practices of being on the down low. He said, "I felt a lot of fear of what my father would think about me, about what my friends would say. I grew up in the 80s man. It wasn't cool." Similarly, Bernie did not come out to his family until recently. He attributed this to changing social attitudes toward homosexuality: "Telling my parents earlier wouldn't have gone down well."

Some of the men in these older cohorts were still not out to their family. AJ said, "we're not the kind of family that discusses birds and bees, you know?…We don't discuss sexuality and sex or any of that stuff. It's very, very traditional." This silencing has been easier for AJ because while he has had sex with men, his relationships have been limited to women. Exemplifying the bisexual privilege that we discussed in Chap. 3, AJ was able to have meaningful relationships while avoiding the stigma of coming out to a conservative family.

Others were out only to certain family members. Lee, aged 29 and black, said he was not out to his parents, but his brothers and sisters knew. However, he still maintained a silence about his sexuality with his family, saying, "Just because they know doesn't mean it needs to be talked about," adding that they would, "eventually meet my partner if it was a man who I was in a relationship with." Similarly, JP said:

> I'm not out to my family at all. I dunno how they'd react. I think they wouldn't talk to me for a while, being from a Hispanic family. It tends to be frowned on, so I don't wanna jeopardize the love I got from my family with stuff from my personal life. I don't particularly wanna tell them, because then I would have to change something about my life. I'd have to talk to them different, and they'd talk to me different. I dunno, it would just be totally different. I mean, I am their brother, I am their son, and stuff like that.

However, not all participants had bad experiences. For Shane, aged 28 and black, this was because of his particular familial context. Shane came out to his mother at 17 to a positive reception. "She had an idea about me being bisexual," he said, "because she is bisexual. My dad wasn't really that comfortable with it, but he said 'you're my son and I love you.'"

Ray, who was 25 and Hispanic, said that his mother was confused at first, saying, "You've had girlfriends in the past, I don't understand what this means for your future." Ray said that he had long talks with her in order to explain it. He added that she accepted him and dealt with the change "quickly" once she was knew his perspectives on having bisexual desire. Similarly, while Jonathan, white and 35, said that his father "didn't have a problem," he said that his mother "couldn't rationalize it and wanted to understand if it was nature or nurture."

Anthony said despite having a troubled relationship with his father, his attitude about his bisexuality was strong:

My dad is currently in jail and he wrote a letter to me asking me if I was or not. By then my whole family had known, but he wrote me a long letter and I spoke to him when I went to visit him. It was a weight of my shoulders, and for him to be so understanding made me feel great.

The rest of Anthony's family found out when he was 16. He says he "never mustered up the courage" to tell his mum, but after coming out to his closest cousins "word of mouth spread between the whole family…[and] no-one ever put me down for it."

For some participants, their greater fear of telling family members than friends was not reflected in the reality of how their family responded to the news. For example, when Trenton, white and aged 28, came out at 16 to his cousin, who then told the rest of his family, he described a positive response. "Some were quiet, thinking about it, but I think that was them processing it" he said. "My mum hugged me and said she would like grandkids, but that I had to follow my heart. I think that's what my Dad thought too." Similarly, Drew, aged 30 and black, said, "I worried about my parents, because they're religious – every Sunday at Church, never fail. But they didn't care. After all that fear, it went fine. They were fine with it." These counter-narratives highlight that range of experiences in coming out to family even during homohysteric times, yet the prevailing discourse was one of stigma and bisexual burden.

Furthermore, there was only one participant, AJ, who attributed his negative experiences to his ethnicity. Black and aged 38, he said, "My parents are from a West Indian background. I was born here [in New York] but my parents are from a Caribbean island and it just wouldn't be accepted." Living a double life, he ensures that the friends with whom he is openly bisexual do not come into contact with his family. However, none of the other participants mentioned race as an important component in encountering bisexual burden, and an analysis of race also did not raise significant difference.

Negotiating Bisexuality at Work

Bisexual men must also consider who they come out to at work (Rumens 2013). This is an issue fraught with difficulty and risk as it is still legal to be fired for ones sexuality in many US states, although such practice has been illegal in the UK for several years. Highlighting the uniqueness of the bisexual experience, research finds that while 48% of gay men and 50% of lesbians state that most or all of their colleagues know about their sexuality, just 11% of bisexuals say the same (Pew 2013). These concerns were mirrored by our participants. For example, AJ said that he was completely closeted at work:

I work in financial services in New York City, so it's very much high achievers, and your ability to negotiate and your demands are linked to your personal achievements and whether you're married, so I just steer well clear of that you know.

Robert, who came out to his group of artistic friends in high school, also argued that his bisexuality had hindered his career. Working as a photographer, he said that after telling a gay client he was bisexual, "the next day I had rumors that I was on the down low." In other words, the client perceived Robert's bisexuality to be a fear of 'fully' coming out as gay (Eliason 1997). As a result of this, he concluded that, "sometimes you have to use a little discretion because you can't come out to certain people, they're not going to understand your business." Similarly, JP said:

> [At work,] they tend to not want to know. They get offended, so I keep it to myself. If they have no trouble with me then I have no trouble with them. I don't care though. I mean, I'm just who I am, it's not like I'm looking to get with that guy. I say to myself, if it happens it happens. I don't wanna hit that guy up, if we happen to talk then that's cool. It's not like I go out of my way to keep it hid, but at the same time, I don't really properly tell anyone. I just feel it's easier if they don't know. If they know about what I'm doing then I'd be thinking 'oh man, are they judging me, are they criticizing me, what are they doing?' Right now, it's safe and they don't do that and I don't have to worry about whether they are ok with it.

However, this was not true of all participants, many of whom were open at work. Arthur worked as a dance choreographer and said that he was open about his bisexuality. However, he also encountered aspects of bisexual burden, commenting that "most people assume I am gay at work. I correct them, but I don't fight it… People accept it eventually, but not always at the beginning."

Similarly, Richard, aged 37 and white, worked in a bank and was open to most of his colleagues: "Most know, and it's only the upper level staff, the people who could damage my job or stop me getting promoted that don't know." He added, "They're older, more conservative and straight down the line. Telling them I'm bisexual is just a bigger risk."

Jose was out to his co-workers as well, saying that:

> they know I'm bi, not because I tell them directly, but it happens in day-to-day stuff. Like, I'll say a guy is attractive and then a girl later, so they know. You know, 'he's hot, she's hot,' they work out I'm bi."

Given his positive experience, it is worth noting that Jose is 24 years old and thus the youngest participant in the middle cohort.

While some participants spoke about their type of work influencing their disclosure of bisexuality, there were a range of experiences here as well. Highlighting this, Barry, Black and aged 39, was a construction worker, and had had positive coming out experience with his colleagues: "They found out through word of mouth or something, but no bad reactions. People are pretty free, you do what you want." Despite working in a macho environment, he added "the people who I work with, they don't ask about your personal life, they mind their own business."

Bisexual Burden on the Scene

The older bisexual men also experienced prejudice from gay people in the gay scene (McLean 2008). Arthur said, "I tend to just say I'm gay on the scene. It doesn't bother me, it's just easier. There is some hostility toward bisexuals from gay guys, in the same way from the straights." Richie, Hispanic and aged 32, complained about the presumption of homosexuality in gay bars:

> I wish people would realize that just because you're in a gay bar, it doesn't mean that you're gay. I go to straight bars as well, but I have more fun in a gay bar because it's more relaxed. In the gay bar, people think I'm gay; in the straight bar, they think I'm straight. We need a bisexual bar!

Several participants commented that they would tell people in gay bars that they are gay to avoid bisexual burden. For example, Anthony said, "To say you're bi is not necessarily taboo, but I feel like I have to explain myself if I do. So I just identify myself as gay—it's easier." Richard also said, "I say I'm gay. When I say I'm bi, gay guys are like 'seriously, why would you do that?'"

Clark, 40 and white, said that there was a gay bar he frequented in Salt Lake City:

> You don't really stand a chance of being thought anything but gay once you go in. The idea, I think, is that you can pick up on women elsewhere, so if you are going to go into a gay bar you are there to pick up on guys.

"I guess it's the way it is," he added. "If you go to a gay bar, you will be thought gay." This framing of gay space as solely for same-sex sexual encounters (see Ghaziani 2014) speaks to how many participants experienced gay cultures as monosexist.

A minority of participants also commented on how they perceived their lack of attractiveness had impacted upon them. For example, Barry, aged 39 and black, said when talking about not feeling comfortable in new settings, and particularly on the scene. He said: "But look at me. I'm outa shape, and I can't afford good clothes. Would you want to come over and talk to me?" Similarly, Arnold, black and aged 40, said, "I've always felt left out. I'm not an attractive guy, and that's crippled me a bit, you know?" He said this went back to his school days: "I was awkward, kinda fat and I just always wanted to be liked by these attractive people. But at the same time, I knew I couldn't talk to them. That's stuck with me, even today."

However, some participants highlighted that being homosexualized by monosexist standards was not universal. For example, while Richie experienced some negativity in his regular gay bar from "a group of guys who have their clique," he said that it was not a major issue. He added, "I've been at certain bars where people have said, 'hey, you're checking out that woman' and a gay friend has said 'yeah, she's hot.'" Suggesting a generational component, he added, "I chat to the younger guys a lot – they're more open and talkative and comfortable with themselves than I was at 21."

Finally, there was strong support among participants for the notion that younger generations of gay men were more accepting of bisexuality (see this chapter). Arthur was explicit, stating that "the younger generation is more accepting of it all than the older generation." Similarly, AJ said, "The older the man gets the more he thinks you're willing to settle on being gay, that you'll just say 'ok' and end up just being with men." This supports recent research that finds approximately two thirds of bisexual and gay men perceive each other as sharing common concerns in their daily lives (Pew 2013), as well as our findings in the following chapter.

Heterosexism

In addition to finding that they generally had negative experiences of being bisexual, there was also elevated personal heterosexism among men of the older cohort (Della et al. 2002). For example, Andy, whose family reacted badly to his disclosure, commented: "I don't throw it in their face. I don't see a reason to make an issue of it." When asked if he discusses female partners with his parents, he answered, "Yeah, sometimes" but said that "it's not appropriate" to discuss male partners with his family. Andy thus adopted a *don't ask, don't tell* policy with his parents: "They don't say anything about it, but they accept it because I'm their son. And I respect their opinion."

Similarly, Darryn, the black male who realized he was bisexual at 15 but did not come out until 28, suggested that his bisexuality was "personal." Adopting a defensive demeanor, he said: "I keep it to myself. We don't need that in our lives, making it harder for ourselves by being all in your face about it."

Some participants also reflected particular stereotypes that form bisexual burden. JP, for example, suggested that young bisexual men today should "make sure they really do know they are bi, that it's not just a phase. That happens a lot, people not actually being bi when they say they are." John also argued that "some of these guys who say they are bisexual. They're not bisexual, they're just horny."

Robert also maintained heterosexist perspectives, particularly related to gendered behaviors and his ideas of how gay men act. Explaining why his friends reacted positively to his coming out, he said:

> I never carried myself in a flamboyant manner. I think there's only judgment when people come out if they sort of posturize it, and make it a national event. You have to be able to keep it personal, that's what you like. And what I like may not be what you like, so I should keep that to myself and not walk around snapping my fingers and being flamboyant to the world like this is me, 'cause the world don't agree.

While this stigmatization of campness was a strong theme in the narratives of the men from these cohorts, there were those who eschewed this position, particularly among the men of the middle cohort. For example, Tyrone, black and aged 34, said, "Some of my friends think I purposefully act gay, but you know I'm a camp guy. That's me, and I like it." Similarly, Sean, white and aged 25, frequented gay bars in

LA. He said, "I didn't really come out to my family, I just emerged. I'm so camp they knew I wasn't straight, so it was more me telling them that I might have a girlfriend at some point." He continued, "I think they had spoken about me being gay already, so it took them a little while to get their head around me being bisexual."

While Sean's camp gendered behaviors had positive effects, this was not the case for Chris, Hispanic and aged 28:

> People assumed I was gay because I'm really feminine, and it took a while for people to get that I'm bi. My dad couldn't understand why I'd be open about being bi if I could just like girls. He was accepting and stuff, I just guess he didn't really understand it all. Things are good now though.

Misogyny

In addition to exhibiting heterosexist behaviors, several men whose adolescence was in the 20th century expressed misogynistic attitudes (Mac an Ghaill 1994). Freddie, a Hispanic male aged 37, spoke about his inability to "pull" women in straight clubs: "I'll go up to a girl, ask to buy her a drink, and she'll say no. I'll be like, "what are you doing here, bitch?"" Likewise, AJ spoke aggressively about women: "Sex with men is great, but women can be bitches. You know, not letting you do what you want. Men are easier."

Several other participants in this cohort used the terms "bitch," "slut" or "whore" during interview, although it was "bitch" that was used most frequently about women. For example, Riccardo, aged 38 and Hispanic, was sat in the coffee shop while being interviewed and commented about the waitress, "bitch forgot my coffee."

Given that these men have lived through feminist advances in US and UK culture, it could have been expected that their attitudes toward women would have improved (see also Pallotta-Chiarolli 2015). Given this use of language among some of the men – and predominantly the American men – these misogynistic behaviors and attitudes highlight the importance of growing up in homohysteric cultures in their formative years (Plummer 2010). That is, misogyny has been documented as raising a man's masculine capital in a homohysteric culture, helping avoid homophobic stigma (Anderson 2005; Floyd 2000). It seems that they have internalized these social practices even when their masculine identities are no longer questioned in the same way.

The Importance of the City

Our focus throughout our study has been on bisexual men's experiences in metropolitan cities. The nature of the contemporary city – where people within it include residents, tourists, visitors from the suburbs and those living in the city only temporarily – means that we have not developed a research design that effectively analyzes differences between cities and suburban or rural areas. Even so, several participants who grew up in rural areas spoke about their hometowns as homophobic and dangerous places. For example, George, white and aged 28, went to college in Georgia, calling it "the bible belt." He said, "I was there just after the sodomy law had been dropped. People got beat up for being gay you know. It was a nasty time, so I just dated girls then."

Richard, aged 37 and white, came from the South as well. He concurred, saying that "people are a little freaked out about homosexuality there." He added, "The last time I experienced it was in Kentucky. I had two straight-acting drag friends and would go to their shows on occasion. There'd be people outside of the clubs shouting abuse at you and sometimes trying to start fights. But that's part of being in the south." Richard suggested that the cultural lag between the south and the rest of the country still exists. "It hasn't really changed in the south," he said. And while this statement is not supported by the narratives of some of our younger cohort (see this chapter), who had positive experiences coming out in the American South, it speaks to the perception of non-metropolitan areas in this cohort.

Barry, Black and aged 39, lived in New York, but grew up in Indiana. He described the move from Indiana to New York as centrally important in his life, escaping the perceived closed-mindedness of rural America. He said:

> So all my family are in Indiana. You get the idea of what that means. Now, they all know I like guys and girls, and my mom and dad are old-fashioned so they don't say anything about it. It's a small-minded town. But they accept it because I'm their son.

Here, Barry used the associations with Indiana to serve as a placeholder for experiences of sexual prejudice. This divide is further evidenced when he discussed his positive experiences in New York:

> My friends out here are all cool with it. You know, it's a lot more open out here. I've been out here about four years, and that's one of the reasons I came out here, because I knew people were more open to that kind of lifestyle. I could be myself without feeling I was hiding anything.

Summarizing his experiences, Barry said:

> I'm pretty happy with the life I've lived... But it's also been rough going for me at the beginning, because no one really accepted it back where I come from. I know I lost a lot of friends that way, but I stuck with my guns, and ever since I moved to New York it's been a lot smoother. I'm pretty happy these days and things are cool.

There is a similar though less pronounced recognition of the importance of geography in the UK. A "north/south divide" is said to exist, where the north is seen as marginalized from the dominance of the south, with wealth and privilege divided unequally between the two. One older participant in the UK spoke about moving first to Brighton and then to London to avoid the homophobia of his hometown in the north. Ed, aged 38 and white, said:

I grew up in a northern mining town. They weren't that open there, you didn't go round listening to [David] Bowie or anything like that. I moved down south at 18, to Brighton first of all and just got a bar job. Then I moved to London to have that big city experience. I loved both – just so much sexual diversity and freedom to be who you want to be.

This support for the city was a theme across most of the older cohorts, particularly in America (Ghaziani 2014). Tyrone, 34 and black, summarized this viewpoint, saying "being in the city is great, it's just very accepting." Thus, despite us not finding significant differences within each cohort according to social experiences of being bisexual, the men from rural areas used their location as one of the ways of understanding their negative experiences.

Conclusion

Our research shows that bisexual men whose adolescence occurred in the latter part of the 20th century experienced discrimination, oppression and bisexual burden when coming out (see also Weinberg et al. 1994). However, our research found a multiplicity of experiences, with family and friends sometimes being supportive and even welcoming the news. It is also important to recognize that the homophobia, bisexual burden and sexual prejudice of the 20th century likely impacted upon our participants in a range of ways. While this occurs in explicit ways, including stories of rejection and abuse from friends and family, we also found it led some participants to espouse heteronormative views and maintain misogynistic attitudes.

We attribute the greater variability in experiences than traditionally found in the literature to two key issues. First, we recruited men from the liberal cities of New York, Los Angeles and London. Second, our innovative recruitment strategy did not rely on bisexual communities and LGBT networks where those who had negative experiences are likely to congregate (McCormack 2014). It is possible that in the 1980s and 1990s the experiences of bisexuality were more diverse but, because of pervasive homophobia, the better experiences were more insulated as people maintained a level of privacy related to their sexual identity (Seidman 2002).

The third factor in why we found a range of experiences is that it is quite likely that participants' experiences have improved across time, as homophobia has decreased (Keleher and Smith 2012). It might be the case that some of our participants who reported positive experiences may respond differently now than they would have done if interviewed in the 1980s. While retrospective interviews are recognized as a valid way of understanding past experiences (Rivers 2001), it is also important to recognize that more recent positive experiences may blur how people recall past negative ones.

While the literature has clearly demonstrated that coming out is a social process (Plummer 1995), it is also worth noting the dual meaning of that terminology. First is the recognition that coming out occurs over an extended period of time; second is that coming out is part of a process of constructing and maintaining an identity to make sense of sexual desires at variance with broader societal norms (Coleman-Fountain 2014; Savin-Williams 1998).

We suggest that coming out needs to be complicated further: that our participants consider coming out to family, friends and colleagues to be distinct things—less a process and more *different* but related social acts (see also Baldwin et al. 2014). This explains why some participants were still not out to parents and even wider family, and how others came out to their family only after a significant period. Significantly, very few of the participants identified as closeted if they were only out to a few people. They still described themselves as being "out" or "openly bisexual," and provided reasons why they were not out to family or colleagues at work.

Chapter 9
Coming Out in the 21st Century

The ways in which sexual minority youth identify has been the topic of much discussion in recent years. In 2005, Ritch Savin-Williams heralded the arrival of the "new gay teenager" who was defined not by difference as the gay and bisexual youth of the 20th century were (Flowers and Buston 2001), but by an ordinariness of experience that meant that "being labeled as gay or even being gay matters little" (p. 1). These changes in how sexual identities are mediated correspond with research that has documented a significant liberalization in attitudes toward homosexuality (Keleher and Smith 2012).

Our own research has contributed to this literature, documenting the positive effects on both gay men (Anderson 2005, 2011) and heterosexual men (Anderson 2009, 2014; McCormack 2012a, 2014). Indeed, one of our motivating factors for this book was to investigate how this social trend manifests in the lives of bisexuals. Our age cohort design enabled us to examine for this social change, and we found a significant improvement in coming out experiences for the youngest group of bisexual men (see also Morris et al. 2014; Savin-Williams 2005).

In this chapter, we examine how our participants in the youngest cohort experience the social world, and how their coming out experiences have improved compared to men of the older cohorts. The collective experience of the 18–23 year old bisexual men was substantially more positive than those in the two older groups. While many participants still spoke of coming out as an important milestone, it was frequently experienced as a positive and even enjoyable event. Like the other cohorts, these men's experiences were still diverse, but collectively, they are much improved compared to those who came out in the twentieth century for these men in Los Angeles, New York and London.

Acceptance and Inclusion Among Friends

The experiences of coming out to friends outside of school were almost entirely positive for this cohort (McCormack 2012b). For example, Kevin's disclosure of bisexuality was not an issue for his close friends. Black and aged 19, Kevin said, "No one judged me. We'd been hanging out for years so they knew I was a good lad and they had got to know that already. They understood that my sexuality didn't affect the type of person I was." He added that he did not have significant problems with people outside his close friendship groups either:

> I'm sure there have been some people who might've avoided talking about it, but as far as bullying or harassment go, no never. I've always believed that if someone feels slightly uncomfortable with it, then it's their problem not mine. Eventually people like that soften up.

Lewis, white and aged 21, came out to his friends a year ago, and their reactions ranged from "slightly puzzled" to positive:

> They were shocked, yeah, and some were a little weird and awkward, but no one was like outwardly negative or hostile…And you might think that's not really acceptance, but for those people I've told it has gone better than I thought it'd go.

Jared, white and aged 21, commented that most people, "seemed to like it that I was so relaxed about my sexuality," adding that there was "not really an issue" and that he lived "pretty much a taboo-free existence." As Laurie, white and aged 19, commented, "No one has ever tried to change me from being bi. It's not about being bi, gay or straight. It's about being comfortable in who you are."

The strategic nature of coming out, highlighted by scholars in the past (Savin-Williams 1998), was still present for some participants. For example, Neil, aged 18 and white, who came out when living in Louisiana, said, "I came out to my friends when I was 17. The best one is first of all, then the others. It was harder to come out back home, and so I came out to fewer people, but everyone here [in New York] knows I'm bisexual."

Angelo had the worst experience in this cohort in coming out to friends, saying that they started to call him "faggot." He added that while several of his peers acted like this, more were accepting and "would be like, 'oh that's cool.'" Interestingly, despite his relatively negative experiences, Angelo commented that he was happy about coming out, adding, "It was like everything was free off my shoulders. I had no burdens, no secrets; I was just letting the world know who I am, and what I'm proud of."

Even so, while overt forms of marginalization or oppression were almost entirely absent from these participants' narratives, elements of bisexual burden remained for some. Brian, black and aged 23, for example, commented that several of his gay friends dismissed his bisexuality, saying "A lot of the guys are like 'yeah, you're gonna be gay one day.'" Attractive and popular, he added "Several of the girls still hope I'm straight. It's stupid. I mean, they could still date me."

When participants experienced negative reactions, these were less intense and occurred for a shorter period than for men of the older cohorts. For example, Mike, aged 18 and white, said that he first came out to his best friend:

> I was 16 at the time and we'd tell each other anything. I made it clear to him that I wasn't attracted to him.... At first he freaked out, as I had been his best mate for 5 years. He got over it quickly though. He's cool now, very cool. We're still best friends.

Jacob, who came out when he was 20, was only out to a few friends. He did not attribute this to a homophobic culture but feeling "just awkward, you know." He described coming out to his best friend as "a little weird at first, but I wasn't attracted to him at all, and eventually he got over it and recently it's been like it was before." He added, "He was accepting of it right away, and he wasn't condescending, but it was a bit awkward." Similarly, Ryan, black and 18, came out to his friends from home a few months prior to interview: "They're trying to be cool and I appreciate that, but you can tell they're still a little uncomfortable about it. Still, they're still my friends and we chat like we used to." Thus, what counted as more positive experiences for the oldest cohort were on the negative end of the spectrum of experiences for the youngest cohort.

While many participants were speaking of coming out experiences from many years previously, David, a slender, quiet Hispanic youth aged 19 had come out to his friends just four days prior to the interview. His experience, not influenced by the passing of time, exemplified the transition away from coming out as a momentous life event for this cohort (Savin-Williams 2005). He said:

> I came out to several different groups, and the first person was Ray. He's my gay friend, and the more I hung around with him, the more I thought "you know what, I really can't do it anymore," and so I came out. I just said, "Ray, I'm bisexual." He gave me a high five, and that was that.

David commented that seeing Ray come out in an "understated" way helped him think about his own sexuality, saying, "He doesn't act particularly gay or anything, but if people ask him he's totally open about being gay. I looked at how accepting people were about him, and I decided that I wanted that for myself."

David then came out to the group of friends that he was socializing with when he approached us to be interviewed. He said:

> Nobody saw me any differently. We were just lazing about, and I said to the group, 'Hey guys I guess you should know that I'm bisexual.' They were fine with it. I wasn't worried at all about telling them as they have gay friends. Besides, I think they kind of already noticed something, maybe me checking out guys occasionally. But yeah they asked a few questions – if I was happy – and then we just carried on with our night.

Coming Out to School

Most of the men in the youngest cohort were still in an educational setting, rather than at work. Given this, we focused our questions for the youngest cohort on coming out at school. Having already discussed coming out to friends outside of school, it is important to note that half of the participants in this cohort reported being out to the great majority of students in their year at their schools. Given that schools have traditionally been hostile environments for sexual minority youth (Elia 2014; Epstein and Johnson 1998), this is significant. With men in the older two age cohorts, only a small number of participants came out while still at school; most remained closeted to the broader school population. For the youngest cohort, fifteen participants came out publically at school, and several did so to large groups of students at once (see also McCormack 2012b)—in essence, coming out *to* the school community. This is exemplified by the coming out narrative of white 18 year-old high school student, Paul. Aged 16 and white, he was scheduled to give a talk in front of his high school:

> I was stood in front of my classmates and announced I was bisexual right there. I'd thought about it for a long time, and I read out this speech about homophobia and the impact it was having on our society. My hands were sweating. I never expected what would happen next.

Paul described how, as he finished, his classmates stood and applauded him as he left the stage. Following this, Paul helped set up the first Gay-Straight Alliance at his school (see also Miceli 2005).

Joseph, aged 20 and Hispanic, came out in less dramatic fashion. Coming out to his school mates aged 17, he said, "I was worried, so I came out to people in lots of separate groups, over a couple of days." Even so, the response he received was similar to Paul's. Believing now that his fears of coming out were exaggerated, Joseph commented that he was out to everyone at his school, and accepted among his peers: "They were like 'whatever, he's cool.'"

While coming out to the whole school community marks a significant shift in experiences in the literature (c.f. Epstein and Johnson 1998), these narratives still only accounted for a minority of our participants in this age cohort. Fifteen participants still only came out to close friends, rather than the broader school community. For example, Saul, aged 19 and black, said that he "only told close friends. The others, I think they probably assumed that I am gay, with how I carry myself and act. But I didn't tell *everyone* I was bi." He added:

> I grew up in New Jersey, and my friends accepted me as bisexual rather than thinking I was straight or gay. It was fine you know, no issues at all. My friends were excited about it actually, I think because it made me different and edgy, I guess. It is different from my classmates.

These responses may be in part attributable to the increasing inclusivity of certain school cultures (McCormack 2012a). Indeed, Liam, white and aged 21, highlighted the benevolent culture that was fostered by his school, saying:

> I went to an artsy fartsy private high school. One of the classes I took was human sexuality, and I learnt about all these terms. Pan, trans, everything. It helped me become a social engineer, and be aware of this stuff. It was really influential in my life actually.

Similarly, Jared, white and aged 21, linked his positive experiences of being bisexual to social trends related to sexuality more generally. He said:

> When I came out, there was a more experimental stage in the world. Girl power was this thing, but I think everything has become a lot more sexy in the past 10 years. Women have become more sexualized, and it's a great time to be a bi guy, and enjoy both.

However, other participants experienced bisexual burden in their broader school community. For example, Ben, white and aged 22, said that while people accepted his bisexuality, several classmates would ask him if he was confused or was "really gay." After coming out to close friends, Angelo, Hispanic and aged 18 and a linebacker on his school football team, said his teammates gave a mixed reaction, including some using the term faggot as discussed earlier. Even so, the over-riding theme of his narrative in school was of inclusion:

> Most of the guys said things like 'way to go' and congratulated me for being who I want to be... Todd, the biggest guy on the team, was very supportive. And then the other guys were supportive too, particularly after I explained to them what it was all about. I still play on the team now, and it's totally fine. Same team, same people, same friends, ya know, never got made fun of after that.

Jackson, white and aged 21, also played sport at college, being on the soccer team. He said he experienced "banter" which described as containing "no malice." He said, "I didn't get a sense of it being aggressive at all," adding that "a lot said 'that's so gay,' but that doesn't mean anything. I never took offense at it, and consider those guys friends" (see also McCormack 2011a for discussion of the changing nature of the phrase *that's so gay* and how it no longer connotes homophobia).

Another significant finding is that the experiences of the youngest cohort did not vary notably between the UK and the US. In the UK, Pete, aged 18 and black, said, "I just told my mates that I was bi. I was pretty popular before that and if anything it just made me cooler." Similarly, Harry, aged 22 and white, said, "I came out at 14. A teacher was talking about sex education, and I just said I was attracted to both sexes. She smiled, said 'that's fine,' and carried on with the lesson." He added, "Maybe one or two friends asked me questions about whether I'd change my mind. But when I said 'no' they were happy with it."

Yet these narratives were not more positive than men from the youngest cohort in New York and Los Angeles. Consider, for example, Paul, the 18 year old who came out in assembly at his high school aged 16 to applause and support; Joseph, who experienced no prejudice or marginalization when he came out to various groups of friends at his school aged 17; and the other ten participants who came out to friends while still at school. While 9 out of the 10 participants in the youngest cohort in the UK coming out while still at school may point to the more positive attitudes in the UK, these are not sizeable differences.

Inclusive Families

It is significant that a large proportion of participants in this cohort had come out to their parents. We cannot make definitive claims about comparisons with the other cohorts regarding the age of coming out, as we were not able to recruit those aged 18–23 who will come out in the future. Even so, the large proportion of participants who have discussed their bisexuality with their parents corresponds with research that has found sexual minorities coming out younger and to more diverse set of people (Riley 2010).

The social change is further demonstrated by the positive reactions of many participants' parents. For example, Joey, white and aged 18, came out to his parents after coming out at school. "They were fine with it. They just weren't that bothered. They said 'whatever makes you happy,' and that did." Terrance, black and 23, said, "My parents have been really accepting…If I'm happy and I've got a good future, that's all they care about."

Angelo, aged 18 and Hispanic, came out to his parents at 17. He said that after initial hesitancy, his parents responded well:

> There was a weird look on their face when I first said it. They went to their room and talked about it, and they came back and said 'look son, if this is what turns you on then go ahead.' They said 'everyone is each to their own,' ya know, and that if that's what I wanted to do then they accepted it fully.

He attributed this positive reaction in part to having both a lesbian and gay cousin in the family. He commented how they helped him come to terms with being bisexual, saying, "I sat down with both of them and they said 'ok, maybe other people are going to react and ask you questions but you gotta be yourself.'" This proved useful for Angelo when members of his extended family talked to him about his sexuality, saying, "They questioned me. They kinda tested me on it, but because I was true to myself they started to see that this is who I am. This is who I am and I'm proud of it. That was the bottom line."

Some participants spoke of parents being accepting but still felt there were issues involved. For example, Mike said:

> I think my parents don't really care either. My dad seems cool with it, ever since I told him, he's been ok. I do feel like there's a tang of disappointment he feels for me though… My mum loves me regardless.

Participants with religious families did not report this having a negative impact. For example, Sam, aged 23 and Hispanic, said that "My family is Catholic, but it wasn't a big hurdle for them." Likewise two English participants spoke about their parents being in the Church of England (protestant), with Laurie, white and 19, saying that "it's not a problem at all. My parents have the Vicar round for dinner and he asks if I have a boyfriend or girlfriend. I think he does that to show he's cool with it." It is of course possible that religious views influenced attitudes toward bisexuality more broadly, particularly in the US given the religiosity of the country, but religion was not a negative influence in the narratives of men of the youngest cohort. While we did not explicitly ask about religion or devoutness, while this issue inductively emerged for some of our older participants it did not with men of the youngest cohort.

While the overarching theme of those who belong to the youngest cohort is one of acceptance (see also Gorman-Murray 2008), some men of this cohort did experience negative reactions (Cohler and Hammack 2007). For example, Marco, Hispanic and 18, told his parents six months prior to the interview. He said, "It was kinda weird at first my mom and dad said 'look, I think you're going through a phase.' Mom said that I was confused, and I said 'no I'm not. This is who I am. Accept it.'" Marco described how his parents gradually became more accepting, saying that "things between us are cool now." In addition to just one other participant sharing Marco's experiences, it is notable that this cohort felt able to come out while still living at home in a manner that the older cohorts did not.

Other participants were not out to all their family. They had made this decision because they had reservations about particular family members' reactions. For example, Cole, aged 18 and white, had come out to his sister but not his parents: "My sister was fine about it and she says I should come out to my parents. She says they'll be fine, but I'm so nervous about it." Similarly, Jackson had also avoided coming out to his family despite being out to all his friends. He said, "You know man, there's just no point. I mean, it'll be stress and at the moment I'm dating this girl, so there's no need." Similarly, Neil was not out to his family, saying that he "just didn't want them to know."

Ryan first came out at 17 but was not out to his parents. He highlighted the importance of local culture in this regard. Having attended a small, private Christian school, Ryan said the "life-script" was clear: "Get a wife. Have children. That's what you have to do." After moving to New York for college, he decided to come out to a number of people: "I'm out here at college, and to my sister back home, but not my parents," he said. When asked about his sister's reaction, he explained, "She has more of the attitude of people in New York, like 'Ok, whatever, it's no big deal.'"

Despite some research showing elevated levels of homophobia among ethnic minorities (Negy and Eisenman 2005), positive experiences were found across ethnic groups with little variation between them (see also Grov et al. 2006). Tyler, 19 and Hispanic, had a positive coming out experience. Telling his Grandma, who he lived with at the time, that he was bisexual, he said, "She was like 'Oh, okay.' We chatted for a bit about it and she was amazing. Then she hugged me."

Eroding Heterosexism

The positive experiences of the younger bisexual men had beneficial consequences on their lives, particularly related to their gendered behaviors. The younger bisexual men appeared more confident, socially competent, and at ease discussing their sexuality during interview compared to the older two cohorts; they also exhibited softer masculinities (see McCormack and Anderson 2010a). This is unlikely to be related to interviewer characteristics, given the age range of interviewers and no discernible differences between each interviewer's data. Compared to the older bisexual men, the younger cohort were less concerned with being socially perceived as heterosexual or "straight acting." Several men in this cohort also exhibited camp mannerisms, and frequently used gay terminology.

Several of those in this cohort frequently attended the gay scene, enjoying the environment and being open about being bisexual. For example, Jeremy, aged 23 and white, said:

> I was in dance competitions in high school and I met my first boyfriend at one of them. There was something wrong with my car and he offered to fix it. He introduced me to the gay scene and things like that. I was able to let down my barriers and just enjoy it. My bisexuality is not something that's really brought up in the gay bars. I don't hide anything about it, if I see a hot women then I will say it. A lot of older gay people have told me that it is a phase that I am going through leading to gayness. There are times were I fluctuate but it depends on my mood.

These younger bisexual men also maintained less heterosexist views, and this was evident in their experiences with gay people. Interestingly, there was a diversity of views regarding how gay people responded to disclosure of bisexuality, and how it compared to straight people's reactions. For example, Mike argued that gay people were more accepting of his bisexuality than straight people, saying, "they accept my notion of who I am more than other people. It's straight people that question it. Gay people are a lot more accepting." Similarly, David said, "I find being bi so easy on the scene, it's just accepted."

Cooper, white and 22, suggested that older gay men did not believe in bisexuality:

> A gay guy kept telling me that I just hadn't properly come out yet. This came from a couple of straight girls as well. When I think about it actually, quite a lot of the gay guys tell me that it's just a phase. These seem to be the older guys that say this. I would say 30 years and older hold this view. They always just say it's a stepping stone to being gay. My straight guy friends my own age just don't mind at all.

Supporting this, Liam, said, "Bisexuals ride a line to begin with. Straights think you get the forbidden fruit, but gay guys say 'you're not really gay.'" Liam's experiences, however, were complicated by his co-identification of being both bisexual and polyamorous. He added, "It's the polyamorous bit that hurts people, people who are into monogamy. That's the thing that causes the problems!"

Concerning the notion that a generational divide exists in relation to bisexual men's interactions with gay men, several participants commented about distance with older men and how they understood bisexuality. Laurie said:

> I don't like the older generation. I know my peers are cool with my sexuality, I'm just not so sure about older people. I know there'd be a level of understanding, but I'd rather just skip it.

Brian also found overt forms of bisexual burden with older generations, saying "A lot of people are like 'you're either gay or straight.' It's mainly older people, like 35 to 40, and they hit on me, but don't believe I'm bi." While happening occasionally with people his own age, Brian said "not nearly as much," adding that his straight male peers "really don't care at all."

These views were supported by some of the older cohorts as well. For example, Arthur, aged 42, said that "young people seem very open about it all." Ricky, aged 33, went into more detail:

> The kids today are so much more open and accepting…There are gay athletes, singers, everything. It shows that it's not uncommon or abnormal to be gay. Having said that, I don't think there is the same level of recognition for bisexual people, and there are stereotypes about that. But yeah, I wish I was coming out now.

This generational difference was also supported by our own experiences when visiting gay venues in these cities and chatting to men about why we were in town. In areas with a predominantly youth scene, people just responded that they approved of our research—or asked questions about it. However, in some venues with an older demographic, discussion of our research project were often met with disbelief or humor. One older man told us that we were studying something that did not exist, while others called out clichés about bisexuality, including statements like "bi today, gay tomorrow."

Similarity Between City and Countryside

The more inclusive experiences of the youngest cohort existed across geographic regions (see Chap. 8). Despite this, participants still spoke about the benefits of living in a metropolitan city. For example, Laurie, from London, spoke about moving away from a small northern town. Disclosing his bisexuality to family and close friends at home, and having good experiences, he said he was out to "just about everyone" in London. He added:

> Since I've been here, things have been really positive. I'm really enjoying my time here and the people I'm meeting. It's good to be out with people around me that are comfortable and supportive, and just to be able to relax and make gay and bi friends. I do still wonder if it's a factor of my environment, because I've felt it much easier to be myself in the city.

Without experiencing overt homophobia or biphobia in his home town, Laurie still felt more "at home" in London.

Some participants had experienced palpable differences between the city and their hometown. For example, William, white and 22, spoke about being bisexual in Wyoming, when he returned from university in New York to work on a farm over the summer. While he was open about his bisexuality, he spoke about emphasizing his attraction to women in a way that he did not have to in New York, saying, "I thought I wouldn't get any male bonding if I didn't chat about that."

Similarly, Neil, white and 18, grew up in Louisiana. Attending university in New York City, he said that it "regularly comes up [in New York] and that's great." He added, though, that "it was harder to come out [in Louisiana] because in general people are less cool with it. Here, it was a lot easier." Not out to his parents, he also said that the one negative reaction was from a female friend's mother in Louisiana: "she didn't like it, you could just kinda tell." Still markedly different from the experiences of the older cohorts, the rural seemed to color the experiences of some participants.

Much of this improvement in the city was related to participants feeling more relaxed. For example, Cole, aged 18 and white, also lived in New York, attending university as well. He said:

> I feel so much more comfortable here. People are much more open here, whereas back home, it always has a negative connotation. Here, nobody cares what you are – gay, straight, whatever. I feel like I can be a successful person and participate here as a bi man, but not at home. It was super conservative, just horrible.

Further highlighting the difference between the rural and the metropolitan city, Cole added:

> Even just the mention of the word back home would be people putting it down. Not being nasty to me, but people aren't very open about sexuality at all. Back home, I only knew one gay dude, whereas here I know tons of people who are gay and bisexual and everyone is very accepting of it.

While Cole's narrative could relate to being away from home rather than the city, other participants attributed sexual open-mindedness to living in the city. Ray, aged 25 and Hispanic, grew up in New York City until the age of 20 and had lived in Los Angeles for the past five years and regularly frequented the gay scene. He attributed his metropolitan upbringing to his positive views related to sex:

> Because I am from New York City and I live in L.A., I think there is more openness to people. I think there are straight men who are open to kink, and they just want to be whipped and there is a gay man nearby. Does that mean they are gay? No, they just want to get off. But that's L.A. for you. Honey, we're not in Kansas anymore.

Some participants, however, did not experience their hometowns negatively. Joey, for example, was 18 and a "fresher" at a university in London. He said, "I'm from [names village in north east England]. I came out at school and had a great time, no-one cared." Even so, he also spoke of the benefits of living in London: "It was fine up there, but the nearest person on my Grindr in London is a meter away not a mile. Sex is easy to come by down here." Thus, for Joey, the benefits of living in the city were primarily about facilitating social and sexual encounters with other sexual minorities.

Conclusion

Research into the experiences of bisexual men has previously demonstrated that discrimination and stigmatization are integral components of their lives (e.g. Burleson 2005); something that we found to be broadly true with the older cohorts, although these groups were not without positive experiences as well—particularly with the youngest people of the middle cohort.

Given the positive experiences of the cohort whose adolescence occurred in the 21st century, we suggest there is a generational difference in the coming out experiences of these bisexual men compared to those who had their adolescence in the 1980s or 1990s. Specifically, the experiences of the younger cohort of bisexual men from these three cities are markedly more positive than those of the older two cohorts: they suffered less marginalization and harassment from peers and family members.

The different experiences and behaviors of the cohorts is also supported by the fact that, despite being the shortest age span, the youngest group was the easiest group for which to recruit participants. Evidencing this, during the time we recruited participants, it would have been possible to interview an additional 20 bisexuals aged 18–23, as well as bisexual youth aged under 18 (the youngest person to approach us was aged 14). We could have recruited an additional two participants from the middle age category, but we had to extend the data collection period to ensure we recruited sufficient men for the oldest cohort. In other words, just as Pew (2013) found younger men more willing to label themselves bisexual, far more younger men willing to be interviewed than older in our research. Part of this may be attributable to the fact that forty dollars or twenty pounds is worth more to young people in general; but considering that the oldest bisexual to approach us was 54, a component does seem to be that youth are more likely to be open with their bisexual identity than older men.

There is significant explanatory power in the fact that homohysteria had markedly decreased during the adolescence of the 18–23 year old men (Keleher and Smith 2012). Ghaziani (2014: 9) frames this period as "post-gay," arguing that it can be characterized by a "dramatic acceptance of homosexuality and a corresponding assimilation of gays and lesbians into the mainstream." We argue that this impacts positively upon bisexual men, which corresponds with research documenting a multiplicity of experiences of LGB youth (Gorman-Murray 2008; Riley 2010; Savin-Williams 2005).

However, given the intersection of gender and sexuality, the expansion of gendered behaviors for American and British men in contemporary culture is also salient in understanding these changes (Anderson 2009). With homohysteria decreasing and heterosexual men both esteeming the provision of emotional support between friends and being increasingly inclusive of sexual minorities (Anderson 2014; McCormack 2011), it is likely that it is the combination of expanded sexual and gender spheres that results in these improved experiences; particularly for bisexual men who do not embody orthodox notions of masculinity.

The difference in levels of misogyny and heterosexism between cohorts is also a significant finding. We explain this through homohysteria and masculine overcompensation thesis (Willer et al. 2013). This contends that men react to insecurity about their own gender identity through extreme behaviors that connote masculinity, and that these acts are traditionally misogynistic and homophobic (Schrock and Schwalbe 2009). Having grown up in a homohysteric culture, it appears that men of the oldest cohort could have felt the need to prove their masculinity to overcompensate for their bisexuality, while those of the youngest cohort did not. In other words, men who had grown up when a macho masculinity was esteemed felt the need to prove their masculinity, while those whose adolescence was in a period of low homohysteria and more diverse masculinities did not (Anderson 2009). This, again, supports the notion that it is levels of homohysteria that has resulted in the cohort differences evident in this research—the combination of attitudes toward homosexuality and changes in gendered behaviors (Adams 2011; Morris et al. 2014).

Chapter 10
Bisexual Relationships

Alongside the stigma of being non-heterosexual, bisexuals are subject to unique forms of stigmatization that other sexual minorities do not experience (see Chap. 4). These stereotypical views impact the bisexual life in multiple ways, including within relationships. Klesse (2011) documents some of the ways that bisexuals have experienced discrimination and bigotry from their own romantic partners, highlighting that bisexuals are frequently viewed as undesirable partners because they are deemed unlikely to be satisfied with a relationship with just one person—that they need both men and women. Eliason (1997) also highlights that stereotypes about bisexuals are more focused on sexual acts than are stereotypes about gays and lesbians. Yet bisexuality becomes a particularly pertinent issue because it troubles the very notion of monogamy by contesting the idea that a couple in monogamous love do not have desire for others—given that a bisexual is perceived to not be fully satisfied sexually because of their desires for both sexes (Schmookler and Bursik 2007).

Bisexuality is also marginalized by social understanding of relationships by monosexist attitudes (Garber 1995). That is, there is a tendency to label a relationship between two men as "gay" and one between a man and a woman as "straight," or "heterosexual." As a result, research has shown that some bisexuals feel that they lose their sexual identity in a relationship. This perceived cultural impossibility of a bisexual relationship can be seen as a further burden on bisexuals, in addition to having to deal with partners who may hold stereotypes about bisexuals themselves. However, not all relationships that bisexuals encounter are like this, and there is growing awareness that relationships can take a number of forms that recognize sexual diversity (Pallotta-Chiarolli 2014).

This chapter examines the bisexual men's experiences of relationships across age cohorts. We examined for social openness about bisexuality within relationships, the level of social acceptance of it, and the prevalence of monogamist attitudes. We show that the negative impact of bisexual burden on bisexual men's lives is less than has previously been found (Burleson 2005), and we attribute much of this to our sampling procedures, alongside a cohort effect within our sample.

© Springer International Publishing Switzerland 2016
E. Anderson and M. McCormack, *The Changing Dynamics of Bisexual Men's Lives*, Focus on Sexuality Research, DOI 10.1007/978-3-319-29412-4_10

We also asked men about their beliefs and practices concerning non-monogamies. While we found some desire for non-monogamies in-line with other research (McLean 2007), our participants mostly ascribed to socially acceptable monogamist ideals. Given that bisexual activist communities often consist of people who ascribe to alternative and polyamorous cultures (Burleson 2005), we contend that our different findings are primarily a result of our recruitment procedure.

Increased Personal Acceptance

Our participants reported increased acceptance in their disclosure of bisexuality to romantic partners than traditionally described in the literature (McLean 2004). While we later document evidence of a cohort effect, the experiences were more positive in all cohorts than what is documented in earlier literature (Klesse 2011). Like many participants, Colin, aged 32 and white, was open with his wife about his bisexuality in the early stages of his relationship. He said of his heterosexual wife, "She knows I am bisexual. It doesn't put a strain on the relationship at all… she asks about what I get turned on by in guys and stuff." Colin added that his wife finds it enjoyable to bond with him over checking other guys out. "We talk about it all the time," he said, laughing, "but she has horrible taste in men." Similarly, Andrew, aged 30 and white, was out to his long-term, heterosexual, girlfriend. He said that although she identified as heterosexual, she had some sexual experience with women when she was younger. It was after her disclosure of her sexual history that he discussed his bisexuality, telling her that it was more than an experimental desire: "I told her…about six months in. I told her I liked guys and girls, and she was cool with it. She said, 'As long as you make me happy and treat me good, I'm not worried about it.'"

Other men from all three age cohorts discussed their openness with heterosexual women (see also Pallotta-Chiarolli 2014), and some gay men as well. Accordingly, whereas the literature finds many bisexuals experiencing significant prejudice from partners (Hartman-Linck 2014; Klesse 2011), just one man experienced this in our sample. AJ, aged 38 and black, spoke of bisexuality as a "lonely journey," because he had been mostly single. He said that his relationships "kinda blow up." While AJ clarified that he was mostly interested in dating women, he also had a number of relationships with men. "It's the same with the guys I date," he said. "I've been rejected by a bunch of gay men who are just like, 'I don't wanna deal with bisexual stuff.'"

While many men we interviewed had failed relationships, and others experienced bisexual burden in particular forms, AJ was the only participant that attributed relationship break-ups to his bisexuality. Bisexual men in our sample did not report having difficulty in finding people to date or marry. However, the majority of older men tended to disclose their bisexual identities only when in serious, long-term relationships, as opposed to disclosing while in the early days of dating.

Matthew, 41 and white, said that his wife knew he was bisexual, but that he only told prior partners once they were "serious." He added:

> It's just not the first thing you say on a date, is it? There are many things you don't talk about on a first date: Politics, religion, and people you have previously dated, or had sex with. Being bisexual is one of those things. You just don't blurt it out early on.

When Matthew was asked how long he normally waited before telling his previous partners about it, he replied that it was different for men and women: "For men I have always told them right up front. I don't, I mean I didn't, want them to think that I was gay." Matthew paused for a moment and reflected upon what he had just said:

> It's more complicated with men...I'm not out on the gay scene. I've never gone to gay bars. So women just think I'm straight and that's easier. If I want to do something with a guy though, I've got to tell him 'hey, I'm not straight' and then when I do that, because I'm now telling, I tell them that I'm bisexual.

Connor, 38 and white, was also reserved about telling romantic partners that he was bisexual. "I want them to get to know me first," he said. "Being bisexual is only a small part of me." When asked what things he liked for potential dates to know about himself, he said:

> Who I am, what makes me tick. It's not all about occupation; that comes up in the first few minutes with almost anyone you meet. It's about how I feel about things and what other areas of interest we might have in common.

This finding, that men of the oldest cohort withheld discussions of their bisexuality until the later stages of a forming relationship, also highlights change within our sample. Men of the youngest cohort tended to come out early in dating, suggesting less concern about how this would be perceived by their partners. There were no examples of younger men hiding their bisexuality from those they dated. For example, Cole, 18 and white, had been in two relationships with gay men since arriving in New York. He said, "One for a month, the second was two months. They knew about me being bi and were pretty relaxed about it." He added, "It says on my Facebook, my friends know, I can hardly hide it, not that I would ever try to."

Similarly, Angelo, aged 18 and Hispanic, had been in a relationship with a woman for two months. He said she knew that he is bisexual, and he was open about being attracted to men and women equally: "She knows that, and she doesn't care that I was having a relationship with a boy for a while before."

That men of this youngest cohort disclosed their sexual identity earlier into relationships than reported by the men of the older cohort is evidence of a lessening of the influence of bisexual burden in their lives. Supporting this, while the youngest cohort did not have the same level of experience of long-term relationships because of their youth, change was also evident in their relationship ideation.

Like Sam, many participants in the youngest cohort expressed an equal desire to be in a relationship with a man or a woman. For example, Jacob, aged 21 and white, said: "I really don't have any hang ups over who I'm gonna end up with. Like, if I meet a guy who I'm in love with, then I'll be with a guy, and if it's a girl then I'll be with a girl." And Anthony, white and aged 34, was open with all his ex-partners, both male and female—documenting the improvement compared with what the literature traditionally shows (Weinberg et al. 1994).

Remnants of Bisexual Burden Among Romantic Partners

While participants' experiences of disclosure in relationships were improved on what the literature has traditionally said, alongside evidence of a cohort effect, elements of bisexual burden remained for some (Hartman-Linck 2014; Pallotta-Chiarolli in press). While in the minority, some of these attributed worse attitudes to that of heterosexual women while others to gay men. For example, aged 21 and white, Jacob's experience of relationships included openness with his female partner about bisexuality, but his narrative also indicated that her response was problematic. Having recently ended the long-term relationship that he started in high school, he said:

> She knew about me being bisexual. I came out to her while I was figuring it out, so she knew... She was a religious girl, and she was kind of weird about it. It's like now she thinks you're looking at other girls *and* at guys. But she didn't tell me I wasn't or anything like that. She just got more jealous.

Most of the other participants who indicated that their partners had difficulty with their bisexuality also attribute this to female partners. A recurring theme in participants' narratives was that heterosexual women were threatened by the idea that their bisexual lover might desire men more than them, leave them or cheat on them. For example, Ray, aged 25 and Hispanic, who believed that straight women were not open to the idea of bisexual men, said, "They say if you're into guys then you're gay, and if it's women you're straight. Straight women like straight men I guess."

Sam, aged 23 and Hispanic, also had similar experiences with girls, saying, "My girlfriend liked it because the thought she could turn me straight, and it would prove her own sexual power." This was true of older men as well. Arthur, aged 42 and white, said that, "I feel women get really angry over [men's] bisexuality."

Similarly, George, aged 28, white and from the American south, had negative experiences when coming out to his female partner. He said:

> My girlfriend was telling me once about some semi-lesbian experience that she'd had, trying to turn me on. So I told her I'd had same-sex experiences as well, but she was horrified and instantly left. She had no interest in dating me anymore, because I was bisexual.

William also spoke of prejudice from female sexual partners, who did not believe he was bisexual, saying, "I don't think that the girls I get with really believe that I can be bisexual. I think that they believe in the theory of it, but I don't think they actually believe in it."

However, we do not draw firm conclusions about heterosexual women being more closed off to bisexual men than gay men are. This is because the men of the youngest cohort—the cohort that came out to partners early into their relationships—had started dating women first. Many of them thus came out as bisexual for the first time, or figured out that they were bisexual, while dating women. This is a different context and dynamic to their experiences with dating men, which tended to happen at a later age and outside of school.

While we cannot provide conclusions about the nature of responses by male and female romantic partners, it is evident that men in the younger cohort were more likely to be out about their bisexuality earlier into a relationship, and appeared more willing to date men as well as women. There was a lessening of bisexual burden, although it persisted for some. These experiences are more positive than other literature would suggest (McLean 2004; Rust 2009), which we attribute to our sampling procedures, but there is also evidence of a cohort effect in our data—although this is less pronounced than coming out in general.

Decreasing Heteronormativity

In addition to finding that younger bisexual me were more likely to come out as bisexual early into a relationship compared to older bisexual men, our interviews also suggest that same-sex relationships tended to be viewed as more problematic with the older cohort, and less stereotyped by the younger cohort. In other words, heteronormativity appears to be decreasing with younger age cohorts of bisexual men. We measure this difference in two ways: thoughts on having children and gendered preferences of partners.

Men of the older cohort idealized heteronormative relationship types for their ability to produce children (Pennington 2009). For example, JP, 31 and Hispanic, said his ideal relationship would be with a woman, "so I can have a family." He did not seem to consider the possibilities of adoption, surrogacy and shared parenting. Matthew, 41 and white, said, "I want to have kids and I can't have that with a guy, obviously." Robert, aged 42 and white, has been in a relationship with a woman for nine years. When asked why he chose to date a woman instead of a man he said it was because he felt that his masculinity is enhanced when dating a woman because of his virility: "With a woman I can make a child. I'm not sterile."

While some younger bisexual men expressed interest in dating women over men, this was not based on desire for children. When asked about children, they answered that there were alternative routes to having them. Ben, 21 and white summarized many of the attitudes of this generation by simply saying, "We can adopt." Ryan, Saul, Laurie and others under 21 gave a similar response.

Gendered Preferences

Another example of the change in heterosexist attitudes is how men of each cohort expressed a gendered preference in their partners. While several men in the older cohort either had been or were in long-term relationships with women, the men who expressed preference for same-sex relationships often used a significant degree of misogyny in their reasoning. For example, Arthur, aged 42 and white, said, "I gravitate toward men. We're okay with each other playing around, but women are more clingy. They can be bitches, particularly if you want an open relationship, they just say no." Similarly, Anthony said, "I lean towards relationships with men because girls are a little too emotional for me, a little too high maintenance." JP said, "I like dating women because that just feels right, you know? Men are your friends, women are girlfriends." Likewise, AJ spoke aggressively about women: "Sex with men is great, but women can be bitches. You know, not letting you do what you want. Men are easier."

These overtly negative reactions were not present with men of the youngest cohort. When men expressed a preference for men rather than women, their rationales were not rooted in sexism or misogyny. For example, Paul, 18 and white, said that he relates better to men. "They are just easier to get along with. So although I'm attracted to women, I can't really see myself marrying one." While many men in the youngest cohort expressed similar opinions, Anthony, 34 and white, was the oldest participant to do so in this manner. He said that where he used to date women more, he recently found himself interested in partnering with men. "Women are a little too high maintenance for me, particularly as I'm pretty high maintenance myself." He added, "Ultimately, I just think 'yeah, I need to date a guy." When asked if he thought he would be able to marry and make a family with a guy when he was a teenager he replied, "Absolutely not. Culture has changed for the better."

Of course, many men in the youngest cohort still expressed a preference for women. For example, Terrance, aged 23 and black, said, "I think I'll date women more. Some guys can be just too much, a real pain in the ass." He added, "I've always had more girlfriends than guy friends, so it fits that I'd have a girlfriend as well." Similarly, Frank, aged 20 and Hispanic, said, "I see guys as more friends, but with girls it can go more romantic. That may change, but at the moment, but I don't have that lovey-dovey feeling with guys."

Overall, the younger cohorts exhibited more openness to relationships with men, and discussed potential relationships with less heterosexist perspectives and from earlier relationship onset. Part of this might be attributed to the fact that they are not thinking about children and families, but given that having children is a foundational principle of heterosexual coupledom, it highlights that, at least in their youth, they are willing to eschew heteronormative ideals, and instead date whomever they feel they will have the best emotional and sexual relationship with. They have cultural and legal permission to do so; and, increasingly, medical technologies to normalize their relationships with family life.

Liam highlighted this awareness. He said: "I'd sort of like for their genetics to be my own." Identifying as polyamorous and using bisexual as a shorthand label, he did not see same-sex relationships as prohibiting genetic children. He said:

> I know it's easier to make a family with a woman, but it's not the only way. Gay couples have kids all the time these days and they do it with their own sperm if they want to....I want kids of my own, so if I partner with a woman and she's fertile, fine we'll do it that way. But if I partner with a guy, then we'll do surrogacy.

Liam's narrative highlights that bisexual youth have greater opportunities in a range of spheres. The differences in experience are not solely the result of an absence of homophobia, biphobia or bisexual burden, but also an expansion of social opportunities: they can marry, have children, and be esteemed members of their communities. In other words, these young men are no longer structured into heterosexist attitudes the way older generations were (Hartman-Linck 2014).

Monogamism

While we found a lessening of bisexual burden in relationships, the majority of men we interviewed remained in favor of monogamy. Few of our participants desired polyamory or open relationships. This contrasts previous research on bisexuality and non-monogamies (see McLean 2004; Moss 2012; Weinberg et al. 1994). Instead, the majority across cohorts idealized monogamy and sought sexual fidelity in their coupled relationships.

John, aged 38 and white, had been in a long term relationship with both men and women. He was hoping to marry his current male partner, saying "The writing is on the wall. Soon we will be able to marry, and at that point, yeah we will." But despite wanting to marry, John was one of the few men we interviewed who rejected monogamy: "I've been with the same guy for 12 years and it's great. I'm not a big believer in monogamy, I just don't think it's natural and being a man, gay or straight, we're gonna fuck everything and anything."

Conversely, most of our participants said that monogamy was their preferred relationship type, and critiqued those who did not ascribe to it. One participant said that if you "aren't doing monogamy than you aren't doing a relationship." He added, "I don't get what the point of being in a relationship is if you want to have sex with other people." Openly recognizing desire for other people was seen as deeply problematic for a large section of participants, particularly among the oldest cohort.

Filipe, 39 and Hispanic, felt that monogamy was important to him because he could not handle the jealousy of his partner sleeping with others. Married to a woman, he said, "I need to feel that I am the most important person in the world to her and she needs to know that I view her the same. I would be incredibly jealous if we opened up the relationship. I just couldn't handle it." Similarly, Ricardo, 38 and Hispanic, said, "I'm not opposed to people doing what they want, but for me, monogamy is a character test of love. If I don't love him or her enough, I will want sex with someone else." When asked if he thought those in open relationships did not love their partners as much as those in monogamous relationships he answered, "I think that's probably true. Yes."

Despite the fact that most of the men interviewed did not want open relationships for themselves, many refrained from criticizing those that did. Paul, 18 and white, said, "I don't judge people who want that. Whatever they want to do is fine, but it's not for me and I can't see it working well." Tyler, 19 and Hispanic, said "It wouldn't work for me. No way. If others want to do that shit, hey, who am I to judge, but I won't do it."

Trenton, 28 and white, talked positively about open relationships, even though he would not want one himself. "I think it's important for people to do what will make them happy," he said. "If being in an open relationship makes two people happier, then that's what they should do." He added, "It's not for me, but then again lots of things aren't. I don't judge it, and I don't think other people should either."

Other participants expressed curiosity about open relationships. Tiago, 33 and Hispanic, had little to say about open relationships, instead asking the interviewer, "How does that work?" After a discussion about open relationships he replied, laughing, "Maybe I should give this more thought." Similarly, Cooper, 22 and white, said, "I think it might be hard, but then again, I can see the appeal of it. I'm not in the position to try one now, but yeah, I think I could consider this at some point."

Despite these narratives of tolerance, and some men expressing interest in open sexual relationships, only a few men discussed polyamory within this context. Liam, white and aged 21, identified as polyamorous but had yet to experience a relationship of that kind. Nicholas, 32 and black, summarized the little positive sentiment toward polyamory. "Whatever you need to do; whatever you are called to; whether that be with men or women, or both together as long as everybody is a consenting adult I have no issues with it whatsoever." We only discussed polyamory when raised by the interviewee, so it is possible that some participants did not volunteer the information—but this silencing would speak to a stigma around the relationship that is not documented on research with bisexual activist communities.

Our findings thus contest other research that has documented that bisexuals are more likely to be in nonmonogamous relationships than the general population (Klesse 2005; McLean 2004) and that bisexuals practice a range of relationship types. Weinberg et al. (1994) documented bisexuals engaging in "swinging, sexual triads, group sex parties…casual sex with friends, and anonymous sex," as well as practicing open (nonmonogamous) relationships with one primary partner. There was little evidence for this with our participants. Whereas others have described open and polyamorous relationships being highly prevalent within bisexual cultures (Monro 2015), we suggest this is because nonmonogamous bisexuals are more inclined to join bisexual groups than bisexuals who seek monogamy. Thus, we again attribute the difference in findings to our sampling method.

Conclusion

In this chapter we showed that multiple narratives emerged in our data related to disclosing and maintaining a bisexual identity, and there was no hegemonic relationship experience for these men. Significantly, there is evidence that coming out was, in general, an easier process for the younger participants in these three cities—a notion further supported by several older participants also commenting that it was easier to be bisexual today (Evans and Broido 1999). Younger men had more confidence in announcing their bisexual identities earlier into relationships; and they also reported that their bisexual identities were more generally accepted by their partners, both male and female, than older bisexual men experienced (Hartman-Linck 2014).

This pattern emerged between the older and middle cohort; but was most striking with the youngest cohort, aged 18–23. One reason might be that a majority of those in the very youngest cohort had not had a significant relationship that lasted more than a few months. Still, the fact that the youngest cohort were coming out to partners in a matter of weeks rather than months or years, suggests that bisexual burden seems impact less on the youngest cohort of bisexual men than when our older cohort were of the same age. We suggest that this is a reflection of the cultural progress toward sexual minorities more broadly (see McCormack and Anderson 2014).

Younger bisexual men were also less heteronormative in their desires for dating women than the older cohort. We suggest that this is attributable to the generational nature of sexualities (Plummer 2010), whereby older bisexual men grew up in a culture where gay adoption and equal marriage neither existed nor seemed possible in the future. This is compared with the youngest cohort who are aware of same-sex parenting, and for whom debates about same-sex marriage have been part of the political landscape when growing up (Weeks 2007).

Finally, we found that monogamy was valued by all three cohorts of the bisexual men that we interviewed to a greater extent than traditionally found in the literature (Burleson 2005). Thus, consistent with other recent research on non-monogamy among straight and gay men (Anderson 2012; LaSala 2005), this research on bisexual men finds that despite the growing acceptance of sexual diversity in a range of forms, monogamy is still socially esteemed. The marked difference from this and other literature on non-monogamies among bisexual men is most likely an artifact of our sampling procedures—finding bisexual men who are more integrated into mainstream society than those who are located within bisexual activist communities (Klesse 2007).

Of course the relevance of our findings is primarily for bisexual men who are public about their sexuality and who live in relatively liberal metropolitan cities. Notwithstanding these important limitations, our research is evidence that bisexual organizations are not representative of the broader bisexual population (McCormack et al. 2014; Pew 2013), and our results contribute to the debate about the problems of recruiting sexual minorities from particular groups and communities (McCormack 2014a; Savin-Williams 2001).

Chapter 11
Conclusions

Social and scientific understandings of bisexuality have taken a complicated, controversial, and circuitous path toward how people conceive of bisexuality today. When Kinsey argued that sexuality was more flexible, fluid and diverse than a conservative form of heterosexuality, he and his colleagues were advancing a radical thesis for a time where heterosexuality was near-compulsory (Kimmel 1994; Plummer 1999). But while his work had extraordinary reach for sexualities scholarship, many people did not know about it. Of those that did, it is likely that many either did not understand the implications of his findings, or simply refused to believe them. It has taken more than fifty years for bisexuality to gain the social legitimacy that we document exists among young men today.

The purpose of this book was to develop a critical account of this trend and determine the influence of decreasing homophobia on bisexual men's lives. Examining the lived experiences of openly bisexual men whose birth dates spanned three decades, we were able to draw out similarities and differences in their lived experiences and how these have changed according to the time of their adolescence. This novel approach permitted us to powerfully capture the positive impact that declining homophobia and homohysteria has had on the lives of bisexual men in Los Angeles, New York and London.

This research not only illustrates longitudinal, cohort change concerning bisexuality and social acceptance, it also constitutes the first large-scale qualitative investigation of bisexual men that does not recruit from bisexual activist or social community groups. Research on bisexuality is limited because it is almost exclusively conducted on these networks, or broader LGBT groups. Almost all of the extant research fails to capture bisexual men who are not part of these support networks or friendship collectives. This is a significant problem because these groups are far less representative of bisexuals more generally than is true for gay and lesbian groups (Pew 2013).

Given that these types of sampling procedures do not accurately reflect the totality of bisexuals' experiences, the data collected for this book eschewed such approaches. We did not use recruitment procedures that relied on, or even

© Springer International Publishing Switzerland 2016
E. Anderson and M. McCormack, *The Changing Dynamics of Bisexual Men's Lives*, Focus on Sexuality Research, DOI 10.1007/978-3-319-29412-4_11

privileged, bisexual or LGBT groups, nor did we use our own networks or snowball sampling. Instead, we adopted a fresh and innovative approach to data collection, capitalizing on the more inclusive cultures of these contemporary, metropolitan cities in a way that was likely not possible in the 1980s and 1990s. We publically recruited bisexual men from busy pedestrian areas of Los Angeles, New York and London and called out that we were looking to interview bisexual men. This simple and effective recruitment strategy permitted us to source men in a way that matched our pre-determined requirements.

We coupled this innovative research design with a holistic approach to understanding the lives of bisexual men. While basing our work in the theories and methods of sociology, we engaged with the literature on bisexuality from across the disciplines. This is necessary to develop a broader understanding of the issues related to bisexual men's lives. Still, the driving thesis of our empirical research is that society is hugely influential in how sexual identities are lived and experienced, and this is why we developed an age cohort analysis to examine how decreasing homohysteria influenced the lives of bisexual men. By adopting this research design, we have shown that progress toward the acceptance of bisexuality as a legitimate sexuality has been slow, but that there has been significant improvement in recent years. In the following sections, we examine the implications of our work for society, the study of bisexuality, and sociology as a discipline.

The Presence of a Generational Cohort Effect

Using the interview data of 90 bisexual men recruited from the metropolitan cities of Los Angeles, New York and London, we explored how bisexual men experienced their lives and to what extent they suffered biphobia and bisexual burden (see Chap. 3). This included examining for negative stereotypes about bisexual identities from both gays and straights, including being seen as confused or in a transitional phase, being promiscuous, sex-crazed and unable to love, as well as being thought unable to do monogamy. These and other aspects of bisexual burden have been repeatedly shown to bear a social cost for being openly bisexual, traditionally influencing bisexuals to selectively disclose their identities (McLean 2007).

The principal finding of our work is that there has been significant improvement for bisexual men in how disclosure of their identities is received by others, and the options available to them in how they identify and live their lives (c.f. Herek 2002; Klein 1993; Mohr et al. 2001). While this has occurred across cohorts, there is a clear generational effect with younger men having improved experiences compared to the older men in our sample. The bisexual men who belonged to the youngest cohort – those aged 18–23 at the time of data collection – enjoyed much greater acceptance among their friends, family and peers than men whose adolescence was in the last two decades of the 20th century. Given that societal attitudes toward bisexuality have been closely linked with society's disposition toward homosexuality (Kangasvuo 2011), the decline in homophobic attitudes and behaviors has seen a corresponding shift in how bisexuals experience navigating their lives within what is still a heterosexist and monosexist society.

We documented a number of ways in which the younger bisexual men had more positive experiences than those men in the older cohort. We interviewed all participants about multiple aspects of their lives, but it was the coming out experiences and negotiation of a public bisexual identity that best illuminated this key sociological trend.

The younger men suffered less marginalization and harassment from peers and family members, and had more positive experiences of relationships. Not only did we find more positive experiences in coming out at school, many of the youngest cohort came out *to* the school community and were socially rewarded for doing so. Many participants still felt that coming out was an important milestone in their social lives, but it was frequently experienced as an enjoyable event. Some even reported that it made them more popular. In other words, bisexual burden had dissipated for most of these young men.

Conversely, we found that that the experiences of those whose adolescence occurred in the mid-late 1980s broadly mirrored that described in the literature on bisexuality. The experiences of these 30 men found significant elements of bisexual burden. These men often faced rejection from their peers and delayed coming out to their family or colleagues out of fear (Weinberg et al. 1994). The men in the middle cohort had a more diverse set of experiences. There was a tendency for the younger men in this cohort to have experiences that were closer to men of the youngest cohort, and the older men in this cohort to have experiences that were closer to men of the oldest cohort.

In addition to the presence of the generational cohort effect, it is also important to recognize improvement in our oldest sample compared to earlier research (e.g. Weinberg et al. 1994). These men would have had their adolescence when that data was collected, so their experiences could have been expected to be similar to those documented in that literature. That our findings are more positive could have two explanations: (1) that men spoke more positively about past experiences having felt their lives improve over the past two decades, whereas they would have spoken more negatively if interviewed contemporaneously; (2) that it is an effect of our sampling procedures, with many of our participants in the oldest cohort not attending bisexual community groups in the 1980s or 1990s. While it is impossible to determine the precise balance of these reasons, we suspect it is more to do with sampling than change in recall (see Rivers 2001 regarding stability of recall related to homophobic bullying). Either way, it has not just become easier for bisexuals of younger generations; there has been improvement from what has previously been shown in the literature across age groups. This supports quantitative research which shows that not only have attitudes toward homosexuality improved with each subsequent cohort, but that cohorts have also changed/improved their attitudes as well (Clements and Field 2014; Keleher and Smith 2012).

While sexual identities were important to the bisexual men we interviewed, we found that the importance of the label/identity decreased with each cohort. Whereas men of the older cohort better articulated identity politics and the political usefulness of the bisexual label, youth expressed that it was not *the* defining characteristic of their lives (see also Savin-Williams 2005; Ghaziani 2014). This suggests that today's bisexual male youth have profited from the coalitional identity politics of the LGBT movement over the past several decades. The ability to eschew the importance of a sexual identity label serves as proof that the political gains so many fought for have had an effect. Maintaining the ability not to identify is, we argue, one thing that many sexual minority activists have fought for. Given our sampling procedures may have over-sampled men who have an attachment to the label (who respond to our call for *bisexual* men), this means these findings likely under-represent the change in the valuing of sexual identity labels among young people.

Our findings of decreased homophobia, homohysteria and bisexual burden have also translated into less heterosexism among men of the youngest cohort. We found that younger bisexuals were more open-minded in their desires for dating men and women. While we principally attribute this cohort effect to the generational nature of sexualities (Plummer 2010), as well as a lessening of heterosexism more generally, part of this is likely the result of younger bisexual men being less oriented toward kinship and planning a family than the older bisexual men.

We also found some evidence of elevated levels of misogyny among bisexual men of the older cohort compared to those of the younger. While we did not systematically investigate this, misogynistic statements emerged in the context of other questions (see also Pallotta-Chiarolli in press). They did so mostly among men of the older generation, with no men using misogynistic language in the youngest cohort. If these organic statements are reflective of a broader trend, we would explain it through the masculine overcompensation thesis (Willer et al. 2013). This contends that men react to insecurity about their own gender identity through extreme behaviors that connote masculinity, and that these acts are traditionally misogynistic and homophobic (Schrock and Schwalbe 2009). Having grown up in a homohysteric culture, it makes sense that men of the oldest cohort felt the need to prove their masculinity because of their non-heterosexuality. Those of the youngest cohort did not feel the pressure to do so—or those that did had different conceptions of masculinity in which misogyny is not esteemed (Anderson 2014; McCormack 2012). This, again, supports the notion that it is levels of homohysteria that has resulted in the cohort differences evident in this research—the combination of attitudes toward homosexuality and changes in gendered behaviors.

Finally, we found that despite the stereotypes that bisexual men are unable to be monogamous; monogamy was valued by participants across all three cohorts. Certainly, a substantial minority contested monogamy, but it was valued to a greater extent than traditionally found in the literature (e.g. Klesse 2006). Thus, consistent with other recent research on non-monogamy among straight and gay men (Anderson 2012), we found that despite the growing acceptance of sexual diversity in a range of forms, monogamy is still socially esteemed as the primary way to maintain a romantic relationship. We again attribute this difference between our findings and what other research on non-monogamies among bisexuals to sampling procedures. There is substantial evidence that the bisexuals who attend bisexual groups also have significantly more permissive attitudes toward non-monogamy than those who do not (see Burleson 2005; Voss et al. 2014).

Theorizing the Cohort Effect

Our research was systematically designed to explore for generational effects in our data. We developed a cohort design that grouped bisexual men according to the time of their adolescence, and we ensured that we recruited equal numbers of men to each cohort (see Chap. 5). These cohorts were designed to account for different levels of attitudinal homophobia in the broader culture as determined by General Social Survey and British Social Attitudes survey data. While we maintain that our sampling procedures bypass some of the bias of recruiting from pre-existing networks and bisexual groups, an important component of this design is that differences between groups are internal to the sample and are not an effect of sampling.

We found marked improvements in experiences based on this cohort design. There is significant explanatory power in the argument that progress toward the social acceptance of bisexuality is dependent upon attitudes toward homosexuality, particularly in a heterosexist and monosexist society. Yet the driving concept of our thesis was that of homohysteria—the fear of being socially perceived as gay. This is because it is only in homohysteric cultures where homophobia influences gendered behaviors. Our prior research has explicated how decreasing homohysteria impacts on the lives of heterosexual men (Anderson 2009, 2014; McCormack 2012) and gay athletes (Anderson 2011b). Indeed, a large and growing body of academic work shows that homohysteria is rapidly diminishing among youth (e.g. Adams 2011; Dean 2014; Jarvis 2013; Roberts 2013, 2014). With homohysteria decreasing and heterosexual men both esteeming the provision of emotional support between friends and being increasingly inclusive of sexual minorities (see Anderson 2014; McCormack 2011b), it is likely that it is the combination of expanded sexual and gender spheres that results in these improved experiences for bisexual men.

We thus argue that finding a cohort effect in the experiences of bisexual men is best explained by inclusive masculinity theory (Anderson 2009). This theory emerged inductively to understand the ways in which a softening of men's behaviors, including an expansion of homosocial tactility, is linked to decreasing homophobia. It seems likely that these findings can be applied to bisexual youth elsewhere (Morris et al. 2014), and this book provides considerable evidence to support this among bisexual men from metropolitan areas. While the theory has always had an implicit generational component, by focusing on the changing experiences of young men, this book provides a significant development of the theory by recognizing the importance of generation in changing social norms.

However, it is also necessary to consider that the effect of recent legal and cultural changes will be different according to the age of participants. While same-sex couples are permitted to adopt in all three cities in which participants were recruited, and surrogacy and shared-parenting arrangements are increasing cultural options for bisexuals, we contend that this will have more impact on younger men's attitudes and values. Given the generational nature of sexualities, older men have spent the majority of their lives in cultures where this was *not* the case. Older men have been taught biphobic, homophobic and heterosexist attitudes through social norms—these men have to undo these attitudes whereas men from the youngest cohort were never taught such values, at least to the same extent.

There are other conceptual and theoretical tools that help explain the cohort effect and the importance of generations, too. The sexualization of culture and what McNair (2013) calls the pornographication of the society is both predominant on the internet, which is most powerfully taken up by younger people. There is growing evidence that heterosexual men are exploring more areas of their own sexual orientations and routes to sexual pleasure, with a growing openness to sexual identities beyond that of exclusively straight (Branfman et al. in press; Scoats et al. in press). What is clear is that the influence of the internet on sexual norms is not limited to facilitating contact between sexual minorities, but for changing how sexuality is perceived in the 21st century across sexualities and age groups (Waskul 2003).

A key argument in the sociological literature has been the changing nature of sexual and romantic love in recent decades. Giddens (1992) famously discussed the transformation of intimacy and his concept of pure relationships was developed to highlight the increasing importance placed on shared pleasure and emotional support in romantic relationships. Giddens also highlighted how sexual pleasure was increasingly important in these relationships. Other research confirms this (Twenge et al. 2015): Sexual pleasure has become increasingly important component of people's lives. The presence of 'hooking up' cultures (Bogle 2008), pornography is readily available, and a lessening of sexual morality means non-marital sex is increasingly accepted. According to Attwood and Smith (2013: 330), sex has now become a form of serious leisure; it serves as "driver, motivator, consolidator and important means toward intimacy, community [and] social cohesion." Recognition of how our understandings of relationships and sexual activity have changed in recent years provide further clarity on the reasons for the generational cohort effect in our data. Thus, while we primarily use inclusive masculinity theory to explain this social trend, we find support in other theoretical arguments about the changing nature of sexuality in contemporary society.

We are unable to provide a clear answer for the rise in bisexual visibility with this research. We suggest that bisexual visibility occurs through the same mechanisms as gay visibility: the media, the internet, and through contact with bisexuals themselves. Bisexual visibility may well also be entangled with the processes of sexualization (McNair 2013), with men recognizing that their desire to be objectified as sexually desirable could be conceived as a form of bisexuality (Anderson and Adams 2011). While bisexuality continues to be marginalized in what remains a monosexist culture, the gains in visibility and recognition are evident in the narratives of the men of our youngest cohort. Thus, the rise in the visibility of bisexuality is an effect of decreasing homophobia and the one-time rule of homosexuality, as well as a factor in the continuation of the trend.

Intersecting Factors

While we have structured the book around the generational effect present in our research, another significant component we have drawn out is that race did not serve as a useful lens of analysis of participants experiences. As we highlight in the empirical chapters, while participants would often discuss their race, the trends in coming out, identifications and relationships did not change when analyzing within racial groups. This is an interesting finding because research has shown that African-American communities, for example, often have elevated rates of homophobia (e.g. Negy and Eisenman 2005).

A significant factor across all groups, however, was the lack of bisexual friends that these men had. The majority of the older cohort spoke about having no bisexual friends, or at most one or two. Those that had more bisexual friends had attended specific bisexual community groups, whether activist or socially oriented. Similarly, although there were a few participants in the youngest cohort who had bisexual friends, they were still in the minority. The small rise in number of bisexual friends in the youngest cohort is likely attributable to their greater presence on the 'gay' scene. Even so, the lack of bi networks more broadly is another factor that sets them apart from gay men and likely influences their experiences of their bisexual identities (see also Pew 2013).

We also found that geography still had a role to play in the social legitimacy and approval of bisexuality. We documented in Chaps. 9 and 10 that many participants from rural areas in the oldest cohort referenced this as a way of understanding their marginalization when they first came out. Similarly, younger participants from metropolitan cities also commented that they expected rural areas to be less accepting—even though the narratives of the younger men were positive independent of whether they were from rural or metropolitan areas. While discussion of 'gayborhoods' (Ghaziani 2014) was notably absent in these discussions, it was the flexibility, freedom and independence associate with the city that was seen to be important to the men we interviewed.

Our analysis of geography must also extend to the differences between the US and the UK. While the trend of decreasing homophobia is remarkably similar in both countries (see Clements and Field 2014; Keleher and Smith 2012), attitudes toward homosexuality have been consistently better in the UK than in the US. Furthermore, while we have documented the changing nature of heterosexual masculinities in both the UK and the US (Anderson 2009, 2011; McCormack 2012), Anderson (2014) has found significant differences in some forms of behavior—most notably kissing on the lips. Here, Anderson found that in stopping every third male to emerge from a university common area, of those who agreed to be interviewed, 89% of heterosexual male undergraduate kissed a male friend on the lips at some point, only 10% of the same demographic had done so in the United States when employing the same methods across 11 universities; something other research shows is 12% (Esterline and Galupo 2013). Thus, it would seem reasonable to expect significantly more positive experiences in the UK when compared to the US. However, while differences existed, they were not as drastic as might have been expected.

We suggest that the lack of broader difference, particularly in the youngest cohort, along with a more pronounced difference in the middle cohort, may suggest that there is a level of attitudinal homophobia that is required for such attitudes to really influence social life—that once they drop below a certain level; they have less influence on everyday experience. If this is the case, the relevant tipping point would have occurred in the adolescence of the middle cohort for the British men, which would have been in the late 1990s. For men in the US, the improvement seemed to occur only with the youngest men in the middle cohort, as well as those in the youngest cohort. This would place the tipping point of the level of homophobia in the early 2000s. While this is just a hypothesis, it seems to relate to the liberalization of attitudes in both countries (Anderson 2009). Whatever the reason, the fact that it may be better in the UK – but only by a bit – is worthy of further investigation.

There are, of course, additional other forms of analysis that we have not included in this research. As with all research projects we conclude it by wishing that we had done more, asked additional questions, or added more locations of data collection. It might be the case, for example, that a person's level of education plays an important role in the social legitimacy that their stated bisexuality brings to them. Similarly, there might be issues of social class that intersect with geography, race and education in determining the lived experience of bisexual men. Likewise, it is possible that if we had undertaken a detailed life-history of race and religion in interviews, rather than sexuality, we would have revealed subtle ways in which race influenced sexuality. Although it would be more methodologically difficult to study, it would also be of interest to examine for how physical attractiveness, social competency and one's status as trans or cisgender impact upon the perceived legitimacy and experiences of bisexual men.

The relevance of our findings is primarily for bisexual men who are public about their sexuality and who live in relatively liberal metropolitan cities. Yet our research is also evidence that bisexual organizations are not representative of the broader bisexual population (McCormack et al. 2014; Pew 2013), and our results contribute to the debate about the problems of recruiting sexual minorities from particular groups and communities (McCormack 2014a; Savin-Williams 2001). Research on bisexual women continues to suggest that they have more troubled lives than lesbian women even when it uses data from women recruited from bisexual activist organizations (Colledge et al. 2015).

Expanding Sexuality and Death of the One-Time Rule

As society has gained a greater understanding of the flexibility of sexual desires and identities, there has been a corresponding increase in the terminology by which people understand their lives (Kuper et al. 2012). While bisexuality is increasingly coming out of the closet, and the word bisexual remains the most utilized term for those who experience sexual attraction towards both males and females (Rust 2009), other labels are also used to explain these desires. In addition to a range of labels to indicate non-gendered sexual desire (Kuper et al. 2012), Vrangalova and Savin-Williams (2013) find that a 5-category classification model best supports how the majority of people identify in US culture, adding "mostly heterosexual" and "mostly gay/lesbian" to the traditional gay/lesbian, bisexual and heterosexual classificatory system.

Vrangalova and Savin-Williams highlight that this classificatory system is part of a continuum of sexual desire, and this blurring between mostly heterosexual and bisexual is significant. Sexologists have long argued that women have greater capacity for same-sex sexual desire than men (Diamond 2009), yet the erosion of homohysteria enables men to engage in a much wider range of sexual behaviors, too (Anderson 2008). Sexuality is more flexible for some straight men today, and that the one-time rule of homosexuality is no longer valid. There does not appear to be gender difference in the prevalence of "mostly heterosexuals," and the public recognition of the possibilities of men having both same-sex and opposite-sex are markedly increased.

This has implications for bisexuality in that some people who would once have identified as bisexual might now identify as mostly heterosexual. Thus, while initially seeming contradictory, the erosion of homohysteria facilitates greater acceptance of bisexuality as a legitimate and viable sexual identity, while also seemingly reducing the number of people who will identify as bisexual. Furthermore, the erosion of homohysteria may also permit people to intellectually recognize elements of bisexuality in themselves because of the increased cultural permission for homosocial love and tactility among otherwise heterosexual individuals (Anderson and Adams 2011).

Exemplifying this, friendships between females have been described as particularly intense (Hey 1997), Anderson (2014) documents bromances between straight undergraduate men. In forthcoming work, Robinson and Anderson show that heterosexual undergraduate men favor their emotional relationships with other men over their emotional relationships with women. Describing these as "love affairs without sex" (Anderson 2014: 124), the notion of bisexuality is further complicated. Similarly, Luttrell (2012) shows that love, care and solidarity are central parts of young men's friendship dynamics, while McCormack (2013) demonstrates the importance of emotional support in young men's friendships in the UK.

Even so, there remains a strong preference for romantic relationships based on sexual attraction. The conflation of romantic and sexual attraction may be evidence of the continued presence of heterosexual privilege or, more likely, the dominance of monogamism in contemporary culture. Yet the erosion of the one-time rule of homosexuality and the development of bromances between heterosexual men highlights that sexual norms, and thus sexual orientation labels, are in a state of flux. This is easier to understand when a two-dimensional model of sexuality is adopted, rejecting the zero-sum game of sexuality where homosexual desire is seen to diminish the amount of heterosexual desire. It is for this reason that we suggest our sexuality thermometers (see Chap. 3) serve as a more accurate way of permitting people to indicate their sexual desires, without having to label or describe them.

All this means that we are at an interesting juncture for bisexuality research. We have demonstrated that matters are improving for bisexual men and that bisexual burden is less pervasive than in the 1980s and 1990s (Burleson 2005; Klein 1993); yet the propagation of identity categories that people identify as, alongside the lessening of personal importance of these categories among youth (Savin-Williams 2005), means that bisexuality may be becoming less significant as a category of analysis.

The Benefits of Our Recruitment Procedure

In addition to the central empirical finding, we contend that our research provides important methodological impacts in terms of its recruitment procedures. As discussed in Chap. 6, we developed a systematic approach to recruiting our participants; recruiting men from city streets, calling out for participants.

We emphasize the strategic, planned nature of this method. We stayed in each city until we had interviewed 30 men, and stopped recruiting in that city once we had reached our target number. Furthermore, we did not just recruit the first 30 men who approached us in each city. Instead, we designated three age cohorts (18–24, 25–35, 36–42) and interviewed ten men from each cohort in each city. This carefully designed and executed sampling procedure enabled us to make valid inter-cohort comparisons between the groups of differently aged men—the central finding of the book.

We recognize that this approach cannot be extrapolated to other projects without careful consideration. It is hard to envisage the approach working in rural areas where there is not the requisite number of passers-by, just as recruiting participants in homophobic areas would also be problematic. Similarly, research on more sensitive topics might require less public forms of address. As with any methodology, the characteristics of each research agenda must be carefully considered before determining the best form of participant recruitment.

However, there were other benefits of this approach. We recruited a rich diversity of ethnicities in our research. The participants from New York and Los Angeles were roughly a third each white, black, and Hispanic, with some mixed-race participants. Participants from London were predominantly white. This diversity was partly because we were recruiting metropolitan areas where ethnic minorities can be found in higher numbers. However, given critiques of LGBT networks being exclusionary to non-white people, recruiting a diversity of ethnic groups is an important advancement—that race did not prove to be a fruitful category of analysis is an important finding as well.

As experienced ethnographers, we also found recruiting participants in this manner yielded interesting data in itself. We did not include this in the data sections as we were focused on recruiting participants and our observations did not have the methodological rigor that accompanies ethnographic data. Yet our interpretations of recruiting participants only supported our findings: we experienced no harassment on the street, encountered no perceived acts of micro-aggression, such as negative looks or nasty comments, and never felt physical danger. Indeed, the comments we heard were positive—the most memorable was overhearing a young child ask his mother if he was bisexual. The mother's response was, "we don't know what you are yet."

Recommendations for Future Research

Our work contributes toward the sociological understanding of bisexuality by: (1) examining the changing nature of bisexual men's lives through a theoretical lens of decreasing homohysteria; (2) examining how the changing cultural zeitgeist manifests in the lived experience of bisexual men according to their age-cohort; and (3) drawing upon an innovative recruitment method to avoid bisexuals institutionalized into gay or bisexual sub-cultures, thus providing us with an understanding of the increasing ordinariness of openly bisexual men's lives.

Our results call for multiple recommendations for future research on bisexuality and sexual minorities more broadly. The first is to call for a greater diversity of recruitment methods in sexualities research. Our participant recruitment approach bypassed many of the sampling problems that have beset research on sexual minority populations in the past. It also provided us with a racially diverse sample, that we suspect would not have occurred if traditional forms of recruitment had been used. This is not to say no potential weaknesses of this approach exist, but it is to recognize that more diversity in recruitment processes and participants' backgrounds will only strengthen qualitative research on sexualities.

It is our contention that these recruitment strategies should be used more widely in sexualities research. There is a need for greater innovation in participant recruitment procedures (McCormack 2014a), and the persistence of sampling issues in both quantitative and qualitative research on sexualities demands consideration. Given the need for research methods to be sensitive to the social context of any research project, innovation in recruitment processes will need to be developed by experts in the particular field. In a research context where qualitative research is generalized to sub-sections of society, and where the majority of qualitative research excludes particular narratives and experiences, a narrow set of recruitment procedures can have negative consequences. Although new recruitment strategies will require particular scrutiny, they should also be welcomed by the academy as contributing to a more comprehensive understanding of bisexuality, LGBT individuals, and sexuality more broadly conceived.

Our sexuality thermometers may also be a useful tool for conducting research on sexualities in the future. We used a modified Klein-grid in our research, yet found problems with it—participants found it hard to fill out, some seemingly not understanding a range of components, and it is also hampered by adopting a zero-sum game understanding of sexual desire. The sexuality thermometers move us from a one-dimensional model to a two-dimensional one, and also clearly situate sexual desire as a continuum. The thermometers can also be modified to measure romantic attraction, too. It should be very simple for participants to fill out and enables participants to accurately describe the strength of each component of their sexual desire. Those who desire men and women equally will also be able to state this without perpetuating the zero-sum game of sexuality. It is our hope that these methodological innovations will prove useful to scholars researching bisexuality and the field of sexuality studies more generally.

However, we also recognize that this approach does not integrate a measurement of sexual desire toward transgendered people. Weinrich (2014b) highlights that one way to accomplish this is through a 'focusing on the beloved' (p. 554). He argues that by focusing on *attraction to* this ameliorates the problem of trans people having to 'change' sexuality as they transition. Similarly, if this *attraction to* is expanded to include a range of characteristics and attributes (and not just 'male' or 'female') measurement of sexual desire, it conceptualizes sex beyond that of a binary model. Galupo et al. (2014) provide empirical evidence of the problems of the Kinsey scale and Klein grid in this regard, and demonstrate that future methodologies that incorporate such an approach will be important to understand the diversity of sexual orientations and gender identities in society. They also highlight how further research is needed to test such frameworks and we endorse their call for methodological investigations in this area.

While we did not examine psychological dimensions of the men we studied, we hypothesize that bisexual men whose adolescence was in the 21st century will have better mental health outcomes than men who maintained their adolescence in the 20th century. We fully expect future research, with appropriate sampling techniques, to show this trend (see also Mustanski et al. 2010). While we have argued that the elevated rates of mental health issues associated with men's bisexuality is greatly attributed to the institutionalized sampling techniques of most bisexual research (see also Savin-Williams 2001a, b), it is highly unlikely that the impact of the erosion of homophobia, homohysteria, and bisexual burden would not result in improvements in bisexual men's mental health.

Next, the prevalence of monosexism in society is self-evident and the term has some popularity on social media, yet remarkably little research uses the concept as a way to understand bisexual erasure or the privileging of binary understandings of sexuality. Using monosexism alongside our framing of the problems of a zero-sum game of sexuality provides a powerful framework by which to critically interrogate discourses and social norms that erase sexual minorities that do not conform to the gay/straight binary.

Our research also shows that the widely accepted differences between city and country may be less pronounced than in the past. In her book on being a sexual minority in rural America, Gray (2009) argued that life for LGBT youth was worse in rural areas because the gains made in popular culture were not as visible in the countryside as they were the city. She stated that young people in rural areas, "face vastly different access to agencies serving lesbian, gay, bisexual and transgender-identifying youth...[living] beyond the reach of publicly funded LGBT health programs, community-based support agencies, and visible constituencies able to finance, nurture, and augment such services" (p. 9).

However, supporting our findings of generally positive experiences across regions, research shows that gay spaces are gradually emerging across the US. In his book *There goes the gayborhood?*, Ghaziani (2014) argues that we live in a world "not of shriveling sexual and spatial expressions but instead of extraordinary growth and new possibilities" (p. 259). While he uses Boystown in Chicago as a case study, Ghaziani emphasizes that changes are also occurring in small towns and rural areas across America. He argues that "our national landscape today is defined by queer geographies" (p. 259) and he is careful to state that these exist "in the plural" (p. 239).

Our research supports the idea that rural areas are still *perceived* as less hospitable, but the positive experiences of the youngest cohort across many regions also supports Ghaziani's contention regarding the emergence of gay spaces across the US. Further research needs to investigate how the increasingly positive attitudes toward sexual minorities intersect with the divide between the rural and the urban. We predict that the differences will be less pronounced than in the past, but that research in this area will help illuminate ways to contest monosexism and the privileging of heterosexuality in the future.

Finally, we advocate for an approach in the sociology of sexualities that recognizes the generational nature of sexualities. We are indebted to Ken Plummer's (2010) insightful essay on the ways in which generations structure sexualities, and we notice a focus on the importance of generational zeitgeists in recent sociological work on sexualities. While we have conceptualized the 20th century as having eras related to erasure, homohysteria and inclusion, Ghaziani (2014: 9) uses the concept of 'post-gay' as a way of understanding a "new gay paradigm...characterized by a dramatic acceptance of homosexuality and a corresponding assimilation of gays and lesbians into the mainstream" (see also Coleman-Fountain 2014). Similarly, Dean (2014) uses the notion of the closet to highlight different eras related to sexualities. It is clear that future research on sexualities will need to recognize the importance of generation and the historical context of the present moment to develop a rigorous, sociological approach to sexualities.

Implications for Social Policy

Our sociological study of bisexual men's lives has important applications in the realm of social policy. Hearn (2010) highlights how social policy initiatives remain rooted in simplistic understanding of masculinity that focuses on crises in masculinity rather than a critical exploration of social change that is gendered in complex ways. Our perspective is that the further masculinities transition away from the rigid, homophobic, orthodox masculinity of the 1980s, the more men benefit. Indeed, while scholars, journalists and even casual observers of contemporary US and UK culture note that heterosexual masculinities are becoming broader, softer, and more inclusive of diversity, misinterpretations of men's gender as a whole still occur in academia and within social policy initiatives (see Roberts 2014).

This focus on crisis is also found in social policy initiatives on sexual minorities (see Cree et al. 2015). Oftentimes fuelled by gay rights charities who rely on government funding, a victimhood framework is perpetuated that presents sexual minorities as passive victims that are isolated from social change. Here, social policy initiatives are sometimes founded on a particularly horrific example of prejudice, despite this disregarding a broader social trend. Social policy is too frequently influenced by moral panics around particularly traumatic incidents, rather than an evidence based approach that examines issues more dispassionately (Clapton et al. 2013).

It is worth here considering the psychological concept of the availability heuristic (Tversky and Kahneman 1973), which speaks to the ease by which we recall information. It holds that more memorable examples are privileged over more mundane ones. The availability heuristic goes someway to explaining why scholars and politicians often overly-focus on particularly negative or horrific examples rather than the everyday experiences of sexual minorities.

This is not to argue against social policies that target sexual minority populations or bisexual men specifically; but it is to call for an approach that seeks to develop a proactive progressive politics in which advances are recognized as a way to contest the inequalities that persist. The debate about the phrase "that's so gay" exemplifies our concern about this issue. Rather than labelling it a form of homophobic bullying (Charlesworth 2015) and channelling time and funding to contest a phrase that has questionable negative effect, an evidence-based social policy would recognize that the meaning of this phrase is changing and it is no longer a form of homophobic bullying (Lalor and Rendle-Short 2007; McCormack 2011). The focus on the phrase "that's so gay" does not tackle the root causes of homophobia, and diverts focus away from policies and funding that could affect real change—not least a holistic sex education that is integrated across subjects in school curricula (McCormack et al. in press).

Our research also illuminates the divide between research that focusses on bisexual activist groups and bisexuals drawn from the wider population. Small-scale quantitative surveys that rely primarily on LGBT activist groups will not provide solid evidence on which to base good social policy. A recent example of this is a study that used data from a UK gay rights charity's study into women's health (Colledge et al. 2015). Using a self-completion survey with opportunistic, community-based sampling that recruited 937 bisexual-identified and 4769 lesbian-identified women, the authors argue that "bisexual women may be more likely to experience social stress due to the double discrimination of biphobia and homophobia" (p. 1). While the authors recognize the data cannot be generalized to the population, it received a significant level of attention that perpetuated the notion that bisexuals have worse mental health than lesbian women. Given its recruitment techniques, this study provides confirmatory evidence that bisexual activist communities are far less representative of bisexuals than lesbian groups rather than evidence of a need for social interventions specifically for bisexuals. In short, social policy makers need to be extremely wary of surveys that use convenience samples.

Finally, the finding of a generational cohort effect shows the need for policy makers to pay due attention to the role of age and how that structures experiences of sexuality. King (2015) provides a helpful analysis of how social policy interventions at the local level can improve services for older LGBT adults, recognizing how aging intersects with sexuality to produce specific needs and requirements. Given the generational nature of sexualities, social policy needs to recognize the diversity of needs across age ranges. Just as "that's so gay" means different things to people of differing ages, there will be an array of ways in which targeting people according to their generation will enhance social policy interventions.

We are not advocating against social policy interventions in general – sexuality has tended to be an under-resourced and marginalized area even when the needs is exceptionally high. What we are calling for is not just an evidence-based social policy, but one that is cognizant of the complexity of sexuality, how it is measured and the politics of the claims of victimhood.

In Conclusion

In this book, we have explored the nature of bisexuality, how it is studied, and the experiences of bisexual men in the largest US and UK metropolitan cities. Related to these experiences, our interests have centered on the particular expectations, attitudes and laws related to sexuality, gender, and morality that impact on these men. As sociologists, we have focused on how these men mediate their position in society given their bisexual identities. Drawing on a social constructionist approach that incorporates an interdisciplinary perspective, we have focused on bisexual men's experiences and their everyday lives, which only brings into sharper focus the men's own interrogation of sexual identity categories.

The argument developed throughout the book is that there are generational differences in how bisexuality is experienced, and that it is the social zeitgeist of the culture in which men experienced their adolescence that is the fundamental reason for these generational differences in sexualities. Without rejecting the idea that every individual has their own unique experiences, we found few negative coming out experiences among the younger generation. In short, it is easier to disclose a sexual identity now than it was in the 1980s.

The social progress we document in this research is the result of two factors. First, there is social progress as cultural homophobia decreases. Second, our sampling procedures indicate that recruiting from bisexual activist community groups will skew the data toward more negative experiences. Given that our older cohort's experiences were not as negative as traditionally found in the literature, it seems that some of the difficulties of being bisexual reported in previous literature might be attributed to the sample: calling upon men from recognized LGBT networks, support groups and bisexual communities more specifically. It is known that bisexual communities are not representative of bisexuals more general (Burleson 2005; Munro 2015), and research with bisexuals from these groups have limited generalizability. By locating men off the streets instead, we are able to source bisexual men that have not otherwise been captured by academic research.

Finally, our research also speaks about heterosexual attitudes toward bisexuality. In calling out on busy city streets that we were looking to interview bisexual men, tens of thousands of pedestrians heard our call. From this pedestrian population, women encouraged us to also study women's sexuality; we were approached by gay and straight men telling us that they approved of our research; we overheard one mother's explanation of bisexuality to her young child's question of what 'bisexual' is; we heard lots of joking among straight men that their friend should qualify; and we were critiqued by one academic passing-by who disapproved of our research methods. What was totally missing from the hundreds of short conversations we had with these pedestrians was hostility or prejudice.

Of the tens of thousands that heard us call out for bisexuals, none approached us with homophobia or biphobia; none approached us to say that we should not be announcing bisexuality in front of children; none approached us to say that bisexuality does not exist. Bisexuality has moved from the abstract perversity on Kinsey's pages to social banality on metropolitan city streets.

Appendix 1
Participant List

Older cohort (36–42) 10 each from NY, LA and Lon			Middle cohort (24–35) 10 each from NY, LA and Lon			Younger cohort (18–23) 10 each from NY, LA and Lon		
Marcus	35	White	Louis	24	White	Marco	18	Hispanic
Stephen	36	White	Jose	24	Hispanic	Cole	18	White
Alejandro	36	Hispanic	Jake	24	White	Mike	18	White
Bernie	37	White	Benji	24	White	Joey	18	White
Richard	37	White	Ray	25	Hispanic	Ryan	18	Black
Freddie	37	Hispanic	Sean	25	White	Neil	18	White
Alex	37	White	Ronnie	27	Hispanic	Pete	18	Black
AJ	38	Black	Danny	27	White	Angelo	18	Hispanic
Ed	38	White	Max	27	White	Paul	18	White
John	38	White	Shane	28	Black	David	19	Hispanic
Riccardo	38	Hispanic	Trenton	28	White	Saul	19	Black
Lloyd	38	White	Chris	28	Hispanic	Kevin	19	Black
Connor	38	White	George	28	White	Laurie	19	White
Garret	38	White	Lee	29	Black	Tyler	19	Hispanic
Diego	39	Hispanic	Stefan	30	White	Joseph	20	Hispanic
Andy	39	White	Andrew	30	White	Liam	21	White
Barry	39	Black	Drew	30	Black	Jared	21	White
Jamal	39	Black	Phil	31	White	Jackson	21	White
Thomas	39	White	JP	31	Hispanic	Jacob	21	White
Filipe	39	Hispanic	Richie	32	Hispanic	Ben	21	White
Simon	39	White	Colin	32	White	Lewis	21	White
Arnold	40	Black	Nicholas	32	Black	William	22	White
Vernon	40	White	Carl	32	White	Harry	22	White
Clark	40	White	Ricky	33	Hispanic	Cooper	22	White
Matthew	41	White	Bill	33	Black	Leonard	22	Black

(continued)

(continued)

Older cohort (36–42)			Middle cohort (24–35)			Younger cohort (18–23)		
10 each from NY, LA and Lon			10 each from NY, LA and Lon			10 each from NY, LA and Lon		
Arthur	42	White	Tiago	33	Hispanic	Frank	23	Hispanic
Robert	42	White	Syrus	33	Black	Sam	23	Hispanic
Darryn	42	Black	Anthony	34	White	Jeremy	23	White
Robin	42	Mixed	Tyrone	34	Black	Terrance	23	White
Ramone	42	Hispanic	Jonathan	35	White	Brian	23	Black
Mean age:	39		Mean age:	29		Mean age:	20	

Appendix 2
Paradigmatic Perspectives on Sexual Desire

Intellectual thinking into the nature of what it means to be homosexual, heterosexual, or bisexual is heavily contested. The great problem with these debates within sociology is that the discussion of the role of society and biology in the etiology of sexuality is then taken as evidence of one ideological position. There are two loosely defined, paradigmatic ideologies to this—biological determinism and social determinism. Despite excellent work that highlights the melding of social and biological forces in the construction of the taxonomies of sex and sexuality (e.g. Fausto-Sterling 2000), the renunciation of biology appears to be a shibboleth for some sociologists of gender and sexuality.

It is important to understand some of the history of these debates. Prior to the 1980s, and certainly by the 1990s, a pragmatic and traditional approach to understanding sexuality in the form of essentialism entered the social sciences through gay and lesbian studies, capitalizing on the success of identity politics for liberation from oppressive cultural norms (Norton 2010). However, this was replaced by the more abstract discipline of poststructural or queer theorizing. While both schools of thought sought for the repeal of homophobic social structures, the new approach — based on an extreme form of social constructionism — soon became the hegemonic paradigm for the investigation of our understanding of human sexuality, particularly among sociologists and historians.

In the newer, poststructuralist, approach to this knowledge and practice are constructed, deconstructed, and reconstructed through ideological discourse, narratives, or super-structural 'discourse.' In the former model, oftentimes pejoratively labelled as 'essentialism,' knowledge and practice are instead discovered, repressed, and recovered through history and experience. Norton (2010) argues that whereas queer theorists emphasize discontinuity and revolutionary ruptures, essentialists emphasize continuity and that sexual desires and orientations exist outside of social discourses about them. Some of this was undoubtedly the result of the historical use of male scientists to retain political power and privilege for men (Edley and Wetherell 1995); yet such a critique of contemporary scientists is not valid (see LeVay 2011).

Essentialists maintain that sexual orientation is mostly "hard-wired" or predisposed, likely before birth, and that it exists as that of a combination of physiological, biological, hormonal, and genetic variance that is least shaped, at least initially, by social, environmental, or cultural factors (Savin-Williams 1998). As Norton (2010: p. 7) says, at the core of homosexual desire is, "innate, congenital, constitutional, stable and fixed rather than fluid." This is supported by scientific research (LeVay 2011; Wilson and Rahman 2005). Our figure below highlights that we view essentialist and social constructionist perspectives as closer together than often posited, and that they do not correspond with deterministic thinking.

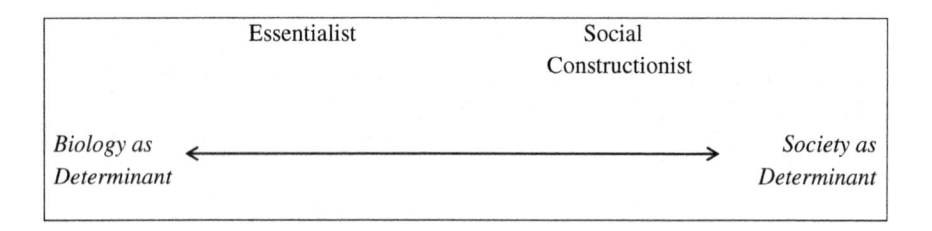

	Essentialist	Social Constructionist	
Biology as Determinant	←	→	*Society as Determinant*

Some who ascribe to this view might also argue that sexual identities exist independently and across time periods, that it is taxonomic, and not simply a matter of semantics. This is to say that biological determinists provide little 'wiggle room' for the influence of culture. We would call this a form of biological determinism, however, that does not account for the potential for different forms of gender or sexuality display and organization.

Yet we also highlight that there are many findings that are hard to explain without a biological component. It is hard to explain, for example, that gay men are more likely to be born into families where they have older brothers, or that lesbians are more likely to be left-handed or have a finger digit length ratio similar to men's not heterosexual women's hands (LeVay 2011). Other studies show that adult gay men have higher rates of gender non-conformity as young kids (Lippa 2005). Gender non-conformity appears to be an excellent example where the potential marriage of the social and biological is rejected in much sociology of sexualities research. Of course, gender non-conformity is inherently social in the sense that it is only through social norms that one can be seen to conform or otherwise. Yet the correlation between gender non-conformity in youth and homosexuality in adulthood has been documented in methodologically rigorous, large scale research. The key point is that the social role in gender non-conformity can co-exist with the recognition that such non-conformity is correlated with same-sex sexual desires.

We highlight here that how the public understands these issues is rather more important than what academics debate. Regardless of the etiology of sexuality, in Western societies (the focus of our work), the population largely, and increasingly, maintains an essentialist and even biological determinist position. In 2011, Lady Gaga released 'Born this Way' that serves as an anthem for today's youth, who maintain that sexual orientation and the sex of whom one loves is not a matter of choice. Gay people are not created by society. There is value in this perspective, as multiple research studies have shown that, regardless of the 'true' etiology of homosexuality, people are more likely to look favorably upon it when they consider it the project of biology and not upbringing. The fascinating thing is that these young people who believe you are "born this way" also eschew sexual identity labels (Savin-Williams 2005)—it seems that they have no difficulty in recognizing the biological and social elements of sexual orientation.

Finally, we highlight that there is fervor among many sociologists who study sexual minorities that sexuality is, without doubt, the product of society. This perspective is, unsurprisingly, more evident among those who earn their Ph.D.s in sociology compared to those who earn their Ph.D.s in other aspects of social sciences, medicine, or biology. However, we also highlight that even here, the majority of sociologists—by far—maintain that homosexuality is the product of biology and not society (Engle et al. 2006). A further problem with those who reject the biological model of sexual orientation is that they have no credible theory about how society constructs sexual orientation.

There is a peculiar argument advanced by some scholars, that because they have been able to choose their sexuality (whatever this means), this proves that sexual orientation is social and not biological. This again smacks of determinist thinking—to recognize that some people may experience sexuality differently from others is fascinating and evidence of the value of sociology and psychology in understanding sexuality. But it is not evidence against the role of biology in the etiology of human sexuality. As Diamond (2009) shows, there are a number of reasons why sexuality may feel like a choice, but it does not preclude the biological origins of sexual desire.

Historically speaking, we suggest that while the rainbow flag is clear indication of global social forces adopting a western notion of gay identity, the underlying range of same-sex attracted customs are predictable even if they are complex and diverse. Just as powerful as Gaga's 'Born this way' anthem, we also endorse the internet meme that homosexuality is natural but homophobia is not.

References

Abes, E. S., Jones, S. R., & McEwen, M. K. (2007). Reconceptualizing the model of multiple dimensions of identity: The role of meaning-making capacity in the construction of multiple identities. *Journal of College Student Development, 48*(1), 1–22.

Adams, A. (2011). "Josh wears pink cleats": Inclusive masculinity on the soccer field. *Journal of Homosexuality, 58*(5), 579–596.

Adams, A., & Anderson, E. (2012). Exploring the relationship between homosexuality and sport among the teammates of a small, Midwestern Catholic college soccer team. *Sport, Education and Society, 17*(3), 347–363.

Adams, A., Anderson, E., & McCormack, M. (2010). Establishing and challenging masculinity: The influence of gendered discourses in organized sport. *Journal of Language and Social Psychology, 29*(3), 278–300.

Afary, J. (2009). *Sexual politics in modern Iran*. Cambridge: Cambridge University Press.

Alexander, J., & Anderlini-D'Onofrio, S. (Eds.). (2014). *Bisexuality and queer theory: intersections, connections and challenges*. London: Routledge.

Almaguer, T. (1991). The cartography of homosexual desire and identity among Chicano men. *Differences, 3*, 75–100.

American Psychological Association. (2008). *Answers to your questions: For a better understanding of sexual orientation and homosexuality*, Washington, DC. Retrieved from www.apa.org/topics/sorientation.pdf

Andersen, B. L., Cyranowski, J. M., & Aarestad, S. (2000). Beyond artificial, sex-linked distinctions to conceptualize female sexuality: Comment on Baumeister (2000). *Psychological Bulletin, 126*, 380–384.

Anderson, E. (2002). Openly gay athletes contesting hegemonic masculinity in a homophobic environment. *Gender and Society, 16*(6), 860–877.

Anderson, E. (2005a). *In the game: Gay athletes and the cult of masculinity*. New York: SUNY Press.

Anderson, E. (2005b). Orthodox and inclusive masculinity: Competing masculinities among heterosexual men in a feminized terrain. *Sociological Perspectives, 48*(3), 337–355

Anderson, E. (2008). "Being masculine is not about who you sleep with..:" Heterosexual athletes contesting masculinity and the one-time rule of homosexuality. *Sex Roles, 58*(1–2), 104–115.

Anderson, E. (2009). *Inclusive masculinity: The changing nature of masculinities*. London: Routledge.

Anderson, E. (2011a). The rise and fall of western homohysteria. *Journal of Feminist Scholarship, 1*(1), 80–94.

Anderson, E. (2011b). Updating the outcome gay athletes, straight teams, and coming out in educationally based sport teams. *Gender & Society, 25*(2), 250–268.

Anderson, E. (2012). *The monogamy gap: Men, love and the reality of cheating*. New York: Oxford University Press.

Anderson, E. (2014). *21st Century Jocks*. Basingstoke: Palgrave MacMillan.

Anderson, E., & Adams, A. (2011). "Aren't we all a little bisexual?": The recognition of bisexuality in an unlikely place. *Journal of Bisexuality, 11*(1), 3–22.

Anderson, E., & McCormack, M. (2014). Cuddling and spooning heteromasculinity and homosocial tactility among student-athletes. *Men and Masculinities.* 10.117/1097184X14523433

Anderson, E., McCormack, M., & Ripley, M. (2014). Sixth form girls and bisexual burden. *Journal of Gender Studies* (ahead-of-print), 1–11.

Appiah, K. A. (2005). *The ethics of identity.* Princeton: Princeton University Press.

Arnett, J. J. (2004). *Emerging adulthood: The winding road from the late teens through the twenties.* Oxford: Oxford University Press.

Asch, S. E. (1946). Forming impressions of personality. *The Journal of Abnormal and Social Psychology, 41*(3), 258.

Aspinall, P. J. (2009). *Estimating the size and composition of the lesbian, gay and bisexual population in Britain. Research Report 37.* Equality and Human Rights Commission.

Attwood, F., & Smith, C. (2013). More sex! Better sex! Sex is fucking brilliant! Sex, sex, sex, SEX. In T. Blackwood (ed.). *Routledge Handbook of Leisure Studies* (pp. 325–342).

Avery, A., Chase, J., Johansson, L., Litvak, S., Montero, D., & Wydra, M. (2007). America's changing attitudes toward homosexuality, civil unions, and same-gender marriage: 1977–2004. *Social Work, 52*(1), 71–79.

Bailey, J. M. (2009). What is sexual orientation and do women have one? In *Contemporary perspectives on lesbian, gay, and bisexual identities*, pp. 43–63. New York: Springer.

Bailey, J. M. (2015). A failure to demonstrate changes in sexual interest in pedophilic men: Comment on Mueller et al. (2014). *Archives of Sexual Behavior 44*(1), 249–252.

Bailey, J. M., Kirk, K. M., Zhu, G., Dunne, M. P., & Martin, N. G. (2000). Do individual differences in sociosexuality represent genetic or environmentally contingent strategies? Evidence from the Australian twin registry. *Journal of Personality and Social Psychology, 78*(3), 537.

Baker, P. L., & Hotek, D. R. (2011). Grappling with gender: Exploring masculinity and gender in the bodies, performances, and emotions of scholastic wrestlers. *Journal of Feminist Scholarship, 1*, 1–15.

Baldwin, A., Dodge, B., Schick, V., Hubach, R. D., Bowling, J., Malebranche, D., & Fortenberry, J. D. (2014). Sexual self-identification among behaviorally bisexual men in the midwestern United States. *Archives of Sexual Behavior* 1–12.

Barker, M. (2007). Heteronormativity and the exclusion of bisexuality in psychology. In *Out in psychology: Lesbian, gay, bisexual, trans, and queer perspectives* (pp. 86–118).

Barker, M. (2014). Bisexuality. *Encyclopedia of Critical Psychology* 170–175.

Barker, M., Bowes-Catton, H., Iantaffi, A., Cassidy, A., & Brewer, L. (2008). British bisexuality: A snapshot of bisexual representations and identities in the United Kingdom. *Journal of Bisexuality, 8*(1-2), 141–162.

Barker, M., Richards, C., Jones, R. L., & Monro, S. (2011). BiReCon: An international academic conference on bisexuality including the program for BiReCon. *Journal of Bisexuality, 11*(2-3), 157–170.

Barker, M., Yockney, J., Richards, C., Jones, R., Bowes-Catton, H., & Plowman, T. (2012). Guidelines for researching and writing about bisexuality. *Journal of Bisexuality, 12*(3), 376–392.

Barnard, A. (2000). *History and theory in anthropology.* Cambridge: Cambridge University Press.

Barrett, T. (2013). Friendships between men across sexual orientation: The importance of (others) being intolerant. *The Journal of Men's Studies, 21*(1), 62–77.

Baumeister, R. F. (2000). Gender differences in erotic plasticity: the female sex drive as socially flexible and responsive. *Psychological Bulletin, 126*(3), 347.

Baunach, D. M. (2012). Changing same-sex marriage attitudes in America from 1988 through 2010. *Public Opinion Quarterly, 76*(2), 364–378.

References

Beisel, N. K. (1998). *Imperiled innocents: Anthony Comstock and family reproduction in Victorian America*. Princeton: Princeton University Press.

Bergler, E. (1956). *Homosexuality—disease or way of life*. New York: Collier.

Blumstein, P. W., & Schwartz, P. (1977). Bisexuality: Some social psychological issues. *Journal of Social Issues, 33*(2), 30–45.

Bogaert, A. F. (2012). *Understanding asexuality*. Maryland: Rowman & Littlefield Publishers.

Bogle, K. (2008). *Hooking up: Sex, dating, and relationships on campus*. New York: New York University Press.

Boroughs, M., Cafri, G., & Thompson, J. K. (2005). Male body depilation: Prevalence and associated features of body hair removal. *Sex Roles, 52*(9–10), 637–644.

Bostwick, W. (2012). Assessing bisexual stigma and mental health status: A brief report. *Journal of Bisexuality, 12*(2), 214–222.

Boykin, K. (2005). *Beyond the down low: Sex, lies, and denial in Black America*. Cambridge: Da Capo Press.

Branfman, J., Stiritz, S., & Anderson, E. (in press). Relaxing the straight male anus: Decreasing homohysteria around anal eroticism. *Sexualities*.

Brewster, P. W. H., Mullin, C. R., Dobrin, R. A., & Steeves, J. K. E. (2010). Sex differences in face processing are mediated by handedness and sexual orientation. *Laterality: Asymmetries of Body, Brian and Cognition* 16(2), 188–200

Bronn, C. D. (2001). Attitudes and self-images of male and female bisexuals. *Journal of Bisexuality, 1*(4), 5–29.

Brown, L. B. (1997). Women and men, not-men and not-women, lesbians and gays: American Indian gender style alternatives. *Journal of Gay and Lesbian Social Services, 6*(2), 5–20.

Brown, T. (2002). A proposed model of bisexual identity development that elaborates on experiential differences of women and men. *Journal of Bisexuality, 2*(4), 67–91.

Burleson, W. E. (2005). *Bi America*. New York, NY: Harrington Park.

Burleson, W. E. (2008). The kinsey scale and the pashtun: The role of culture in measuring sexual orientation. *Journal of Bisexuality, 8*(3-4), 259–264.

Burstein, P. (1998). Bringing the public back in: Should sociologists consider the impact of public opinion on public policy? *Social Forces, 77*(1), 27–62.

Burton-Nelson, M. (1994). *The stronger women get, the more men love football: Sexism and the American culture of sports*. New York: Harcourt Brace.

Buss, D. M. (1995). Evolutionary psychology: A new paradigm for psychological science. *Psychological Inquiry, 6*(1), 1–30.

Cancian, F. M. (1987). *Love in America: Gender and self-development*. Cambridge: Cambridge University Press.

Cancian, F. M. (1992). Feminist science: Methodologies that challenge inequality. *Gender and Society, 6*(4), 623–642.

Cantor, J. M. (2015). Purported changes in pedophilia as statistical artefacts: Comment on Müller et al. (2014). *Archives of Sexual Behavior, 44*(1), 253–254.

Carey, B. (2005). *Straight, gay or lying: Bisexuality revisited*. New York Times. Available online: http://www.nytimes.com/2005/07/05/health/05sex.html?_r=0

Carrier, J. M. (1989). Sexual behavior and spread of AIDS in Mexico. *Medical Anthropology, 10* (2-3), 129–142.

Carrillo, H. (2002). *The night is young: Sexuality in Mexico in the time of aids*. Chicago, Il: University of Chicago Press.

Carrillo, H. (in press). Straight with a pinch of bi. *Sexualities*.

Carrillo, H., & Fontdevila, J. (2011). Rethinking sexual initiation: Pathways to identity formation among gay and bisexual Mexican male youth. *Archives of Sexual Behavior, 40*(6), 1241–1254.

Chan, C. S. (1995). Issues of sexual identity in an ethnic minority: The case of Chinese American lesbians, gay men, and bisexual people. In *Lesbian, gay, and bisexual identities over the lifespan: Psychological perspectives* (pp. 87–101).

Charlesworth, J. (2015). *That's so gay: Challenging homophobic bullying*. London: Jessica Kingsley.

Charmaz, K. (2014). *Constructing grounded theory*. London: Sage.

Chauncey, G. (1994). *Gay New York: Gender, urban culture and the making of the gay male world 1890–1940*. New York: Basic Books.

Chaves, M. (1989). Secularization and religious revival: Evidence from US church attendance rates, 1972–1986. *Journal for the Scientific Study of Religion, 28*(4), 464–477.

Chivers, M. L., & Bailey, J. M. (2005). A sex difference in features that elicit genital response. *Biological Psychology, 70*(2), 115–120.

Chivers, M. L., Rieger, G., Latty, E., & Bailey, J. M. (2004). A sex difference in the specificity of sexual arousal. *Psychological Science, 15*(11), 736–744.

Clapton, G., Cree, V., & Smith, M. (2013). Moral panics, claims-making and child protection in the UK. *The British Journal of Social Work, 43*(4), 803–812.

Clements, B., & Field, C. D. (2014). Public Opinion toward Homosexuality and Gay Rights in Great Britain. *Public Opinion Quarterly, 78*(2), 523–547.

Coad, D. (2008). *The Metrosexual*. New York: SUNY Press.

Cohler, B. J., & Hammack, P. L. (2007). The psychological world of the gay teenager: Social change, narrative, and "normality". *Journal of Youth and Adolescence, 36*(1), 47–59.

Cohler, B., & Hammack, P. (2009). Lives, times and narrative engagement. *The story of sexual identity: Narrative perspectives on the gay and lesbian life course*, 453–465.

Coleman-Fountain, E. (2014). *Understanding narrative identity through lesbian and gay youth*. Palgrave Macmillan, UK.

Colledge, L., Hickson, F., Reid, D., & Weatherburn, P. (2015). Poorer mental health in UK bisexual women than lesbians: Evidence from the UK 2007 Stonewall Women's Health Survey. *Journal of Public Health, advanced online publication*. doi:10.1093/pubmed/fdu105

Collier, K. L., Bos, H. M., Merry, M. S., & Sandfort, T. G. (2013). Gender, ethnicity, religiosity, and same-sex sexual attraction and the acceptance of same-sex sexuality and gender non-conformity. *Sex Roles, 68*(11–12), 724–737.

Collins, P. H. (1999). *Black feminist thought: Knowledge, consciousness, and the politics of empowerment*. Routledge, London.

Connell, R. (1995). *Masculinities*. Cambridge: Polity.

Conron, K. J., Mimiaga, M., & Landers, S. (2010). A population-based study of sexual orientation identity and gender differences in adult health. *American Journal of Public Health, 100*, 460–467.

Cook, J. A., & Fonow, M. M. (1986). Knowledge and women's interests: Issues of epistemology and methodology in feminist sociological research. *Sociological Inquiry, 56*(1), 2–29.

Corey, D. W., & LeRoy, J. (1963). *The homosexual and his society: A view from within*. USA: Citadel Press

Coutinho, S. A., Hartnett, J. L., & Sagarin, B. J. (2007). Understanding promiscuity in strategic friend selection from an evolutionary perspective. *North American Journal of Psychology, 9*(2), 257–274.

Crawley, S. L., Foley, L. J., & Shehan, C. L. (2007). *Gendering bodies*. USA: Rowman & Littlefield.

Cree, V. B., Clapton, G., & Smith, M. (Eds.). (2015). *Revisiting moral panics*. Bristol: Policy Press.

Crenshaw, K. (1991). Mapping the margins: Intersectionality, identity politics, and violence against women of color. *Stanford Law Review*, 1241–1299.

Cunningham, M. R. (1986). Measuring the physical in physical attractiveness: Quasiexperiments on the sociobiology of female facial beauty. *Journal of Personality and Social Psychology, 50*(5), 925–935.

Cunningham, M. R., Barbee, A. P., & Pike, C. L. (1990). What do women want? Facial metric assessment of multiple motives in the perception of male physical attractiveness. *Journal of Personality and Social Psychology, 59*, 61–72.

References

D'Augelli, A. R., & Patterson, C. J. (1995). *Lesbian, gay, and bisexual identities over the lifespan*. Oxford: Oxford University Press.

D'Augelli, A. R., Grossman, A. H., Starks, M. T., & Sinclair, K. O. (2010). Factors associated with parents' knowledge of gay, lesbian, and bisexual youths' sexual orientation. *Journal of GLBT Family Studies, 6*(2), 178–198.

D'Augelli, A. R., Hershberger, S. L., & Pilkington, N. W. (2001). Suicidality patterns and sexual orientation-related factors among lesbian, gay, and bisexual youths. *Suicide and Life-Threatening Behavior, 31*(3), 250–264.

D'Emilio, J. (1998). *Sexual politics, sexual communities: The making of a homosexual minority in the United States, 1940–1970*. Chicago: University of Chicago Press.

Davis, A. (1981). *Women, race and class*. New York: Random House.

Dean, J. J. (2014). *Straights: Heterosexuality in post-closeted culture*. New York: New York University Press.

Deitcher, D. (2001). *Dear friends: American photographs of men together, 1840–1918*. Abrams: Harry N.

Della, B., Wilson, M., & Miller, R. L. (2002). Strategies for managing heterosexism used among African American gay and bisexual men. *Journal of Black Psychology, 28*(4), 371–391.

Demetriou, D. Z. (2001). Connell's concept of hegemonic masculinity: A critique. *Theory and Society, 30*(3), 337–361.

Derlega, V. J., Lewis, R. J., Harrison, S., Winstead, B. A., & Costanza, R. (1989). Gender differences in the initiation and attribution of tactile intimacy. *Journal of Nonverbal Behavior, 13*(2), 83–96.

Deschamps, C. (2008). Visual scripts and power struggles: Bisexuality and visibility. *Journal of Bisexuality, 8*(1-2), 131–139.

Diamond, L. M. (2000). Passionate friendships among adolescent sexual-minority women. *Journal of Research on Adolescence, 10*(2), 191–209.

Diamond, L. M. (2003). What does sexual orientation orient? A biobehavioral model distinguishing romantic love and sexual desire. *Psychological Review, 110*(1), 173.

Diamond, L. M. (2008). Female bisexuality from adolescence to adulthood: Results from a 10-year longitudinal study. *Developmental Psychology, 44*(1), 5.

Diamond, L. M. (2009). *Sexual fluidity: Understanding women's love and desire*. USA: Harvard University Press.

Diamond, L. M., & Wallen, K. (2011). Sexual minority women's sexual motivation around the time of ovulation. *Archives of Sexual Behavior, 40*(2), 237–246.

Doan, L., Loehr, A., & Miller, L. R. (2014). Formal rights and informal privileges for same-sex couples: Evidence from a national survey experiment. *American Sociological Review, 79*, 1172–1195.

Dodge, B., Sandfort, T. G., & Firestein, B. (2007). *A review of mental health research on bisexual individuals when compared to homosexual and heterosexual individuals* (pp. 28–51). Becoming visible: Counseling bisexuals across the lifespan.

Dube, E. M. (2000). The role of sexual behavior in the identification process of gay and bisexual males. *The Journal of Sex Research, 37*(2), 123–132.

Dworkin, S. L. (2012). Sample size policy for qualitative studies using in-depth interviews. *Archives of Sexual Behavior, 41*(6), 1319–1320.

Dyer, R. (1997). *White: Essays on race and culture*. London: Routledge.

Edley, N., & Wetherell, M. (1995). *Men in perspective*. London: Pearson Education.

Elia, J. P. (2014). Bisexuality in education: Exploring the experiences, resourcing, and representations of bisexual students, bisexual parents, and educators in educational systems—A discussion. *Journal of Bisexuality, 14*(1), 146–150.

Eliason, M. J. (1997). The prevalence and nature of biphobia in heterosexual undergraduate students. *Archives of Sexual Behavior, 26*(3), 317–326.

Engle, M. J., McFalls, J. A., Gallagher, B. J., & Curtis, K. (2006). The attitudes of American sociologists toward causal theories of male homosexuality. *The American Sociologist, 37*(1), 68–76.

Epstein, B. J. (2014). "The case of the missing bisexuals": Bisexuality in books for young readers. *Journal of Bisexuality, 14*(1), 110–125.

Epstein, D., & Johnson, R. (1998). *Schooling sexualities*. Buckingham: Open University Press.

Epstein, D. (1997). Boyz' own stories: Masculinities and sexualities in schools [1]. *Gender and Education, 9*(1), 105–116.

Epstein, D., & Johnson, R. (1994). On the straight and narrow: The heterosexual presumption, homophobias and schools. *Challenging lesbian and gay inequalities in education*, 197–230.

Epstein, R., McKinney, P., Fox, S., & Garcia, C. (2012). Support for a fluid-continuum model of sexual orientation: A large-scale Internet study. *Journal of Homosexuality, 59*(10), 1356–1381.

Esterberg, K. G. (1994). Being a lesbian and being in love: Constructing identity through relationships. *Journal of Gay & Lesbian Social Services, 1*(2), 57–82.

Esterline, K. M., & Galupo, M. P. (2013). "Drunken curiosity" and "Gay chicken": Gender differences in same-sex performativity. *Journal of Bisexuality, 13*(1), 106–121.

Evans, N. J., & Broido, E. M. (1999). Coming out in college residence halls: Negotiation, meaning making, challenges, supports. *Journal of College Student Development, 40*(6), 658–668.

Fahs, B. (2009). Compulsory bisexuality? The challenges of modern sexual fluidity. *Journal of Bisexuality, 9*(3–4), 431–449.

Fallowfield, J. L., Hale, B. J., & Wilkinson, D. M. (2005). *Using statistics in sport and exercise science research*. Punjab: Lotus Pub.

Fausto-Sterling, A. (1993). The five sexes. *The Sciences, 33*(2), 20–24.

Fausto-Sterling, A. (2000). *Sexing the body*. New York: Basic Books.

Fazio, R. H., & Olson, M. A. (2003). Implicit measures in social cognition research: Their meaning and use. *Annual Review of Psychology, 54*, 297–327.

Feingold, A. (1992). Good-looking people are not what we think. *Psychological Bulletin, 111*(2), 304.

Firestein, B. A. (Ed.). (2007). *Becoming visible: Counseling bisexuals across the lifespan*. USA: Columbia University Press.

Fisher, H. (2000). Lust, attraction, attachment: Biology and evolution of the three primary emotion systems for mating, reproduction, and parenting. *Journal of Sex Education and Therapy, 25*(1), 96–104.

Flanders, C. E., & Hatfield, E. (2012). Social perception of bisexuality. *Psychology & Sexuality*, (ahead-of-print), 1–15.

Flowers, P., & Buston, K. (2001). "I was terrified of being different": Exploring gay men's accounts of growing-up in a heterosexist society. *Journal of Adolescence, 24*(1), 51–65.

Floyd, K. (2000). Affectionate same-sex touch: The influence of homophobia on observers' perceptions. *The Journal of Social Psychology, 140*(6), 774–788.

Fox, R. C. (1991). *Bisexuality and sexual orientation self-disclosure*. USA: California Institute of Integral Studies.

Frank, D. J., Camp, B. J., & Boutcher, S. A. (2010). Worldwide trends in the criminal regulation of sex, 1945 to 2005. *American Sociological Review, 75*(6), 867–893.

Frank, E. (2014). Groomers and consumers: The meaning of male body depilation to a modern masculinity body project. *Men and Masculinities*. doi:10.1177/1097184X14539509

Frederick, D. A., & Haselton, M. G. (2007). Why is muscularity sexy? Tests of the fitness indicator hypothesis. *Personality and Social Psychology Bulletin., 33*(8), 1167–1183.

Frederick, D. A., Fessler, D. M., & Haselton, M. G. (2005). Do representations of male muscularity differ in men's and women's magazines? *Body Image, 2*(1), 81–86.

Freud, S. (1905) (1953). Three Essays on the Theory of Sexuality. In *The standard edition of the complete psychological works of sigmund freud* (Vol. 7, pp. 123–245). London: Hogarth.

Galupo, M. P. (2007). Friendship patterns of sexual minority individuals in adulthood. *Journal of Social and Personal Relationships, 24*(1), 139–151.

Galupo, M. P., Mitchell, R. C., Grynkiewicz, A. L., & Davis, K. S. (2014). Sexual minority reflections on the Kinsey scale and the Klein sexual orientation grid: Conceptualization and measurement. *Journal of Bisexuality, Advanced online publication.* doi:10.1080/15299716. 2014.92955

Gangestad, S. W., & Simpson, J. A. (2000). The evolution of human mating: Trade-offs and strategic pluralism. *Behavioral and Brain Sciences, 23*, 573–644.

Gangestad, S. W., Bailey, J. M., & Martin, N. G. (2000). Taxometric analyses of sexual orientation and gender identity. *Journal of Personality and Social Psychology, 78*(6), 1109.

Garber, M. B. (1995). *Vice versa: Bisexuality and the eroticism of everyday life.* USA: Simon & Schuster.

Gates, G., & Newport, F. (2013). *LGBT percentage highest in D.C., lowest in North Dakota.* Available at: http://www.gallup.com/poll/160517/lgbt-percentage-highest-lowest-north-dakota.aspx

Gates, G. J. (2011). *How many people are lesbian, gay, bisexual and transgender?* Williams Institute: UCLA.

Gear, S., & Ngubeni, K. (2003). Your brother, my wife: Sex and gender behind bars. *SA Crime Quarterly, 4*, 11–16.

George, S. (1993). *Women and bisexuality.* London: Scarlet Press.

Gerritsen, J., Van Der Made, F., Bloemers, J., Van Ham, D., Kleiverda, G., Everaerd, W., et al. (2009). The clitoral photoplethysmograph: A new way of assessing genital arousal in women. *The Journal of Sexual Medicine, 6*(6), 1678–1687.

Ghaill, M. A. (1994). *The making of men: Masculinities, sexualities and schooling.* Open University Press.

Ghaziani, A. (2014). *There goes the gayborhood?* USA: Princeton University Press.

Giddens, A. (1992). *The transformation of intimacy: Sexuality, love and intimacy in modern societies.* Cambridge: Polity.

Glaser, B., & Strauss, A. (1967). *The discovery grounded theory.* Chicago: Aldin.

Gonsiorek, J. C., Sell, R. L., & Weinrich, J. D. (1995). Definition and measurement of sexual orientation. *Suicide and Life-Threatening Behavior, 25*(s1), 40–51.

Gorman-Murray, A. (2008). Queering the family home: narratives from gay, lesbian and bisexual youth coming out in supportive family homes in Australia. *Gender, Place and Culture, 15*(1), 31–44.

Gorman, B. K., Denney, J. T., Dowdy, H., & Medeiros, R. A. (2015). A new piece of the puzzle: Sexual orientation, gender, and physical health status. *Demography 52*(4), 1–26.

Gottzén, L., & Kremer-Sadlik, T. (2012). Fatherhood and youth sports a balancing act between care and expectations. *Gender & Society, 26*(4), 639–664.

Gough, B., Hall, M., & Seymour-Smith, S. (2014). Straight guys do wear make-up: Contemporary masculinities and investment in appearance. *Debating Modern Masculinities: Change, Continuity, Crisis?* 106.

Gray, M. L. (2009). *Out in the country: Youth, media, and queer visibility in rural America.* New York: NYU Press.

Green, H. B., Payne, N. R., & Green, J. (2011). Working bi: Preliminary findings from a survey on workplace experiences of bisexual people. *Journal of Bisexuality, 11*(2-3), 300–316.

Green, I. A. (2007). Queer theory and sociology: Locating the subject and the self in sexuality studies. *Sociological Theory, 25*(1), 26–45.

Greenberg, D. F. (1988). *The construction of homosexuality.* Chicago: University of Chicago Press.

Griffin, P. (1998). *Strong women, deep closets: Lesbians and homophobia in sport.* USA: Human Kinetics Publishers.

Grov, C., Bimbi, D. S., NaniN, J. E., & Parsons, J. T. (2006). Race, ethnicity, gender, and generational factors associated with the coming-out process among gay, lesbian, and bisexual individuals. *Journal of Sex Research, 43*(2), 115–121.

Guittar, N. A. (2013). The queer apologetic: Explaining the use of bisexuality as a transitionaliIdentity. *Journal of Bisexuality, 13*(2), 166–190.
Guittar, N. A. (2014). *Coming out: The new dynamics*. Boulder Co: First Forum Press.
Hall, L. A. (2013). *Sex, gender and social change in Britain since 1880*. Basingstoke: Palgrave MacMillan.
Halperin, D. M. (2012). *How to be Gay*. USA: Harvard University Press.
Haltom, T., & Worthen, M. (2014). Male ballet dancers and their performances of heteromasculinity. *Journal of College Student Development, 55*(8), 757–778.
Hammack, P. (2014). Introduction in A. Evans & S. Riley. *Technologies of sexiness: Sex, identity, and consumer culture*. New York: Oxford University Press.
Hammack, P. L., & Cohler, B. (2009). Narrative engagement and stories of sexual identity. *The story of sexual identity: Narrative perspectives on the gay and lesbian life course*, 1.
Harbeck, K. M. (1992). *Coming out of the classroom closet: Gay and lesbian students, teachers, and curricula*. London: Routledge.
Hargreaves, J., & Anderson, E. (Eds.). (2014). *Routledge handbook of sport, gender and sexuality*. London: Routledge.
Harris, J., & Clayton, B. (2007). The first metrosexual rugby star: Rugby union, masculinity, and celebrity in contemporary Wales. *Sociology of Sport Journal, 24*(2), 145.
Harris, M. (1964). *Patterns of race in the Americas*. New York: Walker.
Harris, W. C. (2006). "In my day it used to be called a limp wrist": Flip-floppers, nelly boys, and homophobic rhetoric in the 2004 US presidential campaign. *The Journal of American Culture, 29*(3), 278–295.
Hartman, J. E. (2011). Finding a needle in a haystack: Methods for sampling in the bisexual community. *Journal of Bisexuality, 11*(1), 64–74.
Hartman-Linck, J. E. (2014). Keeping bisexuality alive: Maintaining bisexual visibility in monogamous relationships. *Journal of Bisexuality*, (just-accepted), 14(2), 177–193.
Hatzenbuehler, M. L. (2009). How does sexual minority stigma "get under the skin"? A psychological mediation framework. *Psychological Bulletin, 135*(5), 707.
Hayfield, N., Clarke, V., Halliwell, E., & Malson, H. (2013). Visible lesbians and invisible bisexuals: Appearance and visual identities among bisexual women. *Women's Studies International Forum* 40 (Sep-Oct), 172–182.
Hearn, J. (2010). Reflecting on men and social policy: Contemporary critical debates and implications for social policy. *Critical Social Policy, 30*(2), 165–188.
Hemmings, C. (2002). *Bisexual spaces: A geography of sexuality and gender*. UK: Psychology Press.
Herdt, G. (1981). *Guardians of the flutes: Idioms of masculinity*. Nova York: McGraw Hill.
Herdt, G. (2001). Social change, sexual diversity, and tolerance for bisexuality in the United States. *Lesbian, gay, and bisexual identities and youth: Psychological perspectives*, 267–283.
Herdt, G., & Boxer, A. M. (1993). *Children of horizons: How gay and lesbian youth are leading a new way out of the closet*. Boston: Beacon.
Herdt, G., & McClintock, M. (2000). The magical age of 10. *Archives of Sexual Behavior, 29*(6), 587–606.
Herek, G. M. (2002). Heterosexuals' attitudes toward bisexual men and women in the United States. *Journal of Sex Research, 39*(4), 264–274.
Herek, G. M. (2004). Beyond "homophobia": Thinking about sexual prejudice and stigma in the twenty-first century. *Sexuality Research & Social Policy, 1*(2), 6–24.
Herz, R. S., & Cahill, E. D. (1997). Differential use of sensory information in sexual behavior is a function of gender. *Human Nature, 8*, 275–286.
Herz, R. S., & Inzlicht, M. (2002). Sex differences in response to physical and social factors involved in human mate selection: The importance of smell for women. *Evolution and Human Behavior, 23*(5), 359–364.
Hey, V. (1997). *The company she keeps: An ethnography of girls' friendships*. London: McGraw-Hill.

References

Hubbard, K., & de Visser, R. (2014). Not just bi the bi: The relationship between essentialist beliefs and attitudes about bisexuality. *Psychology and Sexuality*. doi:10.1080/19419899.2014.987682

Hyde, J., & Jaffee, S. R. (2000). Becoming a heterosexual adult: The experiences of young women. *Journal of Social Issues, 56*(2), 283–296.

Ibson, J. (2002). *Picturing men: A century of male relationships in everyday American photography*. Washington, DC: Smithsonian Institution Press.

Israel, T., & Mohr, J. J. (2004). Attitudes toward bisexual women and men: Current research, future directions. *Journal of Bisexuality, 4*(1-2), 117–134.

Jackson, S., & Scott, S. (2010). Rehabilitating interactionism for a feminist sociology of sexuality. *Sociology, 44*(5), 811–826.

Jarvis, N. (2013). The inclusive masculinities of heterosexual men within UK gay sport clubs. *International Review for the Sociology of Sport*. doi:10.1177/1012690213482481

Jensen, K. L. (1999). *Lesbian epiphanies: Women coming out in later life*. London: Routledge.

Johnson, D. K. (2004). *The lavender scare: The cold war persecution of gays and lesbians in the federal government*. USA: University of Chicago Press.

Johnson, J. M. (2002). In-depth interviewing. *Handbook of interview research: Context and method*, 103–119.

Jones, R., & Clarke, G. (2007). The school experiences of same-sex attracted students in the 14-to 19-year-old secondary sector in England: Within and beyond the safety and tolerance framework. *Journal of Gay & Lesbian Social Services, 19*(3–4), 119–138.

Jourard, S. M. (1971). *Self-disclosure: An experimental analysis of the transparent self*. New York: Wiley.

JWT. (2013). *The state of men*. Available online: http://www.jwtintelligence.com/wp-content/uploads/2013/06/F_JWT_The-State-of-Men_Trend-Report_06.04.13.pdf

Kahn, J. G., Gurvey, J., Pollack, L. M., Binson, D., & Catania, J. A. (1997). How many HIV infections cross the bisexual bridge? An estimate from the United States. *AIDS, 11*(8), 1031–1037.

Kangasuvo, J. (2011). "There has been no phase in my life when i wasn't somehow bisexual": Comparing the experiences of finnish bisexuals in 1999 and 2010. *Journal of Bisexuality, 11* (2-3), 271–289.

Keleher, A., & Smith, E. R. (2012). Growing support for gay and lesbian equality since 1990. *Journal of Homosexuality, 59*(9), 1307–1326.

Kimmel, M. (1994). Homophobia as masculinity: Fear, shame, and silence in the con-struction of gender identity. *Theorizing Masculinities*, 119–141.

Kimmel, M. (1996). *Manhood in America: A cultural history*. New York: Free Press.

King, A. (2015). Prepare for Impact? Reflecting on knowledge exchange work to improve services for older LGBT people in times of austerity. *Social Policy and Society, 14*(1), 15–27.

King, A. (in press). Talking 'bout my generation? The decline of homophobia debate and older lesbian, gay and/or bisexual people. *Sociological Review*.

Kinnish, K. K., Strassberg, D. S., & Turner, C. W. (2005). Sex differences in the flexibility of sexual orientation: A multidimensional retrospective assessment. *Archives of Sexual Behavior, 34*(2), 173–183.

Kinsey, A. C., Pomeroy, W. B., & Martin, C. E. (1948). *Sexual behavior in the human male*. Philadelphia: Saunders.

Klein, F. (1993). *The bisexual option*. New York: Harrington Park Press.

Klesse, C. (2005). Bisexual women, non-monogamy and differentialist anti-promiscuity discourses. *Sexualities, 8*(4), 445–464.

Klesse, C. (2006). Polyamory and its 'others': Contesting the terms of non-monogamy. *Sexualities, 9*(5), 565–583.

Klesse, C. (2011). Shady characters, untrustworthy partners, and promiscuous sluts: Creating bisexual intimacies in the face of heteronormativity and biphobia. *Journal of Bisexuality, 11* (2-3), 227–244.

Komarovsky, M. (1974). Patterns of self-disclosure of male undergraduates. *Journal of Marriage and the Family*, 677–686.

Kong, T. S., Mahoney, D., & Plummer, K. (2002). Queering the interview. *Handbook of interview methods sage* (pp. 239–258). CA: Thousand Oaks.

Kontula, O., & Haavio-Mannila, E. (2004). Renaissance of romanticism in the era of increasing individualism. In Duncombe, K. Harrison, G. Allan, & D. Marsden (Eds.), *The state of affairs, explorations in infidelity and commitment* (pp. 79–102). Marwah, NJ: Lawrence Erlbaum.

Kreager, D. A., & Staff, J. (2009). The sexual double standard and adolescent peer acceptance. *Social Psychology Quarterly, 72*(2), 143–164.

Kunzel, R. G. (2002). Situating sex: Prison sexual culture in the mid-twentieth-century United States. *GLQ: A Journal of Lesbian and Gay Studies*, 8(3), 253–270.

Kuper, L. E., Nussbaum, R., & Mustanski, B. (2012). Exploring the diversity of gender and sexual orientation identities in an online sample of transgender individuals. *Journal of Sex Research, 49*(2–3), 244–254.

Lalor, T., & Rendle-Short, J. (2007). 'That's so gay': A contemporary use of gay in Australian English. *Australian Journal of Linguistics, 27*(2), 147–173.

Lancaster, R. N. (1986). Comment on arguelles and rich's "homosexuality, homophobia, and revolution: Notes toward an understanding of the cuban lesbian and gay male experience, Part II". *Signs*, 188–192.

Lancaster, R. N. (1988). Subject honor and object shame: The construction of male homosexuality and stigma in Nicaragua. *Ethnology*, 111–125.

Langer, G. (2013). *ABC. Washington post poll: Gay marriage: Poll tracks dramatic rise in support for gay marriage*. Available online: http://abcnews.go.com/blogs/politics/2013/03/poll-tracks-dramatic-rise-in-support-for-gay-marriage/

Lalumière, M. L. (2015). The lability of pedophilic interests as measured by phallometry. *Archives of Sexual Behavior, 44*(1), 255–258.

LaSala, M. C. (2005). Monogamy of the heart: Extradyadic sex and gay male couples. *Journal of Gay & Lesbian Social Services, 17*(3), 1–24.

Laumann, E. O., Gagnon, J.H., Michael, R.T. & Michaels, S. (1994). *The social organization of sexuality: Sexual practices in the United States*. USA: University of Chicago Press.

LeVay, S. (2011). *Gay, straight, and the reason why: The science of sexual orientation*. UK: Oxford University Press.

Levy, A. (2006). *Female chauvinist pigs: Women and the rise of raunch culture*. USA: Simon & Schuster.

Lewis, R. A. (1984). Emotional intimacy among men. *The gender gap in psychotherapy* (pp. 181–193). US: Springer.

Lippa, R. A. (2005). *Gender, nature, and nurture*. London: Routledge.

Lippa, R. A. (2007). The preferred traits of mates in a cross-national study of heterosexual and homosexual men and women: An examination of biological and cultural influences. *Archives of Sexual Behavior, 36*, 193–208.

Lippa, R. A. (2008). Sex differences and sexual orientation differences in personality: Findings from the BBC internet survey. *Archives of Sexual Behavior, 37*(1), 173–187.

Lippa, R. A. (2013). Men and women with bisexual identities show bisexual patterns of sexual attraction to male and female "swimsuit models". *Archives of sexual behavior, 42*(2), 187–196.

Lippa, R. A., Patterson, T. M., & Marelich, W. D. (2010). Looking at and longing for male and female "swimsuit models" men are much more category specific than women. *Social Psychological and Personality Science, 1*(3), 238–245.

Lipman-Blumen, J. (1976). Toward a homosocial theory of sex roles: An explanation of the sex segregation of social institutions. *Signs, 1*(3), 15–31.

Loftus, J. (2001). America's liberalization in attitudes toward homosexuality, 1973 to 1998. *American Sociological Review*, 762–782.

Lottes, I. L., & Grollman, E. A. (2010). Conceptualization and assessment of homonegativity. *International Journal of Sexual Health, 22*(4), 219–233.

Lovelock, J. M. (2014). Using the Klein sexual orientation grid in sociological studies. *Journal of Bisexuality*, (just-accepted), 14(3-4), 457-467.

Lowenberg, B. J., & Bogin, R. (1976). *Black women in nineteenth century American life.* USA: University Pennsylvania Press

Lübke, K. T., & Pause, B. M. (2015). Always follow your nose: The functional significance of social chemosignals in human reproduction and survival. *Hormones and Behavior*, 68, 134–144

Lugg, C. A. (1998). The religious right and public education: The paranoid politics of homophobia. *Educational Policy*, 12(3), 267–283.

Luttrell, W. (2012). Making boys' careworlds visible. *Thymos: Journal of Boyhood Studies*, 6(2), 186–202.

Magrath, R., Anderson, E., & Roberts, S. (2013). On the door-step of equality: Attitudes toward gay athletes among academy-level footballers. *International Review for the Sociology of Sport.* Advanced online publication 10.1177/1012690213495747

Mark, K., Rosenkrantz, D., & Kerner, I. (2014). "Bi"ing into monogamy: Attitudes toward monogamy in a sample of bisexual-identified adults. *Psychology of Sexual Orientation and Gender Diversity*, 1(3), 263.

Martikainen, P., & Valkonen, T. (1996). Mortality after death of spouse in relation to duration of bereavement in Finland. *Journal of Epidemiology and Community Health*, 50(3), 264–268.

Martins, Y., Preti, G., Crabtree, C. R., Runyan, T., Vainius, A. A., & Wysocki, C. J. (2005). Preference for human body odors is influenced by gender and sexual orientation. *Psychological Science*, 16(9), 694–701.

Martos, A. J., Nezhad, S., & Meyer, I. H. (2015). *Variations in sexual identity milestones among lesbians, gay men, and bisexuals.* DOI: Sexuailty Research and Social Policy, Advanced online publication. doi:10.1007/s13178-014-0167-4

Masters, W.H. & Johnson, V.E. (1979). *Homosexuality in perspective.* USA: Littlebrown & Co.

Matsuda, W. T., Rouse, S. V., & Miller-Perrin, C. L. (2014). Validation of the attitudes regarding bisexuality scale: Correlations with ratings of a positive media image of bisexual men and women. *Journal of Bisexuality*, (just-accepted), 14(2), 265–276.

McAndrew, F. T., & Milenkovic, M. A. (2002). Of tabloids and family secrets: The evolutionary psychology of gossip. *Journal of Applied Social Psychology*, 32(5), 1064–1082.

McCall, L. (2005). The complexity of intersectionality. *Signs*, 30(3), 1771–1800.

McCormack, M. (2011a). Mapping the terrain of homosexually-themed language. *Journal of Homosexuality*, 58(5), 664–679.

McCormack, M. (2011b). 'Hierarchy without hegemony: Locating boys in an inclusive school setting. *Sociological Perspectives*, 54(1), 83–101.

McCormack, M. (2012a). *The declining significance of homophobia: How teenage boys are redefining masculinity and heterosexuality.* New York: Oxford University Press.

McCormack, M. (2012b). The positive experiences of openly gay, lesbian, bisexual and transgendered students in a Christian sixth form college. *Sociological Research Online*, 17(3), 5.

McCormack, M. (2013). Friendship dynamics and popularity hierarchies among inclusive men. *Revista Canaria de Estudios Ingleses*, 66, 37–48.

McCormack, M. (2014a). Innovative sampling and participant recruitment in sexuality research. *Journal of Social and Personal Relationships*, 31(4), 475–481.

McCormack, M. (2014b). The intersection of youth masculinities, decreasing homophobia and class: an ethnography. *The British Journal of Sociology*, 65(1), 130–149.

McCormack, M., & Anderson, E. (2010a). 'It's just not acceptable any more': The erosion of homophobia and the softening of masculinity at an English sixth form. *Sociology*, 44(5), 843–859.

McCormack, M., & Anderson, E. (2010b). The re-production of homosexually-themed discourse in educationally-based organised sport. *Culture, Health & Sexuality*, 12(8), 913–927

McCormack, M., & Anderson, E. (2014a). The influence of declining homophobia on men's gender in the United States: An argument for the study of homohysteria. *Sex Roles*. *71*(3–4), 109–120

McCormack, M., & Anderson, E. (2014b). Homohysteria: Definitions, context and intersectionality. *Sex Roles*, *71*(3–4), 152–158

McCormack, M., Wignall, L. & Morris, M. (in press). Gay guys using gay discourse: Friendship, shared values and the intent-context-effect matrix. *British Journal of Sociology*.

McCreary, D. R. (1994). The male role and avoiding femininity. *Sex Roles, 31*(9-10), 517–531.

McLean, K. (2004). Negotiating (non) monogamy: Bisexuality and intimate relationships. *Journal of Bisexuality, 4*(1–2), 83–97.

McLean, K. (2007). Hiding in the closet? Bisexuals, coming out and the disclosure imperative. *Journal of Sociology, 43*(2), 151–166.

McLean, K. (2008). Inside, outside, nowhere: Bisexual men and women in the gay and lesbian community. *Journal of Bisexuality, 8*(1–2), 63–80.

McNair, B. (2002). *Striptease culture*. London: Routledge.

McNair, B. (2013). *Porno? Chic!*. London: Routledge.

Meyer, I. H. (2003). Prejudice, social stress, and mental health in lesbian, gay, and bisexual populations: Conceptual issues and research evidence. *Psychological Bulletin, 129*(5), 674.

Meyer, I. H., & Wilson, P. A. (2009). Sampling lesbian, gay, and bisexual populations. *Journal of Counseling Psychology, 56*(1), 23.

Miceli, M. (2005). *Standing out, standing together*. New York: Routledge.

Mock, S. E., & Eibach, R. P. (2012). Stability and change in sexual orientation identity over a 10-year period in adulthood. *Archives of Sexual Behavior, 41*(3), 641–648.

Mohr, J. J., & Rochlen, A. B. (1999). Measuring attitudes regarding bisexuality in lesbian, gay male, and heterosexual populations. *Journal of Counseling Psychology, 46*(3), 353.

Mohr, J. J., Israel, T., & Sedlacek, W. E. (2001). Counselors' attitudes regarding bisexuality as predictors of counselors' clinical responses: An analogue study of a female bisexual client. *Journal of Counseling Psychology, 48*(2), 212.

Møller, A. P., & Alatalo, R. V. (1999). Good genes effects in sexual selection. *Proceedings of the Royal Society of London Biologial Sciences, 266*, 85–91.

Monro, S. (2015). *Bisexuality: Identities, politics and theories*. Basingstoke: Palgrave MacMillan.

Morin, S. F., & Garfinkle, E. M. (1978). Male homophobia. *Journal of Social Issues, 34*(1), 29–47.

Morris, M., McCormack, M., & Anderson, E. (2014). The changing experiences of bisexual male adolescents. *Gender and Education, 26*(4), 397–413.

Moses, R. (2013). Millenial men aren't what they used to be. *AdWeek*. Available online http://www.adweek.com/news/advertising-branding/millennial-guys-are-turning-makeup-150313

Mosher, W. D., Chandra, A., & Jones, J. (2005). *Sexual behavior and selected health measures: Men and women 15-44 years of age, United States, 2002*. Atlanta, GA: US Department of Health and Human Services, Centers for Disease Control and Prevention, National Center for Health Statistics.

Moss, A. R. (2012). Alternative families, alternative lives: Married women *doing* bisexuality. *Journal of GLBT Family Studies, 8*(5), 405–427.

Mulick, P. S., & Wright, L. W, Jr. (2002). Examining the existence of biphobia in the heterosexual and homosexual populations. *Journal of Bisexuality, 2*(4), 45–64.

Müller, K., Curry, S., Ranger, R., Briken, P., Bradford, J., & Fedoroff, J. P. (2014). Changes in sexual arousal as measured by penile plethysmography in men with pedophilic sexual interest. *The Journal of Sexual Medicine, 11*(5), 1221–1229.

Muòoz-Laboy, M. A. (2004). Beyond 'MSM': Sexual desire among bisexually-active Latino men in New York City. *Sexualities, 7*(1), 55–80.

Nardi, P. M. (1999). *Gay men's friendships: Invincible communities*. USA: University of Chicago Press.

Nardi, P. M., Sanders, D., & Marmor, J. (1994). *Growing up before Stonewall: Life stories of some gay men*. London: Routledge.

References

Negy, C., & Eisenman, R. (2005). A comparison of African American and White college students' affective and attitudinal reactions to lesbian, gay, and bisexual individuals: An exploratory study. *Journal of Sex Research, 42*(4), 291–298.

Netzley, S. B. (2010). Visibility that demystifies: Gays, gender, and sex on television. *Journal of Homosexuality, 57*(8), 968–986.

Norton, R. (1992). *Mother clap's molly house: The gay subculture in England, 1700–1830*. London: GMP.

Norton, R. (2010). *F-ck Foucault: How eighteenth-century homosexual history validates the essentialist model*. Paper presented at Homosexualities: From Antiquity to the Present. USA: UCLA

Nussbaum, M. (2010). *Not for profit. Why democracy needs the humanities*. NJ: Princeton University Press.

Page, B., & Shapiro, R.Y. (1992). *The rational public: Fifty years of opinion trends*. USA: University of Chicago Press.

Page, E. (2007). *Bisexual womens' and mens' experiences of psychotherapy* (pp. 52–71). Becoming invisible: Counseling bisexuals across the lifespan.

Page, E. H. (2004). Mental health services experiences of bisexual women and bisexual men: An empirical study. *Journal of Bisexuality, 4*(1-2), 137–160.

Pahl, R. (1995). *After success: Fin-de-siecle anxiety and identity*. Cambridge: Polity Press.

Pallotta-Chiarolli, M. (2014). "New rules, no rules, old rules or our rules": Women designing mixed-orientaiton marriages with bisexual men. In M. Pallott-Chiarolli & B. Pease (Eds.), *The politics of recognition and social justice*. London: Routledge.

Pallotta-Chiarolli, M. (2015). The problem is that he's a man, not that he's bisexual": Women discussing bi-masculinities and bi-misogyny. In M. Flood & R. Howson (Eds.), *Engaging men in building gender equality*. London: Cambridge Scholars Publishing.

Pallotta-Chiarolli, M. (in press). *Women in relationships with bisexual men: Bi men by women*. New York: Lexington Books.

Paul, J. P. (1984). The bisexual identity: An idea without social recognition. *Journal of Homosexuality, 9*(2–3), 45–63.

Pearcey, M. (2005). Gay and bisexual married men's attitudes and experiences. *Journal of GLBT Family Studies, 1*(4), 21–42.

Pennington, S. (2009). Bisexuals "doing gender" in romantic relationships. *Journal of Bisexuality, 9*(1), 33–69.

Penton-Voak, I. S., Little, A. C., Jones, B. C., Burt, D. M., & Perrett, D. I. (2003). Measures of human female condition predict preferences for sexually dimorphic characteristics in men's faces. *Journal of Comparative Psychology, 117*, 264–271.

Peplau, L. A., & Garnets, L. D. (2000). A new paradigm for understanding women's sexuality and sexual orientation. *Journal of Social Issues, 56*(2), 330–350.

Perrett, D. I., Burt, D. M., Penton-Voak, I. S., Lee, K. J., Rowland, D. A., & Edwards, R. (1999). Symmetry and human facial attractiveness. *Evolution and Human Behavior, 20*(5), 295–307.

Pew. (2013a). *Growing support for gay marriage: Changed minds and changing demographics*. Washington, DC: Pew Research Center.

Pew. (2013b). *A survey of LGBT Americans: Attitudes, experiences and values in changing times*. Available online: http://www.pewsocialtrends.org/2013/06/13/a-survey-of-lgbt-americans/

Piontek, T. (2006). *Queering gay and lesbian studies*. USA: University of Illinois Press.

Pitts, M., & Rahman, Q. (2001). Which behaviors constitute "having sex" among university students in the UK? *Archives of Sexual Behavior, 30*(2), 169–176.

Pleck, J. H. (1975). Masculinity—Femininity. *Sex Roles, 1*(2), 161–178.

Plummer, D. (1999). *One of the boys: Masculinity, homophobia, and modern manhood*. New York: Harrington Park Press.

Plummer, D. (2014). The ebb and flow of homophobia: A gender taboo theory. *Sex Roles, 71*(3–4), 126–136.

Plummer, K. (1995). *Telling sexual stories*. Lonon: Routledge.

Plummer, K. (2010). Generational sexualities, subterranean traditions, and the hauntings of the sexual world: Some preliminary remarks. *Symbolic Interaction, 33*(2), 163–190.

Pollack, W. (1999). *Real boys: Rescuing our sons from the myths of boyhood*. UK: Macmillan.

Pompili, M., Lester, D., Forte, A., Seretti, M. E., Erbuto, D., Lamis, D. A., et al. (2014). Bisexuality and suicide: A systematic review of the current literature. *The Journal of Sexual Medicine*. Advanced online publication, 11(8), 1903–1913.

Popkins, N. C. (1998). *Natural characteristics that influence environment: How physical appearance affects personality*. Available online: http://www.personalityresearch.org/papers/popkins2.html

Pronger, B. (1992). *The arena of masculinity: Sports, homosexuality, and the meaning of sex*. USA: Macmillan.

Pryor, J., DeAngelo, L., Blake, L., Hurtado, S., & Tran, S. (2011). *The American freshman: National norms fall 2011*. Los Angeles: HERI, UCLA.

Putnam, R. D. (2000). *Bowling alone: The collapse and revival of American community*. USA: Simon & Schuster.

Ramazanoglu, C. (2002). *Feminist methodology: Challenges and choices*. London: Sage.

Rhodes, G., Yoshikawa, S., Clark, A., Lee, K., McKay, R., & Akamatsu, S. (2001). Attractiveness of facial averageness and symmetry in non-Western populations: In search of biologically based standards of beauty. *Perception, 30*(5), 611–625.

Rich, A. (1980). Compulsory heterosexuality and lesbian existence. *Signs*, 631–660.

Rieger, G., & Savin-Williams, R. C. (2012). The eyes have it: Sex and sexual orientation differences in pupil dilation patterns. *PloS one, 7*(8), e40256.

Rieger, G., Chivers, M. L., & Bailey, J. M. (2005). Sexual arousal patterns of bisexual men. *Psychological science, 16*(8), 579–584.

Rieger, G., Rosenthal, A. M., Cash, B. M., Linsenmeier, J. A., Bailey, J. M., & Savin-Williams, R. C. (2013). Male bisexual arousal: A matter of curiosity? *Biological Psychology, 94*(3), 479–489.

Riley, B. H. (2010). GLB adolescent's "Coming out". *Journal of Child and Adolescent Psychiatric Nursing, 23*(1), 3–10.

Rivers, I. (2001). Retrospective reports of school bullying: Stability of recall and its implications for research. *British Journal of Developmental Psychology, 19*(1), 129–141.

Rivers, I. (2011). *Homophobic bullying: Research and theoretical perspectives*. UK: Oxford University Press.

Roberts, S. (2013). Boys will be boys…won't they? Change and continuities in contemporary young working-class masculinities. *Sociology, 47*(4), 671–686.

Roberts, S. (Ed.). (2014). *Debating modern masculinities: Change, continuity, crisis?* Basingstoke: Palgrave Macmillan.

Robinson, J. P., & Espelage, D. L. (2011). Inequities in educational and psychological outcomes between LGBTQ and straight students in middle and high school. *Educational Researcher, 40*(7), 315–330.

Rosenbluth, S. (1997). Is sexual orientation a matter of choice? *Psychology of Women Quarterly, 21*(4), 595–610.

Rosenthal, A. M., Sylva, D., Safron, A., & Michael Bailey, J.(2012). The male bisexuality debate revisited: Some bisexual men have bisexual arousal patterns. *Archives of Sexual Behavior*, 41(1), 135–147.

Rostosky, S. S., Riggle, E. D., Pascale-Hague, D., & McCants, L. E. (2010). The positive aspects of a bisexual self-identification. *Psychology & Sexuality, 1*(2), 131–144.

Rubin, G. (2012). *Deviations: A Gayle rubin reader*. Durham: Duke University Press.

Rullo, J. E., Strassberg, D. S. & Miner, M. H. (2014). Gender-specificity in sexual interest in bisexual men and women. *Archives of Sexual Behavior*, iFirst.

Rumens, N. (2013). *Queer company: the role and meaning of friendship in gay men's work lives*. Farnham: Ashgate.

References

Russel, S. T., & Seif, H. (2010). Bisexual female adolescents: A critical analysis of past research, and results from a national survey. *Journal of Bisexuality, 10*(4), 492–509.

Rust, P. C. (1992). The politics of sexual identity: Sexual attraction and behavior among lesbian and bisexual women. *Social Problems*, 366–386.

Rust, P. C. (2000). Bisexuality: A contemporary paradox for women. *Journal of Social Issues, 56*(2), 205–221.

Rust, P. C. (2002). Bisexuality: The state of the union. *Annual Review of Sex Research, 13*(1), 180–240.

Rust, P. C. (2009). Bisexuality in a house of mirrors. In B.J. Cohler & P. Hammack (Eds) *The Story of Sexual Identity* (pp. 107–130).

Sanders, S. A., & Reinisch, J. M. (1999). Would you say you had sex if..? *Jama, 281*(3), 275–277.

Sanderson, S. K. (2001). Explaining monogamy and polygyny in human societies: Comment on Kanazawa and Still. *Social Forces, 80*(1), 329–335.

Savin-Williams, R. C. (1998). *And then I became gay: Young men's stories*. London: Routledge.

Savin-Williams, R. C. (2001a). Suicide attempts among sexual-minority youths: Population and measurement issues. *Journal of Consulting and Clinical Psychology, 69*(6), 983–991

Savin-Williams, R. C. (2001b). A critique of research on sexual-minority youths. *Journal of Adolescence, 24*(1), 5–13

Savin-Williams, R. C. (2005). *The new gay teenager*. USA: Harvard University Press.

Savin-Williams, R. C. (2014). An exploratory study of the categorical versus spectrum nature of sexual orientation. *The Journal of Sex Research, 51*(4), 446–453.

Savin-Williams, R. C., & Joyner, K. (2014). The dubious assessment of gay, lesbian, and bisexual adolescents of Add Health. *Archives of Sexual Behavior, 43*(3), 413–422.

Savin-Williams, R. C., & McCormack, M. (under review). An exploratory study of exclusively gay, primarily gay, and mostly gay young men. *Archives of Sexual Behavior*

Savin-Williams, R. C., & Vrangalova, Z. (2013). Mostly heterosexual as a distinct sexual orientation group: A systematic review of the empirical evidence. *Developmental Review, 33*(1), 58–88.

Savin-Williams, R. C., Joyner, K., & Rieger, G. (2012). Prevalence and stability of self-reported sexual orientation identity during young adulthood. *Archives of Sexual Behavior, 41*(1), 103–110.

Savin-Williams, R. C., Rieger, G., & Rosenthal, A. M. (2013). Physiological evidence for a mostly heterosexual orientation among men. *Archives of Sexual Behavior, 42*(5), 697–699.

Schmitt, D. P. (2004). Patterns and universals of mate poaching across 53 nations: The effects of sex, culture, and personality on romantically attracting another person's partner. *Journal of Personality and Social Psychology, 86*(4), 560.

Schmookler, T., & Bursik, K. (2007). The value of monogamy in emerging adulthood: A gendered perspective. *Journal of Social and Personal Relationships, 24*(6), 819–835.

Schrock, D., & Schwalbe, M. (2009). Men, masculinity, and manhood acts. *Annual Review of Sociology, 35*, 277–295.

Schwartz, P. (1995). The Science of sexuality still needs social science. The Scientist. Available online: http://www.the-scientist.com/?articles.view/articleNo/17270/title/The-Science-Of-Sexuality-Still-Needs-Social-Science/

Scoats, R. (in press) Inclusive masculinity and Facebook photographs amongst early emerging adults at a British University. *Journal of Adolescent Research*.

Scoats, R., Joseph, L. and Anderson, E. (in press). "I don't mind watching him cum": Heterosexual men, threesomes and the erosion of the one-time rule of homosexuality. *Sexualities*.

Sears, J. T. (1991). *Growing up gay in the South: Race, gender, and journeys of the spirit*. New York: Harrington Park Press.

Sears, J. T. (2014). Becoming and being: Bisexuality and the search for self. *Journal of Bisexuality, 14*(1), 3–6.

Seidman, S. (2002). *Beyond the closet: The transformation of gay and lesbian life*. UK: Psychology Press.

Sell, R. L. (1997). Defining and measuring sexual orientation: A review. *Archives of Sexual Behavior, 26*(6), 643–658.
Semlyen, J., Killaspy, H., Nazareth, I., & Osborn, D. (2007). *A systematic review of research on counselling and psychotherapy for lesbian, gay, bisexual & transgender people*. Lutterworth: British Association for Counselling & Psychotherapy.
Sheff, E. (2010). Polyamorous women, sexual subjectivity and power. *Journal of Contemporary Ethnography, 34*(3), 251–283.
Shepard, B. (2009). History, narrative, and sexual identity. In *The story of sexual identity: Narrative perspectives on the gay and lesbian life Course* (p. 23).
Sherkat, D. E., Powell-Williams, M., Maddox, G., & De Vries, K. M. (2011). Religion, politics, and support for same-sex marriage in the United States, 1988–2008. *Social Science Research, 40*(1), 167–180.
Shilts, R. (2007). *And the band played on: Politics, people, and the AIDS epidemic* (20th-Anniversary Edition). UK: Macmillan.
Slater, A., Von der Schulenberg, C., Brown, E., Badenoch, M., Butterworth, G., Parsons, S., & Samuels, C. (1998). Newborn infants prefer attractive faces. *Infant Behavior and Development., 21*, 345–354.
Smith, S. J., Axelton, A. M., & Saucier, D. A. (2009). The effects of contact on sexual prejudice: A meta-analysis. *Sex Roles, 61*(3-4), 178–191.
Smith, T. W. (2011). *Attitudes towards same-gender, sexual behavior across time and across countries*. Chicago, IL: NORC.
Smith, T. W., Son, J., & Kim, J. (2014). *Public attitudes towards homosexuality and gay rights across time and countries*. Chicago, IL: NORC.
Snowden, R. J., Wichter, J., & Gray, N. S. (2008). Implicit and explicit measurements of sexual preference in gay and heterosexual men: A comparison of priming techniques and the implicit association task. *Archives of Sexual Behavior, 37*(4), 558–565.
Snowden, R. J. McKinnon, A. & Gray, N. S. (2015). *Automatic evaluation of male and female sexual images in bisexual men: 1: The implicit association test*. Poster presentation at International Academy of Sex Research. Toronto. 12 Aug, 2015.
Spencer, C. (1995). *Homosexuality in history*. Florida: Harcourt Brace.
Spitzer, R. L. (2003). Can some gay men and lesbians change their sexual orientation? 200 participants reporting a change from homosexual to heterosexual orientation. *Archives of Sexual Behavior, 32*(5), 403–417.
Steinman, E. (2011). Revisiting the invisibility of (male) bisexuality: Grounding (queer) theory, centering bisexual absences and examining masculinities. *Journal of Bisexuality, 11*(4), 399–411.
Steinman, E. W., & Beemyn, B. G. (2014). *Bisexuality in the Lives of Men: Facts and Fictions*. UK: Routledge.
Stief, M. C., Rieger, G., & Savin-Williams, R. C. (2014). Bisexuality is associated with elevated sexual sensation seeking, sexual curiosity, and sexual excitability. *Personality and Individual Differences, 66*, 193–198.
Stokes, J., Taywaditep, K., Vanable, P., & McKirnan, D. J. (1996). Bisexual men, sexual behavior, and HIV/AIDS. *Bisexuality: The psychology and politics of an invisible minority*. Newbury Park, CA: Sage.
Storms, M. D. (1980). Theories of sexual orientation. *Journal of Personality and Social Psychology, 38*(5), 783.
Stotzer, R. L. (2009). Straight allies: Supportive attitudes toward lesbians, gay men, and bisexuals in a college sample. *Sex Roles, 60*(1-2), 67–80.
Szalacha, L. A. (2003). Safer sexual diversity climates: Lessons learned from an evaluation of Massachusetts safe schools program for gay and lesbian students. *American Journal of Education, 110*(1), 58–88.
Thomas, M., Bloor, M., & Frankland, J. (2007). The process of sample recruitment: An ethnostatistical perspective. *Qualitative Research, 7*(4), 429–446.

References

Thompson, E. M. (2006). Girl friend or girlfriend? Same-sex friendship and bisexual images as a context for flexible sexual identity among young women. *Journal of Bisexuality, 6*(3), 47–67.

Thompson, E. M., & Morgan, E. M. (2008). "Mostly straight" young women: Variations in sexual behavior and identity development. *Developmental Psychology, 44*(1), 15.

Thornhill, R., & Gangestad, S. W. (1998). Facial attractiveness. *Trends in Cognitive Sciences., 3*(12), 452–460.

Thurlow, C. (2001). Naming the "outsider within": Homophobic pejoratives and the verbal abuse of lesbian, gay and bisexual high-school pupils. *Journal of Adolescent, 24*(1), 25–38.

Trumbach, R. (1998). *Sex and the gender revolution: Heterosexuality and the third gender in Enlightenment London* (Vol. 1). USA: University of Chicago Press.

Tversky, A., & Kahneman, D. (1973). Availability: A heuristic for judging frequency and probability. *Cognitive Psychology, 5*(2), 207–232.

Twenge, J. M., Sherman, R. A., & Wells, B. E. (2015). Changes in American adults' sexual behavior and attitudes, 1972–2012. *Archives of Sexual Behavior*. Advance online publication. doi:10.1007/s10508-015-054-2.

Udis-Kessler, A. (1990). *Bisexuality in an essentialist world: Toward an understanding of biphobia* (pp. 51–63). Bisexuality: A reader and sourcebook.

Urquhart, C. (2013). *Grounded theory for qualitative research: A practical guide*. USA: Sage.

Vaillancourt, T., & Sharma, A. (2011). Intolerance of sexy peers: Intrasexual competition among women. *Aggressive Behavior, 37*(6), 569–577.

Voss, G., Browne, K., & Gupta, C. (2014). Embracing the "and": Between queer and bisexual theory at Brighton bifest. *Journal of homosexuality, 61*(11), 1605–1625.

Vrangalova, Z., & Savin-Williams, R. C. (2012). Mostly heterosexual and mostly gay/lesbian: Evidence for new sexual orientation identities. *Archives of Sexual Behavior, 41*(1), 85–101.

Vrangalova, Z., Bukberg, R. E., & Rieger, G. (2014). Birds of a feather? Not when it comes to sexual permissiveness. *Journal of Social and Personal Relationships, 31*(1), 93–113.

Walls, N. E., Wisneski, H., & Kane, S. (2013). School climate, individual support, or both? Gay-straight alliances and the mental health of sexual minority youth. *School Social Work Journal, 37*(2), 88–111.

Waskul, D. D. (2003). *Self-games and body-play: Personhood in online chat and cybersex*. Switzerland: Peter Lang.

Watson, J. B. (2014). Bisexuality and family: Narratives of silence, solace, and strength. *Journal of GLBT Family Studies, 10*(1–2), 101–123.

Weeks, J. (1985). *Sex, politics and society: The regulations of sexuality since 1800*. London: Routledge.

Weeks, J. (1991). *Against nature: Essays on history, sexuality and identity*. London: Rivers Oram.

Weeks, J. (2007). *The world we have won*. London: Routledge.

Weinberg, G. H. (1972). *Society and the healthy homosexual*. USA: Macmillan.

Weinberg, M. S., Williams, C. J., & Pryor, D. W. (1994). *Dual attraction: Understanding bisexuality*. UK: Oxford University Press.

Weinrich, J. D. (2014a). From the Editor: A sexual orientation quiz. *Journal of Bisexuality, 14*(3–4), 307–313.

Weinrich, J. D. (2014b). Multidimensional measurement of sexual orientation: Ideal. *Journal of Bisexuality, 14*(3–4), 544–556.

Weinrich, J. D. (2014c). Notes on the Kinsey Scale. *Journal of Bisexuality, 14*(3–4), 333–340

Weinrich, J. D., Snyder, P. J., Pillard, R. C., Grant, I., Jacobson, D. L., Robinson, S. R., & McCutchan, J. A. (1993). A factor analysis of the Klein sexual orientation grid in two disparate samples. *Archives of Sexual Behavior, 22*(2), 157–168.

Weiss, J. T. (2003). GL vs. BT: The archaeology of biphobia and transphobia within the US gay and lesbian community. *Journal of Bisexuality, 3*(3–4), 25–55.

Weiss, J. T. (2011). Reflective paper: GL versus BT: The archaeology of biphobia and transphobia within the US Gay and lesbian community. *Journal of Bisexuality, 11*(4), 498–502.

Welzer-Lang, D. (2008). Speaking out loud about bisexuality: Biphobia in the gay and lesbian community. *Journal of Bisexuality, 8*(1-2), 81–95.
West, C., & Zimmerman, D. H. (1987). Doing gender. *Gender & Society, 1*(2), 125–151.
Weston, K. (1994). *Families we choose: Lesbians gays kinship*. New York: Columbia University Press.
Whisman, V. (1996). *Queer by choice: Lesbians, gay men, and the politics of identity*. UK: Psychology Press.
White, J. (2013). Thinking generations. *The British Journal of Sociology, 64*(2), 216–247.
Willer, R., Rogalin, C. L., Conlon, B., & Wojnowicz, M. T. (2013). Overdoing gender: A test of the masculine overcompensation thesis1. *American Journal of Sociology, 118*(4), 980–1022.
Wilson, B. D., Harper, G. W., Hidalgo, M. A., Jamil, O. B., Torres, R. S., & Fernandez, M. I. (2010). Negotiating dominant masculinity ideology: Strategies used by gay, bisexual and questioning male adolescents. *American Journal of Community Psychology, 45*(1–2), 169–185.
Wilson, G., & Rahman, Q. (2005). *Born gay. The psychobiology of sex orientation*. London: Peter Owen.
Worthen, M. G. (2013). An argument for separate analyses of attitudes toward lesbian, gay, bisexual men, bisexual women, MtF and FtM transgender individuals. *Sex Roles, 68*(11–12), 703–723.
Worthen, M. G. (2014). The cultural significance of homophobia on heterosexual women's gendered experiences in the United States: A commentary. *Sex Roles, 71*(3–4), 141–151.
Yip, A. K. (1997). Gay male Christian couples and sexual exclusivity. *Sociology, 31*(2), 289–306.
Yoshino, K. (2000). The epistemic contract of bisexual erasure. *Stanford Law Review*, 353–461.
Zietsch, B. P., Verweij, K. J., Heath, A. C., Madden, P. A., Martin, N. G., Nelson, E. C., & Lynskey, M. T. (2012). Do shared etiological factors contribute to the relationship between sexual orientation and depression? *Psychological Medicine, 42*(03), 521–532.
Zinik, G. (1985). Identity conflict or adaptive flexibility? Bisexuality reconsidered. *Journal of Homosexuality, 11*(1–2), 7–20.
Zivony, A., & Lobel, T. (2014). The invisible stereotypes of bisexual men. *Archives of Sexual Behavior*, 1–12.
Zuhur, S. (2005). Gender sexuality and the criminal laws in the Middle East and North Africa: A comparative study. *Women for Women's Human Rights*, 1–76.

Index

A
Acceptance among friends, 130
Anderson McCormack sexuality thermometer, 40
Anti-gay, 49
Attractions, 21
  emotional, 18, 24, 25
  romantic, 18, 162
  sexual, 19, 24, 28, 66
  sexual attraction, measures of, 32
  social, 18
Authenticity, 59

B
Behavioral Risk Factor Surveillance System (BRFSS), 50, 65
Behavior, sexual, 18, 22
Biphobia, 50, 51, 86
Bisexual burden, 3, 11, 13, 51
  characteristics of, 53
  disloyalty to lesbian and gay community, 61
Bisexual privilege, 65
Bromance, 25
Burden, 144
Burden of bisexuality, 51, 123
  characteristics, 53
  health effects of, 64
  psychological effects of, 64

C
Changing identifications, 101
Challenging identities, 101
City
  coming out in, 137
City streets, research in, 90, 92–94

Cohort analysis, 91–93, 96, 98, 99
Cohort effect, 152
  theorizing, 155
Coming Out in 21st Century
  acceptance among friends, 130
  City and Countryside, similarity, 137
  inclusive families, 134
  to school, 132
Coming Out, with twentieth Century baggage
  burden on the scene, 123
  importance of city, 125
  negotiating at work, 121
  to family, difficulty in, 119
  to friends, 114
Community, 61
Community of bisexuals, 4, 6
Confusion in 20th Century, 102
Countryside
  Coming Out in, 137
  critiquing bisexuality as an identity label, 107

D
Definitional issues, 22
Denial in 20th Century, 102
Desire, 105

E
Emotional orientation, 18, 25
Erasure, 53, 54
Erasure of bisexuality, 58
Eroding heterosexism, 136
Erosion of one-time rule of homosexuality, 83

F
Fear of discrimination, 56
Flexibility, sexual, 45

Functional Magnetic Resonance Imaging (fMRI) technique, 32
Fundamentalist christianity, 76

G
Gay and Lesbian Alliance Against Defamation (GLAAD), 41
Gendered boundaries, 80
Gendered preferences, 146
General Social Survey (GSS), 76
Generational analysis, 99
Generational cohort effect, 152
Generational differences in identity categories, 106

H
Health effects of bisexual burden, 64
Heteronormativity, 145
Heterosexism, 50, 124
Heterosexism role in bisexual erasure, 54
Heterosexual-homosexual rating scale. *See* Kinsey scale
HIV/AIDS, 76
Homoerasure, 73
Homohysteria, 4, 5, 7, 8, 11–13, 71, 75
Homonegativity, 50
Homophobia, 49, 92
Homophobic, 54
Homosexuality, One-Time Rule of, 83

I
Identification, 44
Identity, 16, 17
　orientation and, 17
　self-identity, 29
　sexual, 23
　significance of, 23
　social, 18
Identity categories, 106
Identity label, 107
Implicit Association Task (IAT), 32, 33
Inclusion among friends, 130
Inclusivity, 77
　effects of, 80
Indecision, 60
Innovation, in research methods, 95
Intersectionality, 58
Interview procedure, 96

K
Kinsey, Alfred, 34
Kinsey scale, 11, 34, 35
Kinsey's sampling techniques, 1
Klein sexual orientation grid, 36

L
Love, 24, 27
　desire and, 28
　Romantic Love, 24

M
Masculinity, 70–72, 75–78, 81
Measures of sexual attraction, 32
Men who have Sex with Men (MSM), 58
Methods, sampling, 7, 8
Metrosexuality, 77, 78, 83
Misogyny, 125
Modified Klein grid, 38
Monogamism, 147
Monogamous, inability to be, 62
Monogamy, 22, 26
Monosexism, 3
Monosexual culture, 2–4, 11
Mostly heterosexuals, 88

O
One-time rule, 159
One-time rule of homosexuality, 69
Orientation, 17
Outness, 93

P
Permissiveness, 63
Personal acceptance in relationship…, 142
Pew research, 44
Population-based sampling method, 42
Population, bisexual, 40
Population, sexual minority, 42
Positive experiences, 104, 105
Post-gay, 73
Priming Task (PT), 32
Psychological effects of bisexual burden, 64

Q
Qualitative analysis, 98

R
Realization of bisexuality, 102, 105, 106
Recruitment procedure
　benefits of, 160
Relationships
　burden in, 144
　decreasing heteronormativity, 145
　gendered preferences, 146
　increased personal acceptance, 142
　monogamism, 147
　romantic partners, 144
Repulsion
　sexual, 21

Index

Research on bisexuals
  age brackets for analysis, 92
  evaluation, 95
  importance of generations, 99
  interview procedure, 96
  methods as controversial, 96
  note on Women, 99
  qualitative analysis, 98
  situating the study, 91
Ritual bisexuality, 28
Romance
  bromance versus, 25
Romantic love, 24
Romantic partners, 144

S
Sampling, 89, 90, 93, 95
School, Coming Out to, 132
Segmented identity, 116
Self-erasure, 56
Sex-crazed sexual permissiveness, 63
Sexological approach to bisexuality, 8
Sexology, 2, 9
Sexual attraction, 19
Sexual behavior, 22
Sexual flexibility, 45
Sexual fluidity, 47
Sexual identities among youth, 87
Sexual identity, 23
Sexuality
  components, 17
Sexuality acknowledgement, 104
Sexuality, expanding, 159
Sexuality thermometers, 39
Sexual orientation, 17
Sexual repulsion, 21
Situational bisexuality, 29
Social policy, implications for, 164
Sociology, 9
Stage model of homohysteria, 72
Stigma, 50, 52, 53, 55, 63, 65
Surveying bisexuality, 34, 37

T
Thermometers, sexuality, 39
Types of bisexuality, 28
Typologies of sexuality, 17

Y
Young bisexual Men and clarity of desire, 105

Z
Zero-sum game of sexuality, 36